RENAISSANCE RHETORIC

Renaissance Rhetoric

Edited by

Peter Mack
Lecturer in English
University of Warwick

St. Martin's Press

First published in Great Britain 1994 by
THE MACMILLAN PRESS LTD
Houndmills, Basingstoke, Hampshire RG21 2XS
and London
Companies and representatives
throughout the world

This book is published in Macmillan's
Warwick Studies in the European Humanities series
General Editors: Tom Winnifrith (1987–90); Michael Mallett (1990–   )

A catalogue record for this book is available
from the British Library.

ISBN 0–333–52354–7

Printed in Hong Kong

First published in the United States of America 1994 by
Scholarly and Reference Division,
ST. MARTIN'S PRESS, INC.,
175 Fifth Avenue,
New York, N.Y. 10010

ISBN 0–312–10184–8

Library of Congress Cataloging-in-Publication Data
Renaissance rhetoric / Peter Mack.
p.   cm.
Includes index.
ISBN 0–312–10184–8
1. Rhetoric—1500–1800.   2. Renaissance.   I. Mack, Peter, 1955–

P301.3.E85R46   1994
808'.009'031—dc20   93–8119
                                                                              CIP

Contents

List of Illustrations

The editor and publishers are grateful to the copyright-holders listed below for permission to print the illustrations:

Introduction

Over the past fifty years there has been a tremendous resurgence of interest in the history and theory of rhetoric. The study of rhetoric now plays a part in a wide range of academic disciplines: art history, classical studies, composition teaching, cultural studies, law, linguistics, philosophy, psychology, politics, and theology.[1] But rhetoric has probably been most studied in relation to history and literature, particularly within the renaissance period. For this reason the European Humanities Research Centre decided to hold a conference on renaissance rhetoric in July 1991. In the event we were able to assemble a very strong team of specialists in the field. This volume contains the revised texts of the nine papers delivered at the conference.

Larry Green's 'Aristotle's *Rhetoric* and Renaissance views of the Emotions' combines two trends in recent scholarship: studies of the use that renaissance teachers made of classical rhetorical texts[2] and studies of the impact of Greek rhetoric.[3] Through his studies of translations, commentaries and textbooks Green illustrates the understandable difficulties which the Latin rhetorical tradition had in accommodating and exploiting the *Rhetoric*. Green shows that a reading of Aristotle tended to promote more serious consideration of the emotional side of rhetoric, and that the more important contributions tended to come from Southern Europe.

Lisa Jardine's 'Ghosting the Reform of Dialectic' pursues several areas of enquiry that she has pioneered. It illustrates the connection between rhetoric and dialectic, and the modern interest in renaissance dialectic.[4] It examines the connections between reputation, career-building and publishing that she and Tony Grafton have emphasised in their studies of renaissance education.[5] And it reconstructs Erasmus's transactions with friends, assistants, printers and manuscript owners as he saw (or urged) into print his own *De copia*, his two editions of Seneca and his friends' edition of Agricola's *De inventione dialectica*.

Kees Meerhoff's 'The Significance of Philip Melanchthon's Rhetoric in the Renaissance' places Melanchthon's rhetoric textbooks in the context of his contemporaneous lectures on Classical and Biblical texts. Meerhoff shows how Melanchthon continually applies the precepts of rhetoric and dialectic to the practical task of reading and interpreting texts. In so doing he aligns himself with recent studies of renaissance reading.[6] Meerhoff also insists on the connection between the training in classical reading which Melanchthon provided and its application to the reading of scripture, and particularly to St. Paul's letters. Like Jardine, Meerhoff argues that we must break down the disciplinary barriers between rhetoric, dialectic, textual scholarship and theology if we are to understand sixteenth-century humanism.

Dilwyn Knox's 'Order, Reason and Oratory: Rhetoric in Protestant Latin Schools' continues the educational theme. School regulations and extant textbooks indicate the methods of teaching and the materials used. Knox shows how considerations of school organisation and religious reform affected rhetoric teaching. Like Meerhoff, he emphasises the application of rhetorical training to the reading of texts. Knox finds an increasing emphasis on composition in the vernacular, and on *pronuntiatio* which he interprets, drawing on his own earlier work,[7] as a training in comportment.

Brian Vickers founded the International Society for the History of Rhetoric. His publications have introduced the subject of rhetoric to many students of English literature.[8] His contribution offers some 'dispersed meditations' on the rhetoric textbook. He discusses the variety of the textbooks, the motives for their publication and the comparative success of several sixteenth-century rhetorics. He emphasises the importance of studying the manuals in the light of the educational purposes and realities they had to serve. Finally he introduces some examples from Samuel Shaw's *Words Made Visible* (1679), which entertains its audience at the same time as it recalls the basic doctrines of rhetoric and indicates the ethical limitations of the subject.

George Hunter's chapter represents a double return: to the University whose English department he founded in 1965, and to the subject of his postgraduate work in the early 1950s. His 'Rhetoric and Renaissance Drama' argues that we need to make more of a distinction between modern literary criticism and renaissance rhetorical education. The latter's emphasis on practical persuasion makes it the forerunner of the advertising and public relations businesses. Hunter suggests that the English renaissance perceived a large gap between the contingent world of practical action and the absolute world of truth, and that this gap was to some extent bridged by the drama. The audience recognises that the plays take place in a world of verisimilitude, but emotional involvement invites it to extend the observations and judgements of the play into the 'real' world. Hunter's argument makes connections with recent work on declamation.[9]

In my chapter 'Rhetoric in Use: Three Romances by Greene and Lodge' I argue that a rhetorical approach can respond to some of the unusual (and to the reader accustomed to the novel, off-putting) features of these works. Then I compare the rhetoric exploited in the romances with ideas about invention and style that were developed and taught in the sixteenth century.

David Norbrook's 'Rhetoric, Ideology and the Elizabethan World Picture' examines the connections between the theory and teaching of rhetoric (particularly discussions of similitude) and political arguments. He shows that rhetorical education induced an awareness of the power (and also the limitations) of arguments from analogy like those in Ulysses's 'degree' speech in *Troilus and Cressida* and Sir John Davies's *Orchestra*. This leads him to reject arguments, whether traditional or new historicist, which take such analogies as expressions of a fixed Elizabethan mindset.

Pat Rubin's 'Raphael and the Rhetoric of Art' provides this predominantly northern and literary collection with a much needed excursion to Southern Europe and visual evidence. She argues in detail that rhetorical approaches help us to understand Raphael's approach to painting and his admirers' interpretation of his career. Conversely the rhetorical perspective helps her develop new interpretations of some very important paintings. I have placed her essay at the end of the collection to facilitate reference to the plates, which are essential to her argument.

It is a strength of this collection that chapters on the development and teaching of rhetoric are balanced with chapters on its applications and implications. But I am also aware of the omissions: literatures other than English,[10] Italian rhetoric,[11] epideictic rhetoric,[12] letter-writing and sermons,[13] to name only the most obvious areas.

These chapters incorporate many improvements on the versions delivered at Warwick in July 1991, but it will be very hard for them to equal the spirit of cooperative inquiry that we enjoyed then. It is my pleasure to thank the contributors to this volume for their hard work and the other conference participants for the atmosphere they created. I must also thank Marion Franklin, secretary of the European Humanities Research Centre, for her help in organising the conference, Tom Winnifrith former director of the centre and current chairman of the English department, for his enthusiastic moral and financial support from the inception of the project to its completion, and Ruth Robbins who acted as conference assistant and has since helped greatly in the preparation of this volume. I am grateful to Elizabeth Cameron, Cheryl Cave and Pauline Wilson for help in preparing the typescript, and to Margaret Cannon and Keith Povey for seeing it into print.

Notes and References

1. For example, M. Baxandall, *Giotto and the Orators* (Oxford, 1971); R. Barthes, 'L'Ancienne rhétorique: Aide-mémoire', *Communications*, vol. XVI (1970), pp. 172–229, translated in *The Semiotic Challenge* (Oxford, 1988), pp. 13–93; 'Rhetoric of the Image', in S. Heath (ed.), *Image–Music–Text* (Glasgow, 1977), pp. 32–51, Edward P.J. Corbett, *Classical Rhetoric for the Modern Student* (New York, 1965); R. Andrews (ed.), *Narrative and Argument* (Milton Keynes, 1989); D. Leith and G. Myerson, *The Power of Address* (London, 1989); S. Fish, *Doing What Comes Naturally: Change, Rhetoric and the Practice of Theory in Literary and Legal Studies* (Durham, NC, 1989); D. Sperber and D. Wilson, *Relevance: Communication and Cognition* (Oxford, 1986), W. Nash, *Rhetoric* (Oxford, 1990); S. Ijsseling, *Rhetoric and Philosophy in Conflict* (The Hague, 1976); J. E. Seigel, *Rhetoric and Philosophy in Renaissance Humanism* (Princeton, 1968); W. Ong, *Orality and Literacy* (London, 1982); M. Warner (ed.), *The Bible as Rhetoric* (London, 1990), J. Kinneavy, *Greek Rhetorical Origins of Christian Faith* (New York, 1986).
2. J.J. Murphy, 'Quintilian's Influence on the Teaching of Speaking and Writing in the Middle Ages and Renaissance', in R. L. Enos (ed.), *Oral and Written Communication* (London, 1990); L. Green (ed.), *John Rainolds's Oxford Lectures on Aristotle's Rhetoric* (Newark, DL, 1986).
3. J. Monfasani, 'The Byzantine Rhetorical Tradition and the Renaissance', in J. J. Murphy (ed.), *Renaissance Eloquence* (Berkeley, 1983), pp. 174–87; C.W. Wooten, *Hermogenes's On Types of Style* (Chapel Hill, 1987).
4. C. Vasoli, *La dialettica e la retorica dell' Umanesimo* (Milan, 1968); W. Ong, *Ramus, Method and the Decay of Dialogue* (Cambridge, MA, 1956); W. S. Howell, *Logic and Rhetoric in England 1500–1700* (Princeton, 1956); L. Jardine, *Francis Bacon: Discovery and the Art of Discourse* (Cambridge, 1974).
5. A. Grafton and L. Jardine, *From Humanism to the Humanities* (London, 1986), A. Grafton, *Joseph Scaliger: A Study in the History of Classical Scholarship: I, Textual Criticism and Exegesis* (Oxford, 1983).
6. A. Grafton and L. Jardine, ' "Studied for Action": How Gabriel Harvey Read his Livy', *Past and Present*, vol. 129 (1990), pp. 30–78, P. Mack,

'Rudolph Agricola's Reading of Literature', *Journal of the Warburg and Courtauld Institutes*, vol. XLVIII (1985), pp. 23–41.

7. D. Knox, 'Erasmus's *De civilitate* and the Religious Origins of Protestant Civility', in A. Brown and P. Rubin (eds), *The Renaissance Revisited* (Oxford, forthcoming).

8. B. Vickers, *Francis Bacon and Renaissance Prose* (Cambridge, 1968), *The Artistry of Shakespeare's Prose* (London, 1968), *Classical Rhetoric in English Poetry* (London, 1970), *In Defence of Rhetoric* (Oxford, 1988), (ed.), *Rhetoric Revalued* (Binghamton, 1982).

9. For example W. Trimpi, *Muses of One Mind* (Princeton, 1983).

10. For example G. Castor, *Pléïade Poetics* (Cambridge, 1964); A. Gordon, *Ronsard et la rhétorique* (Geneva, 1970); T. Cave, *The Cornucopian Text* (Oxford, 1979); M. Fumaroli, *L' Age de l' éloquence. Rhétorique et 'res literaria' de la Renaissance au seuil de l' époque classique* (Paris, 1980); K. Meerhoff, *Rhétorique et poétique en France au XVIe siècle* (Leiden, 1985).

11. R. Sabbadini, *Il metodo degli umanisti* (Florence, 1922), H. Gray, 'Renaissance Humanism: The Pursuit of Eloquence', in P. O. Kristeller and P. P. Weiner (eds), *Renaissance Essays* (New York, 1968); N. Struever, *The Language of History in the Renaissance* (Princeton, 1970); J. Weinberg (ed.), *Trattati di poetica e retorica del Cinquecento*, 3 vols (Bari, 1970–2); P. O. Kristeller, *Renaissance Thought and Its Sources* (New York, 1979).

12. O. B. Hardison, *The Enduring Monument* (Chapel Hill, NC, 1962); J. W. O'Malley, *Praise and Blame in Renaissance Rome* (Durham, NC, 1979); B. Vickers, 'Epideictic and Epic in the Renaissance', *New Literary History*, vol. XIV (1983), 497–537.

13. J. R. Henderson, 'Erasmus on the Art of Letter-Writing', in Murphy (ed.), *Renaissance Eloquence* (note 3 above); J. N. MacManamon, *Funeral Oratory and the Cultural Ideals of Renaissance Humanism* (Chapel Hill, NC, 1989).

Notes on the Contributors

Lawrence Green is Professor of English at the University of Southern California. He edited and translated *John Rainolds's Oxford Lectures on Aristotle's Rhetoric*. He is preparing a book on Aristotle's *Rhetoric* in the renaissance.

George Hunter was formerly Professor of English at Warwick and Yale. His publications include *John Lyly: The Humanist as Courtier*, *Dramatic Identities and Cultural Tradition* and editions of *All's Well That Ends Well*, *King Lear* and *Macbeth*.

Lisa Jardine is Professor of English at Queen Mary and Westfield College, University of London. Her publications include *Francis Bacon: Discovery and the Art of Discourse, Still Harping on Daughters*; (with A. Grafton) *From Humanism to the Humanities* and (with Julia Swindells) *What's Left*. She is preparing a book on Erasmus.

Dilwyn Knox is Professor of History at Pace University, New York. He is the author of *Ironia: Medieval and Renaissance ideas on Irony*.

Peter Mack lectures in English at the University of Warwick. He is the author of *Renaissance Argument: Valla and Agricola in the Traditions of Rhetoric and Dialectic*.

Kees Meerhoff is Professor of French at the University of Amsterdam. His publications include *Rhétorique et poétique au seizième siècle en France* and numerous studies on renaissance rhetoric. He is preparing a book on Melanchthon.

David Norbrook is Fellow and Tutor in English at Magdalen College, Oxford. He is the author of *Poetry and Politics in the English Renaissance* and the editor (with H. Woudhuysen) of *The Penguin Book of Renaissance Verse 1509–1659*. He is preparing a book on literature and politics in the seventeenth century.

Patricia Rubin is Lecturer in History of Art at the Courtauld Institute, University of London. Her book on Vasari is about to appear.

Brian Vickers is Professor of English in the Centre for Renaissance Studies at ETH, Zurich. Among his books are *In Defence of Rhetoric, Rhetoric Revalued, Shakespeare: The Critical Heritage 1623–1801* (6 vols), *Returning to Shakespeare, The Artistry of Shakespeare's Prose* and *Francis Bacon and Renaissance Prose*.

1

Aristotle's *Rhetoric* and Renaissance Views of the Emotions

Lawrence D. Green

Aristotle's *Rhetoric* was not a major treatise for scholars during the Latin middle ages, who considered it largely as an adjunct to Aristotelian ethics and politics. It was not a major treatise for the early Italian humanists, who knew about the treatise, but who found their principal inspiration for rhetoric in the rediscovered works of Cicero and Quintilian. Nor was it a major treatise for the Greeks of renaissance Byzantium, who viewed Aristotle primarily as a precursor to the principal writers of their own rhetorical tradition.[1]

Yet, despite the minor status of Aristotle's *Rhetoric* at the beginning of the renaissance, by the year 1600 a prodigious amount of material had been published on it; there are successive Greek editions, Greek editions with Latin translations, exclusively Latin translations and several vernacular translations. Each of these types may appear with or without a commentary; sometimes the commentary seeks only to justify the edition or translation, sometimes it seems more important and sometimes it stands alone. And there are numerous paraphrases and digests, both Latin and vernacular. Add to this catalogue the numerous discussions of Aristotle's *Rhetoric* that are found in other rhetorical studies during the renaissance, ranging from discussions of rhetorical theory to analyses of Cicero's speeches, and it becomes clear that the renaissance fascination with the treatise goes beyond simple excitement over another rediscovered classical text.[2]

The *Rhetoric* emerged during the renaissance in a slow and halting fashion. To begin with, the Greek text of the *Rhetoric* had been lost for many centuries. The medieval West had a laconic paraphrase from the Arabic, and there were two principal Latin translations available from the thirteenth century, but the Greek text itself was

1

nowhere to be found. The best-known medieval version was the
translation by William of Moerbeke, which he made while serving
as the Latin Bishop of Corinth. Giles of Rome produced a
commentary based upon Moerbeke, and that commentary is
shaped by scholastic readings of Aristotle's dialectical and ethical
treatises. In the medieval universities the *Rhetoric* was studied
within this same context, and when it appeared with another of
Aristotle's treatises it was usually paired with the *Politics*.

The amount of publication and commentary on Aristotle's
Rhetoric is paltry when compared with the amount of publication
and commentary on Cicero's rhetoric.[3] This is as true in the early
renaissance as in the medieval period, and the imbalance is only
intensified in the renaissance by the discovery of the mature works
of Cicero and of a complete Quintilian. It is into this Latin rhetorical
context that émigré scholars from Byzantium brought a fresh
interest in Aristotle's *Rhetoric*. For the Byzantine Greeks in the East,
Hermogenes was the principal rhetorician, not Aristotle or Cicero.
For the Latins in the West, Cicero was the principal rhetorician,
Hermogenes was unknown and Aristotle was understood in
scholastic contexts. Thus when Greek émigré scholars reintroduced
Aristotle's *Rhetoric* to the Latin West, they took a minor text from
within the Byzantine literary and philosophical tradition, and
helped transplant it very suddenly into a Latin rhetorical and
ethical culture which from the beginning was looking in a different
direction.

These, then, are three principal contexts for the renaissance of
Aristotle's *Rhetoric*. First, an ongoing concern in the Latin West with
the *Rhetoric* as an ancillary treatise on ethics, coupled with an
interest in seeing it allied with dialectical matters. Second, a concern
in the Byzantine world to see all of Greek intellectual work as a
continuum leading to the literary present, a continuum in which
Aristotle was not necessarily a principal. Third, a revivified interest
in the lore of classical rhetoric as articulated by Cicero and
Quintilian, both of whom could be seen as elaborating ideas drawn
from Aristotle and earlier Greek writers.

I do not suggest that these three strands interwove with one
another to form a major renaissance understanding of Aristotle's
Rhetoric. On the contrary, starting with these three concerns the
understandings multiply. The treatise was not an easy one for
renaissance scholars. They disagreed with one another about what
context to place it in, and what perspectives to bring to bear on it.

They disagreed about how to translate the text, and they disagreed about how to understand the text they had translated. They disagreed about how to determine what constituted a good Greek text, they disagreed about what the Greek text said, and then they disagreed about what that Greek text meant.

In the present essay I want to suggest that one of the principal ways in which writers sought to make sense of the *Rhetoric* was as a study of the role of the emotions in persuasion, and more generally as a study of the role of the audience in persuasion. It is an interest different from the ethical concerns which dominated the earlier Latin tradition, but one which is coherent in terms of those concerns. I will trace this particular effort to make sense of the Rhetoric, starting with early instances in George of Trebizond and Juan Luis Vives, before looking at an early Latin commentary and some of the efforts to teach Aristotle's treatise, and I will conclude with a look at some attempts to make sense of troublesome textual details.

I

In 1416 the Greek scholar George of Trebizond was invited to Italy by the Venetian statesman Francesco Barbaro, and in 1433–4 he completed his *Rhetoricorum libri quinque*. The treatise immediately established Trebizond as the leading theorist of rhetoric in the Latin West. Twenty-four manuscripts still survive, the treatise was printed as early as 1472 in Venice, and it was reprinted throughout the next century – in whole, in part and in digest.[4] In *Rhetoricorum libri quinque* Trebizond managed a stunning blend of his own native Greek tradition, stemming from Hermogenes, and his adopted Latin tradition of Cicero and Quintilian. It could not have come at a more opportune time. The prestige of Cicero and Quintilian was well established in the West (despite the fact that extant texts were incomplete and even misattributed), and the rediscovery of complete texts of both rhetoricians at about the time Trebizond arrived in Italy was the cause of enormous excitement among scholars. To this reinvigorated Latin tradition Trebizond added the Greek stylistic doctrines of Hermogenes, who was then still unknown in the West, but who had long been studied in the East. The result was an accommodation of each tradition to the other, which also provided the only Latin source for Hermogenean ideas for decades to come.

If Trebizond had any interest in, or knowledge of Aristotle, much less of Aristotle's *Rhetoric*, there is little trace of it in *Rhetoricorum libri quinque*. Yet, within a decade, Trebizond produced the first renaissance Latin translation of Aristotle's *Rhetoric*. His interest in Aristotle seems to have started only after he had completed *Rhetoricorum libri quinque*. During the years 1438–41, Trebizond attended the Council of Florence, where the Byzantine scholar George Gemistos Pletho delivered an electrifying lecture celebrating the philosophy of Plato, who was nearly unknown in the Latin West, by attacking Aristotle, whom Pletho thought the West overestimated.[5] George of Trebizond afterwards claimed to be offended by this unwarranted attack on the Latin Aristotle by his former fellow-Greek. Two years after the close of the council, Trebizond began work on his Latin translation of Aristotle's *Rhetoric*, and finished it in 1445. A decade after Trebizond completed this translation, he published a spirited defense (actually, a mean-spirited defence) of Aristotle against Plato, and in his comparison of the two he defended Aristotle's *Rhetoric* in words which made Aristotle sound indistinguishable from Cicero and Quintilian.[6] Thus, the course of Trebizond's career argues three coordinate intentions for his Latin translation of Aristotle's *Rhetoric*: first, it advertises Trebizond's intellectual and political allegiance to his new-found patrons by defending the Latin Aristotle against the Greek Plato; second, it stakes out Trebizond's claim as the leading rhetorical scholar in the West; and third, it presents Aristotle to the Latin West in the same kind of intellectual context that had made Trebizond's earlier *Rhetoricorum libri quinque* such a success.

Trebizond's dedicatory prologue to his translation of Aristotle turns away from the literary concerns of his earlier treatise and instead stresses human motivation. Trebizond says that of all of Aristotle's works, and especially of those which address great civic affairs, Aristotle's *Rhetoric* is by far the most useful. The reader of Trebizond's translation will, with the greatest of ease, come to understand much about human affairs, and for the reader who already has some experience of such things there will be a shock of recognition:

For here, everything about the ways of men – in the variety of their ages and fortunes – everything is judiciously laid out, clearly explained, and suitably described, so completely that nothing is missing. Here we can peer into, not just the secrets of Nature (and

Nature is the greatest philosopher of all), but even peer into the hidden minds of men, into the private emotions of men, and we can do so harmlessly.[7]

These are the notes that Trebizond sounds for Aristotle's *Rhetoric* – knowledge of the well-springs of human action, the habits of men, their hidden minds, their private emotions.

The numerous writings of the Spanish humanist Juan Luis Vives almost a century later demonstrate the same focus. In his treatise *De tradendis disciplinis* (1531) Vives declares that it is the responsibility of a conscientious teacher to lecture on Aristotle's *Rhetoric*, not merely because it is 'a work of great ability and art (as is often the case with this author), but also because it is a work of immense usefulness for teaching good sense and prudence about the affairs of public life'.[8] This ringing endorsement will become a cliché as the century wears on, but even at this point the endorsement is not without problems, since it comes at the end of a long list of rhetorical treatises which should be studied first, ranging from those of Cicero, Quintilian and Hermogenes, to less expected works such as Rutilius Lupus, Julius Ruffianus and Sulpitius Victor. Vives thinks that all of these treatises, including Aristotle's *Rhetoric*, are flawed by offering 'confused, disordered and impractical directions'.[9] But as Vives explains elsehere, this is not to take anything away from Aristotle, since Aristotle had taken the subject of rhetoric from its rude, uncertain beginnings and raised it to the highest levels. There is such a difference in rhetorical theory before and after Aristotle that, just as Aristotle is thought to have invented the discipline of dialectic, so also he should be considered the inventor of the discipline of rhetoric. Aristotle's *Rhetoric* seems complete, and as for his discussions of invention, disposition and elocution, there is nothing one could add.[10]

Despite Aristotle's contributions to the technical aspects of rhetoric, which amounted almost to inventing rhetoric, Vives still thinks the inherited rhetorical lore is a mishmash of useless precepts, and that the real value of Aristotle's *Rhetoric* is to be found elsewhere. Vives is scathing in his denunciation of the *tria genera causarum*, of Aristotle's analysis of audiences according to past, present and future concerns, of Aristotle's distinctions about the various ends of oratory, and of Aristotle's division of audiences into judges and so-called spectators. Vives is even more scathing about the inherited lore of Ciceronian rhetoric, and he sees

Aristotle's *Rhetoric* as a corrective to the worst effects of that tradition; in *De ratione dicendi* (1534) he expostulates against those who 'think the whole art of speaking is included in that part which concerns words or schemes, tropes, periods and harmony of diction, which make up not so much the body itself of speaking, as if they were the substance, as the decoration and ornament and form of a speech'.[11] What Vives finds of value in Aristotle is his recognition that rhetoric is based on an understanding of 'the arts, customs, laws, affections and the conduct of civil and human life'.

If we want to see the full impact of Aristotelian rhetorical thinking on Vives, we need to look at his *De consultatione* (1523). There he rejects the soaring emotional appeals of Roman rhetoric as having no place in the art of private consultation,[12] but even as he rejects such overt appeals, he emphasises (in common with his *De ratione dicendi*) the need to understand what George of Trebizond earlier described as the hidden minds of men, the private emotions of men. He explains that when you advise a prince you need both discretion and deference, while avoiding flattery, since flattery might be pleasing in the short term, but eventually it is found out, and you will lose all credibility. And when you instruct a prince you cannot approach him as though he were inexperienced or uninformed, unless, of course, he is a child and you are specifically charged with guiding him.[13] You also need to ascertain

> the nature and character of the person you counsel, and adjust your speech to that nature and character, speaking learnedly with the learned, pointedly with the clever, more plainly and bluntly with the obtuse, adroitly with the disdainful, freely with the trustworthy; let your speech show what you have selected from the character of each.[14]

Your speech must be adjusted not only to the nature and character of the person addressed, but also to his circumstances, and these include considerations as various as age, learning, reputation for wisdom, wealth, familiarity, citizenship, military rank, respect for authority and the extent to which the person is in touch with reality.[15]

The age of the auditor, his condition and state in life, his habits of thought, his predispositions to respond and act: these are the same notes that Trebizond sounded earlier for Aristotle's *Rhetoric*. And in a telling passage, one that has its roots in Augustine, but which will not find its full flower until Bernard Lamy's *L'art de parler* in the seventeenth century,[16] Vives admonishes that the speaker should strive to be make the listener believe that the speaker loves him (*ut amare illum credaris cui consulis*); love for the listener will be seen as loving care for his best interests and make the speaker believable (*fides quae ex amore nascitur*).[17] Once your auditor thinks you love him, you can tell him anything.

II

When we turn to the early commentaries on Aristotle's *Rhetoric*, the main line of the story is much the same. In 1544 Daniele Barbaro published his commentary on the *Rhetoric*, based upon the manuscript translation completed by his uncle Ermolao Barbaro in the preceding century.[18] As far as Daniele Barbaro is concerned, the principal value of Aristotle's treatise lies in what it tells us about the passions and powers of the souls of men, about how to manipulate opinion by manipulating the passions and faculties that determine opinion. Just as medicine guides and influences our bodies (actually, *partes et membra corporum nostrorum*), so also does rhetoric guide and influence our souls.[19] Thus it is incumbent upon us to study Aristotle's theory of how to use the mental dispositions (*sensus animorum*) which determine human action, inflaming or calming men's emotions (*motus*) as needed. In order to do this, one needs to study, first of all, the human soul (*anima*), and next the things of this world (*res*), then speech itself (*oratio*), and finally both *actio* and *pronuntiatio*. By half-steps Daniele moves toward a Ciceronian reconstruction of Aristotle's *Rhetoric*, and the path lies directly through human character and emotions.

Daniele's focus upon the emotions, coupled with his impulse to read the *Rhetoric* in terms of Ciceronian *officia rhetoricae*, leads him to conflate Aristotle's careful distinctions about human motivation as it relates to deliberative and judicial oratory. Daniele draws his principal understanding of states of mind out of Aristotle's discussion of deliberative oratory in Book 1, where Aristotle explores communal attitudes toward political expediency and the common good. He draws the details of his understanding of states of mind out of Aristotle's discussion of judicial oratory in Book 1, where Aristotle delineates the personal motivations which make individual men act unjustly. Neither of Aristotle's discussions is intended as a general discussion of the emotions; that discussion is reserved for Book 2 of the *Rhetoric*. Instead, each of these earlier discussions is circumscribed by the needs of the immediate exploration of why it is that men act in common as they do, and why men act individually as they do. Daniele, in his driving need to develop an overarching theory of rhetoric and the emotions tries to make these two discussions consonant with one another, reading Aristotle's views on rational and irrational desires as support for his own views on intellect and appetite.

The human soul is unitary, we are told, but within that unity are many parts and many feelings. By 'parts' Daniele means the powers and faculties of doing anything. By 'feelings' he means states of mind (*perpessiones*) and emotions (*motus*). Powers are designated in terms of nature, the appetite and the intellect. The only powers which interest Daniele as he tries to make sense of Aristotle's *Rhetoric* are those of the appetite and the intellect, and he is especially interested in the relations among them. 'Appetite', he writes,

> is a kind of power in the soul that can either compel or incite someone to do anything whatsoever; either because the rational intellect demonstrates the desirability of that thing, or because an irrational feeling demands that it be done. The rational intellect is where the Will is placed, while irrational feeling manifests itself in two ways – either it surges on waves of Anger, or else it is aroused by the enticements of Desire. So it is that a singular human being has two counsellors – Anger and Desire, and in these are found both pleasure and pain. Reason tries to steer a middle course, yielding neither to Anger nor Desire; thus it is that Justice, the greatest of all the virtues, is situated in the Will [which is in the realm of Reason].[20]

There are echoes in this passage not only of the *Nicomachean Ethics* and *De anima* (indeed the latter reverberates throughout the commentary), but also of Plato's Phaedran charioteer. When Desire is governed by reason, it yields temperance, liberality and the like, but without reason Desire is impetuous and leads to all the ills depicted in renaissance literature. So also with Anger, which, if it follows right thinking, urges us on to magnificence, loftiness of mind and moral heights, but if Anger ignores reason the vices come in ebbs and flows: 'first Anger fears and then it dares, it is sometimes manic and sometimes depressed, it is often paralyzed and numb, and often active so that it produces all the ugliness of life'.[21]

More complicated for Daniele is the role of the intellect in Aristotle's *Rhetoric*. It is a mental power which can turn toward knowledge and science, or else 'put on its more human face' (*humaniori fronte*) to deal with the affairs and action of men. If the intellect takes this second path, it works in the realm of opinion, and it must rely upon practical discretion and upon art. This distinction leads to a discussion of the role of persuasion, which is nothing other than leading men's opinion. This task properly belongs to the orator, in part because of the nature of auditors, and in part because of the nature of subjects, but mostly because of the constraints of time, 'for it is just not possible, in the brief time allotted to an orator, to teach or educate an auditor about major subjects'.[22] Since the constraints of the situation do not allow for intellectual understanding, 'the speaker who wants to draw opinion must first excite those counselors whom nature placed in our souls, namely Intellect, Anger and Desire, and with these cords the orator draws us along'.[23]

Thus Aristotle's *Rhetoric* turns out to have functions resembling those of Ciceronian rhetoric – that is, teaching, pleasing and moving. The Intellect, Daniele explains, is for teaching, Desire is for pleasing and Anger is for 'excitation'. Subtlety is needed to move the Intellect, since intellect is more lofty than the appetite, while the two parts of appetite, Anger and Desire, are moved by different means, 'force for excitation, gentleness for pleasing'.[24] And this distribution of functions explains why Aristotle's *Rhetoric* has three books: in the first is the theory of teaching, in the second the power of moving, and in the last the rules for pleasing men are gathered. But Daniele's account contradicts itself. He explains that Book 1 deals with invention, that is to say, with Ciceronian 'teaching', and that such invention rests upon the rational faculty – despite the fact that Aristotle explicitly identifies emotional appeals as a source of invention, and these are found in Book 2. Daniele explains that Book 3 deals with speech itself, that is to say, with Ciceronian 'pleasing', and rests upon the power of Desire – despite the fact that Aristotle deals with desire largely in Book 1, not Book 3. Daniele does best with Book 2, which discusses Anger and the other emotions, but even then there are problems. To start with, Anger is only the first of many emotions which Aristotle discusses in Book 2; the other emotions are mildness, love, fear, shame, benevolence and pity. This

Aristotelian list does not include Desire, presumably because
Daniele considers it an appetite, not an emotion in itself, but in
that case, Anger will have to exist simultaneously as an appetite and
as an emotion. If we are to stick with Daniele's earlier allocation of
the three books, then the emotion of Anger will have to be
subsumed under the appetite of Anger, and as an appetite Anger
will have to subsume all the other emotions of Book 2. This would
result in the Aristotelian emotion of 'mildness' (among others) being
subsumed under the appetite of Anger, when in fact mildness is
part of the essential definition of Desire.

How did all this come about? Daniele's difficulties in making
sense of Aristotle stem from his interest in the emotions as the
causes of human action. While Anger indeed is discussed at length
in Book 2 of the *Rhetoric*, Daniele's real starting point is Book 1,
Chapter 6, in which Aristotle discusses deliberative oratory and the
general principles of the good and the expedient, before concluding
that no man knowingly chooses evil for himself, and that therefore
the expedient and the good entail one another – at least, they do so
for the purposes of finding deliberative arguments. Daniele
struggles with Aristotle's chapter by discussing a threefold appetite
of nature, soul and intellect.[25] Aristotle himself does nothing of the
kind at this place, and Daniele's justification seems to come from
later chapters in the *Rhetoric*. In Chapter 11, for example, Aristotle
has his famous discussion of what constitutes the 'pleasant', since all
men seek what is pleasant. In Chapter 11 Aristotle divides the
general notion of desire into two parts, rational and irrational.
Irrational desires are natural desires, that is, they are desires about
which we do not need to think, and over which we have very little
control. Rational desires, on the other hand, are those longings we
have because we are somehow convinced that something is
pleasant.

But Daniele's discussion of appetition is complicated further
when he draws upon a different discussion in Chapter 10, where
Aristotle discusses the nature and the number of the motivations
which cause human action, and this chapter is perhaps Daniele's
most important source within the *Rhetoric*. Aristotle arrives at seven
causes of human action through relentless division and subdivision.
In this scheme, appetite is a subdivision of a subdivision. Appetite
itself is divided into rational and irrational appetites, and these also
are further subdivided, leading ultimately to three of Aristotle's
seven motivations. The first of these three is the rational appetite,

which deals with the nature of the Good and the Pleasant. The human Will is associated with the rational appetite, since no one wills for himself what is not good or pleasant. The second of these three motives is the irrational appetite called Anger, and the third is the irrational appetite called Desire.

Daniele's conflation of Aristotle's separate discussions leads to an account of appetite which is incomprehensible. At times, Daniele's account of the appetite is threefold, embracing intellect as a rational appetite, and anger and desire as irrational appetites. At other times, Daniele's account of appetite is twofold, embracing only anger and desire, with the intellect having somehow a separate existence and operating independently upon the appetites. Not surprisingly, these problems lead to confusions about the soul and the mind, between *anima* and *animus*, with *mens* thrown in for good measure.

Daniele Barbaro has a great deal more to say about the details of Aristotle's text when his commentary gets to particular passages, such as the logical aspects of Aristotle's enthymeme, or the conditions of the *tria genera causarum*, and what he has to say should not be taken lightly. But the overall framework in which his commentary operates is that of this introduction, and his later comments continually return to these initial perspectives on the relations among intellect, anger and desire. The elements of the account are not unusual in themselves; we see similar accounts of reciprocity between the intellect and the emotions in other Renaissance writers, such as Vives and even Agricola, who agrees that Aristotle has very good things to say about the emotions in the *Rhetoric*.[26] But Vives, who has the most to say on this subject, and who himself seems to have known the *Rhetoric* fairly well, never went as far as Daniele Barbaro goes in reconstructing what Aristotle says in order to make the text come out right.

III

Daniele Barbaro was hardly alone in focusing upon the passions in Aristotle's treatise. We have very little direct evidence of how Aristotle's *Rhetoric* was actually discussed in renaissance class-rooms, but what evidence we have strongly suggests a widespread interest in the same concerns which George of Trebizond articulated a century earlier – the well-springs of human action, the habits of men, their hidden minds, their private emotions.

During the 1570s the Greek Reader at Corpus Christi College, Oxford, was John Rainolds, who lectured on the *Rhetoric* as an elective topic; the autograph of his lecture notes is in the Bodleian Library. Rainolds's sympathies as he approaches the *Rhetoric* are clearly Protestant, even puritan, especially when he lectures on Aristotle's understanding of the emotions. Rainolds proceeds with his lectures in much the same way that a published renaissance commentary would, sometimes line by line, and sometimes chapter by chapter. By the end of the academic term Rainolds had only got through Aristotle's first nine chapters, primarily because each chapter served as a starting point for an excursus on Aristotelian philosophy, classical letters and Christian theology – particularly with respect to discourse and correct action. Not surprisingly, Cicero and Quintilian look better to Rainolds than does Aristotle; as Rainolds says in his concluding lecture, 'Eloquence has two parts; the first belongs to life, the second to the tongue. The first without the second does much good; the second without the first does very much more harm. The second we learn from Cicero, the first we should learn from Christ.'[27]

Rainolds explains that Aristotle has many excellent things to say, but Aristotle was willing to degrade himself by pandering to the thoughts and values of the unwashed multitude, so his *Rhetoric* needs to be studied with the greatest circumspection, and as far as ethics go, Christian writings are more dependable.[28] The whole problem for a Christian orator is that the Christian recognises the inadequacy of the human intellect, and how extensively our moral perverseness has corrupted the human Will. Christians already have the revealed truth and the promise of salvation, and yet it is still difficult for Christians to know the right way to act. Thus it is very dangerous for Christians to turn to a pagan, who has neither that truth nor that promise, for advice on how to persuade others to correct action.

Dangerous, but not impossible, and, if done correctly, rewarding. Rainolds assails Aristotle on all aspects of the theory of the *tria genera causarum*, saying that he is wrong about the types of oratory, wrong about the ends of oratory, wrong about the times of oratory and wrong about the variety of auditors.[29] But Rainolds directs most of his attention to Aristotle's discussions about the emotions and the various characters of men. He takes issue with one of the opening sentences of the *Rhetoric* (1354a16–18), in which Aristotle seems to condemn the use of emotional appeals in oratory. Since Aristotle later spends an enormous amount of time discussing the role of emotions in rhetoric, this opening line caused difficulties for many renaissance commentators. Rainolds articulates eleven reasons why Aristotle might conceivably have made this rash statement, and then turns around to refute each of these eleven at great length. 'Now then', says Rainolds,

> to sum up a long discussion in a few words, the passions must be excited, not for the harm they do but for the good, not so they twist the straight but so that they straighten the crooked; so that they ward off vice, iniquity and disgrace; so that they defend virtue, justice and probity.[30]

The position Rainolds finally comes to concerning this part of Aristotle's text is close to the modern critical consensus. What is of more interest, however, is not whether Rainolds was right or wrong, but the intellectual rigor and moral determination with which he had to puzzle out the problem. Aristotle was not only theoretically wrong, but he was also morally wrong to attack earlier rhetoricians who focused on the emotions.

John Rainolds was not the only classroom lecturer who was concerned with the emotions and with defining the characters of audiences. In the Laurentian Library there remain the classroom notes, dated 1586–7, of a set of lectures on Aristotle's *Rhetoric* delivered by Francisco Benci.[31] Benci was a professor of rhetoric, first at Siena and then at Rome, where he later lectured to his Jesuit brethren. The student notes on Benci's lectures indicate what actually was understood in the classroom, flaws and all, rather than simply what was in the master's notes. The manuscript is deceptively titled *In librum secundum rhetoricae Aristotelis*, and internally it looks like scattered bits and pieces of Book 2. But in fact the notes cover a complete reconsideration of character and emotion in the *Rhetoric*, presented to serve the interests and needs of renaissance rhetoricians. All of the *Rhetoric* is represented, not just Book 2, so it is neither the case that we have lost an earlier lecture on Book 1, nor that Benci was unfamiliar with Book 1. The order of the material is important in this manuscript, so let me first recall the general shape of Aristotle's treatise. Book 1 establishes the general definitions and perspectives, discusses the *tria genera causarum* and elaborates the materials proper to each of the three kinds of oratory. Book 2 comes in two parts: the first discusses emotion and character, while the second part discusses enthymemes and commonplaces. Book 3 explores stylistic details along with some mechanics on organising a speech.

Benci's lectures turn this organisation inside out, and they focus upon audience even more than emotion. Benci begins in the middle of Book 2, where Aristotle discusses the characters of audiences according to their ages. First Benci discusses the character of Youth (*Rh.* 2.12), which is an excellent entry point for a set of lectures delivered to young, headstrong, hot-blooded, impatient, amorous and feisty young pupils. In fact, Benci seems to dwell upon the inadequacies of youth, in excess of what Aristotle's text requires. Next comes the character of Older Men (*Rh.* 2.13), done as Theophrastus might have painted Polonius in a cruel moment, followed by the excellent character of men in the prime of life (*Rh.* 2.14). Following the order of Aristotle's text, Benci then covers the Goods of Fortune as they apply to these three characters, ranging over noble birth, wealth and power (*Rh.* 2.15–17). What Benci has done is plunge directly into Aristotle's discussion of character to find the most inclusive statements about the kinds of audiences his students could ever expect to meet: young, middle or old; noble or not, rich or not, powerful or not. This much of Aristotle will remain applicable no matter how many other aspects of his *Rhetoric* may become dated.

Benci next moves across the notorious 'break' in Book 2, Chapter 18, where Aristotle resumes his discussion about enthymemes, which were discussed originally in Book 1. As we read Aristotle's treatise today, this chapter comes as a summary of the *tria genera causarum* and a reprise of what has been discussed in Book 1. But in Benci it instead comes as the very first mention of the *tria genera causarum*, where it shows up in the context of the complete range of possible audiences, and then Benci immediately launches into a very fast summary of the entirety of Book 1. Benci then follows with an equally fast summary of the first nine chapters of Book 2 in which Aristotle discusses each of the emotions at length.

What are we to make of this extraordinary rearrangement and proceeding? Clearly, Benci is completely familiar with all of Aristotle's treatise. Just as clearly, he does not think that Aristotle's discussion of judicial, deliberative and demonstrative rhetoric is all that important. Benci lays out this material accurately, but does not take the time, as many another renaissance commentator will, to try to accommodate renaissance rhetorical practice to Aristotle's *tria genera causarum.* So also with Aristotle's discussion of each of the emotions. What was important to Benci about audiences was elaborated in Aristotle's discussion about the ages and conditions of man. Where Aristotle devotes an entire chapter to each emotion, Benci instead discusses the emotions in the context of the age-group Aristotle suggests as most appropriate: thus the emotion of anger is treated during the discussion of the character of youth. Immediately after these two quick-moving reformulations of Book 1 and half of Book 2, Benci slows down for a very detailed analysis of commonplaces (*Rh.* 2.19), and then proceeds systematically through the remaining chapters of Book 2. In the course of these discussions on fables, maxims, enthymemes and refutations, he has much to say about character and emotions, and relatively little to say about what we might think of as 'logic' or dialectic. He is interested, as he says, in the power and potential of contraries, what we today think of as the 'topical' aspect of Aristotelian enthymemes, and in the impact upon an audience of using shortened and sharpened statements of contraries.[32]

Benci's complete reordering of the *Rhetoric* was not the only way to emphasise the role of emotion and audience. Nathan Chytraeus lectured on the *Rhetoric* at the University of Rostock, apparently using Ermolao Barbaro's translation, and in 1586 he published just his lectures on emotions and character, dismissing all of Book 1 and the second half of Book 2. As Chytraeus reads Aristotle, the character of the audience is paramount, and to it the orator must conform both his own character and the character of his speech.[33]

IV

The materials I have just been discussing were meant for neophytes with Aristotle's *Rhetoric*, where we might expect simplification. But when we turn to the materials intended for experts – to the scholarly editions and commentaries – we find many of the same concerns and an emerging interest in a psychological understanding of the ways of discourse. These concerns often shape the analysis of textual details, and I want now to look at two such details. In Book 1, Aristotle criticises teachers of rhetoric who concentrate primarily on emotional appeals which are ἔξω τοῦ πράγματος, 'extraneous to the πράγματος' (*Rh.* 1354a15). The Greek word πράγματος causes the problem here because the word can mean nearly anything, just like the Latin words *res* and *negotium* which are often used to translate it. In fact, William of Moerbeke uses both Latin words together in his medieval translation of this phrase: *de extrinsecus autem rei plurima negotiantur.*[34] The medieval commentary on Moerbeke by Giles of Rome (ca 1290) manages to preserve Moerbeke's uncertainty: *quae quodammodo sunt extra negotium rhetoricum plura negotiantur.*[35] What, exactly, is this 'thing' – this 'business', this 'subject' – to which emotional appeals are external? Antonio Riccobono, writing in 1588, points out the problem very nicely; the Latin translation *quae sunt extra rem* can mean many things. Some explain it as *extra rhetoricam*, that is, as external to the entire subject of Aristotle's *Rhetoric*. But Riccobono himself prefers *extra causam et quaestionem, qua de agit orator*, that is, as external to the immediate judicial issue confronting the orator at that moment.[36]

George of Trebizond set the early tone for renaissance discussions about emotional appeals at this locus by using the unexplained phrase *quae praeter rem sunt.*[37] Ermolao Barbaro seems to follow along with *res quae extra negotium adhibeantur,*[38] but then Ermolao interpolates his own translation with the explanation that such emotional appeals use artful means to corrupt and suborn the judge.[39] Daniele Barbaro's commentary on Ermolao's translation then explains that emotional appeals do not belong properly to the art of rhetoric, but rather are additions to it. Daniele's explanation then immediately runs foul of itself by legitimising emotional appeals within rhetoric. The art of rhetoric is rational, and it leads opinion. Emotional appeals are used to move from rational opinion to action, and to make up for the mental inadequacies of vulgar auditors.[40]

Commentators today continue to struggle with these same textual details. The representative translation by J. H. Freese, for example, preserves the ambiguity of the Greek ἔξω τοῦ πράγματος with the phrase 'matters outside the subject'.[41] More recently, William Grimaldi has glossed this simple phrase with a two-part expansion as 'those matters extrinsic to the subject of discourse and to the point at issue in the discourse'.[42] Grimaldi solves the problem by accepting both readings at the same time, and in this he follows the renaissance lead of Piero Vettori, who says that emotional appeals *in rebus quae extra causam essent* and that treatises about emotional appeals *implent praeceptis extra rem tradendis.*[43]

At issue, for renaissance and modern commentators alike, is how to reconcile Aristotle's condemnation of emotions in this early

passage with the fact that so much of the *Rhetoric* deals centrally
with the emotions. Much turns on the definition of what constitutes
an emotion, what constitutes a misuse of emotions and what a
legitimate use; and the confident answers of modern commentators
were not always those of their renaissance forbears. Aristotle's
immediate explanation at this point in the text causes as many
problems as it solves; we are told that certain matters are outside the
πρᾶγμα because (and here I use J. H. Freese's translation):

> the arousing of prejudice (διαβολή), compassion, anger, and
> similar emotions has no connexion with the matter in hand, but is
> directed only to the dicast.[44]

The issue of textual detail at this point is how to reconcile the notion
of διαβολή – that is, 'the arousing of prejudice,' or, perhaps better,
'slander' – with the summary phrase 'and similar emotions'. Some
renaissance commentators were not at all troubled. Vettori, for
example, says that 'slander' is not the same kind of thing as
'compassion' and 'anger,' and therefore the summary phrase 'and
similar emotions' simply does not apply to 'slander'.[45] Grimaldi, in
the modern period, is equally untroubled: 'In itself, διαβολή is not an
emotion; it produces an emotion.'[46] But for other writers in the
renaissance, it just was not this simple, and despite the relatively
early date of Vettori's commentary (1548), his authority did not put
the issue to rest.

Marco-Antonio Maioragio, writing about the same time as Vettori
(1547), explains that slander must be understood as a passion of the
mind, as an emotion, and he offers a series of arguments.[47] Antonio
Riccobono, writing four decades later in 1588, still finds it necessary
to refute each of those arguments.[48] Maioragio's first argument is
that whatever agitates the mind is an emotion; slander agitates the
minds of those in whom it is set in motion; therefore slander is an
emotion. Riccobono responds by denying the major proposition,
since emotions are aroused responsively in the mind, and do not of
themselves actively agitate the mind. Maioragio's second argument
is that every violent appetite is a passion; slander is a violent
appetite; therefore slander is a passion. Riccobono cannot deny the
major proposition, since that is a consequence of reading Book 1,
Chapter 10 of the *Rhetoric*, so Riccobono instead denies the minor
proposition: it is true that some violent appetite resides within
slander, but slander itself is not an appetite. This second refutation

is nearly the same as Grimaldi's modern explanation. Maioragio's third argument is equally categorical: that which derives from malevolence is an emotion, and slander derives from malevolence; therefore slander is an emotion. Again, as with the first argument, Riccobono denies the major proposition, saying that while malevolence is indeed an emotion, it is not the case that its derivatives are also emotions. And there are further arguments by Maioragio concerning the derivation of slander, and just what it is that is derived. The last of Maioragio's arguments is a hypothetical, not a categorical syllogism: if engaging in slander constitutes agitation, then slander is an emotion; but the first, therefore the second. Riccobono responds by denying the consequent: it is presumably emotionally distressing to be the object of slander, but it does not follow that slander is emotionally distressing to the slanderer, even if the latter can produce his slander out of emotion.

The question about the word διαβολή is a small textual detail leading to major arguments, and while it is the sort of thing which we today dispense with in a hurry as we move on to what strikes us as more important, in the Renaissance such a dispute was likely to bring the whole enterprise to a halt. Two aspects of this particular debate should be pointed out. First, the ease with which Maioragio, and then in turn Riccobono, slides from categorical syllogisms to hypothetical syllogisms, from the world of peripatetic syllogistic to the world of stoic syllogistic. The relations between these two ways of proceeding have a long history, and I will not broach the problem here other than to say that the conflation of the two has manifold consequences for the renaissance understandings of Aristotelian enthymematic reasoning in the *Rhetoric*. Secondly, as I observed above, Riccobono's second refutation effectively anticipates Grimaldi's modern position, that slander produces emotion without slander actually being an emotion. But two of Riccobono's subsequent arguments – both the third and the last – effectively turn that same argument around, saying that emotion produces slander without slander actually being an emotion. In short, it doesn't much matter to Riccobono which one produces the other, as long as the argument concludes that slander is not an emotion. Riccobono confirms this suspicion when he castigates the author of the *Tabulae Rhetoricae*, who included slander under the heading for πάθη, when what he supposedly meant was the emotion 'hatred'.[49]

It is clear from the vigor of Riccobono's argument that, despite the minuteness of this particular textual detail, the issue itself is important. And indeed it is. There is some sort of relationship between slander and emotion, between διαβολή and πάθη, between social action and private emotion. The relationship troubles Riccobono, and his syllogistic arguments at this locus really do not come to grips with that relationship. He returns to that relationship in his very lengthy commentary on the passions at the beginning of Book 2 of the *Rhetoric*, where he explores peripatetic and stoic conceptions of the emotions. He finally concludes that the stoic conceptions are better for explaining what Aristotle has in mind in the *Rhetoric*. Human emotion, as Riccobono understands it, has a rational aspect to it. Human emotion depends upon some kind of opinion about the present or about the future. Thus human happiness, unlike some mere bestial response, involves a rational thought about what is good in the present, while desire involves a rational thought about what will be good in the future; and conversely with unhappiness and fear.[50] Thus it is for Riccobono that some emotions can legitimately be aroused and not be ἔξω τοῦ πράγματος, since rational thoughts about the question at issue are inextricably bound with human emotions.

V

There are a great many other writers with whom I have not dealt in this chapter – as well as several genres of edition and commentary, along with a good number of problem areas to which I have merely alluded in passing. I want to close by returning to the point from which I started, the emergence of a renaissance interest in the role of the audience in persuasion. It was George of Trebizond who pointed his readers toward the well-springs of human action, the habits of men, their hidden minds, their private emotions. And in this respect the contribution of renaissance perspectives on Aristotle's *Rhetoric* may well be in advance of our own. From the seventeenth century on into the present century, discussions by commentators have neatly distributed Aristotle's three available means of persuasion – logical aspects within the speech itself, emotion within the audience and character for the speaker. Some of the renaissance writers mentioned in this chapter clearly agreed with this distribution. But some of the others saw it quite differently, and thought that Aristotle's *Rhetoric* made no sense if distributed like this. Riccobono, for one, thinks that he is merely summarising the best of received opinion when he looks at character and finds that character, like emotion, is evenly distributed between the speaker and his audience. In Book 1 Aristotle speaks about the character of the speaker (*Rh.* 1.2), in Book 2 he speaks about the character of the audience (*Rh.* 2.12–18), and in Book 3 he speaks about the character of the spoken and written *logos* (*Rh.* 3.8). All three provide persuasive resources for the artful rhetorician.

This very position currently is being debated afresh, and George of Trebizond's overblown claims for the psychological aspects of Aristotle's *Rhetoric* may well prove to be close to the mark, that is, close to our own mark. I do not suggest that we today have an understanding of Aristotle that is sufficiently stable to enable us condemn or applaud renaissance efforts. It was a struggle for renaissance writers to make sense of Aristotle's *Rhetoric*, just as it continues to be a struggle for commentators today.

Notes and References

1. These renaissance traditions are discussed in greater detail in my study on 'The Renaissance Reception of Aristotle's *Rhetoric*', in William Fortenbaugh (ed.), *Rutgers University Studies in Classical Humanities*, vol. 6 (forthcoming). In the present study I indicate within my text the date of the original publication of early materials. All translations, except as noted, are my own.
2. See the census in Paul D. Brandes, *A History of Aristotle's Rhetoric: with a Bibliography of Early Printings* (Metuchen, NJ and London, 1989). Brandes should still be supplemented with F. Edward Cranz and Charles B. Schmitt, *A Bibliography of Aristotle Editions, 1501–1600*, 2nd edn (Baden-Baden, 1984); with the inventories of renaissance Latin commentaries by Charles H. Lohr SJ, in *Studies in the Renaissance*, vol. XXI (1974), *Renaissance Quarterly*, vol. XXVIII (1975), vol. XXXIII (1980), vol. XXXV (1982); and with James J. Murphy, *Renaissance Rhetoric: A Short-Title Catalogue on Rhetorical Theory from the Beginning of Printing to A.D. 1700* (New York and London, 1981).
3. See John O. Ward, 'From Antiquity to the Renaissance: Glosses and Commentaries on Cicero's Rhetorica', in James J. Murphy (ed.), *Medieval Eloquence: Studies in the Theory and Practice of Medieval Rhetoric* (Berkeley, Los Angeles, London, 1978), pp. 25–67.
4. See John Monfasani (ed.), *Collectanea Trapezuntiana: Texts, Documents, and Bibliographies of George of Trebizond* (Binghampton, NY, 1984), pp. 459–61. For Trebizond's place in the history of rhetoric, see Monfasani, *George of Trebizond: A Biography and a Study of his Rhetoric and Logic* (Leiden, 1976).
5. Pletho's controversial lecture was known in the West as 'De Platonicae et Aristotelicae philosophiae differentia'. C.M. Woodhouse has

translated the lecture as *On the Differences of Aristotle from Plato in George Gemistos Plethon: The Last of the Hellenes* (Oxford, 1986). The critical edition by B. Legard, 'Le *De Differentiis* de Pléthon d'après l'autographe de la Marcienne', *Byzantion*, vol. XLIII (1973), pp. 312–43, should still be consulted, as should the earlier edition of 1923. For the history of this controversy, see Deno John Geanakoplos, *Greek Scholars in Venice: Studies in the Dissemination of Greek Learning from Byzantium to Western Europe* (Cambridge, MA, 1962), pp. 85–92, and now Geanakoplos, *Constantinople and the West: Essays on the Late Byzantine (Palaeologan) and Italian Renaissances and the Byzantine and Roman Churches* (Madison, 1989), passim. See also Paul Oskar Kristeller, 'Byzantine and Western Platonism in the Fifteenth Century', *Renaissance Thought and Its Sources* (New York, 1979), pp. 150–68.

6. Those aspects of Trebizond's vituperative *Comparationes Aristotelis et Platonis* (1455) significant for the history of rhetoric are discussed in detail in Green, 'Renaissance Reception'; see note 1 above.

7. George of Trebizond (Georgius Trapezuntius, 1395–1484), *In tres rhetoricorum Aristotelis libros ad Theodecten tralatio*, in *Continentur hoc volumine . . .* (Venice, 1523), p. 109: 'Mirum enim est sic ipsum omnia de moribus hominum per diversas aetates atque fortunas prudenter invenisse, distincte explicasse, ornate conscripisse, ut nihil ab eo praetermissum esse videatur. nec secreta naturae solum, ut summus omnium philosophus, sed abditas quoque hominum mentes, motusque reconditos non iniuria percepisse putetur.' My text is the Aldine edition, but the passage appears in all manuscripts and editions; see Monfasani, *Collectanea*, pp. 90–1; 206–8.

8. Juan Luis de Vives (Johannes Lodovicus Vives, 1492–1540), *De tradendis disciplinis*, in Gregorio Mayáns y Siscar (ed.), *Joannis Ludovici Vivis Valentini Opera Omnia*, 8 vols. (Valencia, 1782–90; reprinted London: Gregg Press, 1964), vol. 6, p. 358: 'opus magni quidem ingenii ac artis, quod in hoc auctore est perpetuum, sed ingentis quoque utilitatis ad sensum et prudentiam vitae communis'.

9. Vives, *De tradendis disciplinis*, in *Opera*, vol. 6, p. 357: 'perturbate, confuseque est olim a majoribus nostris praeceptum, minimeque ad usum congruenter'.

10. Vives, *De Aristotelis operibus censura*, in *Opera*, vol. 3, pp. 36–7: 'Aristoteles vero, ab ultima origine tota hac disciplina repetita, ita perduxit ad summum, ut nihil videatur deesse, explicata inventione, dispositione, elocutione, admista ingenti sententiarum copia, et gravissimis monitis ad usum forensem ac civilem instructa pruden-tia; plane ut dialectices, ita etiam rhetorices inventor existimari debet Aristoteles'. Vives's language in this section is nearly identical to the phrasing used by Trebizond in his prologue to Aristotle's *Rhetoric*; see note 7 above.

11. Vives, *De ratione dicendi*, in *Opera*, vol. 2, p. 92: 'eo sunt falsi, quod arbitrantur universam dicendi artem ea parte concludi, quae est de verbis, velut de schematibus, de tropis, de periodis, et concentu dictionis, quae non tam ad dicendi corpus ipsum, et quasi substantiam faciunt, quam ad dicendi decorem atque ornamenta'. Vives's reference

to the 'body of speaking' reflects the contemporary debates over Aristotle's phrasing in the opening chapter of his treatise; see Green, 'Renaissance Reception'.

12. Vives, *De consultatione*, in *Opera*, vol. 2, p. 254: 'Affectus non sunt in hoc genere, ut in aliis nonnullis, concitandi et perturbandi, propterea quod alienum id videtur a gravitate et probitate, quae in consultationibus exigitur'.

13. Vives, *De consultatione*, in *Opera*, vol. 2, p. 247: 'apud majorem modestius et reverentius, principem praesertim, sed sic ut absit assentatio, quae grata initio, post cognita omnem adimit fidem, neque vero huic ita consulendum, tamquam praecipias imperito, nisi puer sit, et ejus aetatem regas'.

14. Vives, *De consultatione*, in *Opera*, vol. 2, p. 248: 'perspiciendum et ingenium, et mores ejus cui consulis, eisque aptanda oratio, docto docta, ingenioso acuta, hebeti crassior, ac apertior, supercilioso callida, humano liberior fiducia, ut ostendas sumpta ex eis moribus'.

15. Vives, *De consultatione*, in *Opera*, vol. 2, p. 248: 'attemperanda et conditioni ejus qui dicit, non eadem auctoritate aut gravitate juvenis qua senex, ineruditus qua doctus, subnixus sapientiae opinioni ac qui eam non est nactus, pauper qua dives, ignotus qua familiaris, peregrinus qua civis, miles qua dux; in quibusdam sufficit auctoritas, alios vix res ipsa et veritas tuetur'.

16. As translated in the first English edition of *The Art of Speaking* (1676), 'We may say any thing if the person to whom we speak be convinc'd that we love him. Ama, & dic quod vis [Augustine, *In Joannem*, 7.8]'; see John T. Harwood (ed.), *The Rhetorics of Thomas Hobbes and Bernard Lamy* (Carbondale and Edwardsville, 1986), p. 354.

17. Vives, *De consultatione*, in *Opera*, vol. 2, pp. 245, 246. On this point, see Iris Grace Gonzalez, *Juan Luis Vives: His Contributions to Rhetoric and Communication in the Sixteenth Century with an English Translation of 'De Consultatione'* (PhD dissertation, Indiana University, 1973), p. 67. The translation must be used with great care.

18. Daniele Barbaro (Danielus Barbarus, 1514–70), Ermolao Barbaro (Hermolaus Barbarus, 1454–93), *Aristotelis rhetoricorum libri tres, Hermolao Barbaro Patricio Veneto interprete, Danielis Barbari in eosdem libros commentarii* (Basel, 1545).

19. Daniele Barbaro's reading of Aristotle is filtered through unusual readings of both Plato and Cicero. Plato in the *Gorgias* denigrates rhetoric by saying that it has the same relationship to dialectic as the practice of cooking has to the art of medicine. Both rhetoric and cooking represent a kind of flattery, the one of the soul, the other of the palate, and both are, in a sense, immoral cheats. Daniele apparently has confused Aristotle's statements about medicine at *Rhetoric* 1355b28 with Plato's statements in the *Phaedrus*, and tried to ignore Plato's *Gorgias*, all in an effort to put rhetoric on the same footing as medicine as a practical art, in which right thinking (*animae rectum sensum*) is on a par with good health.

20. Barbaro, *Commentarii*, p. 3: 'Animae vis quaedam appetens est, qua quidem ipsa fertur in aliquid, vel incitatur: sed illud aliquid, vel id

intelligitur, quod ratio, et mens ostendit: vel id, quod sensus temerarius exposcit. In priori loco Voluntas est posita, in posteriori duplex Ratio: nam aut irarum fluctu aestuat, aut cupiditatum illecebris commovetur. Hinc illud, quod homo cum unus sit, duos habet consultores, Iracundiam, et Cupiditatem: in quibus voluptas inest, et dolor. Accedit ratio quidem media, quae alio nos modo movet, quam vel ira: vel cupiditas. In voluntate virtutum maxime omnium Iustitia collocatur'.

21. Barbaro, *Commentarii*, p. 4: 'si non obtemperat, adversis vitiorum fluctibus agitata, modo timet, modo audet, interim abiecta, interim elata, saepe nihil commota et quasi stupida omnem vitae turpitudinem gignit'. Daniele Barbaro's account of Anger is complicated by his apparently not being aware of the synonymy in Aristotle's *Rhetoric* between ὀργή and θυμός ('anger' and 'passion'), although Ermolao Barbaro may have realised it. As a result we are not justified, as we are with other commentators, in translating his *ira* as the more general 'violent passion', and this makes for difficulties later.

22. Barbaro, *Commentarii*, p. 5: 'auditor enim non est satis idoneus, ut magnis de rebus, tam brevi tempore, quale est Oratori praescriptum, vel doceatur, vel certus fiat'.

23. Barbaro, *Commentarii*, p. 5: 'Ut ergo opinionem inducat, necesse est ut eos dicendo excitet consultores, quos in animis nostris natura posuit, et insignivit: Mentem scilicet, Iracundiam, et Cupiditatem, quibus quasi nervis, quo velit nos pertrahat, et deducat.'

24. Barbaro, *Commentarii*, p. 5: 'vis in concitando, lenitas in conciliando ponetur'. Barbaro makes no distinction between *delectare* and *conciliare*, leading to such locutions as *conciliando cupiditatem*.

25. Barbaro, *Commentarii*, p. 178, at *Rh.* 1.6.23.

26. Rudolph Agricola (Roelof Huusman, Rodolphus Agricola Phrisius, 1444–85), *De inventione dialectica libri omnes* (Cologne, 1539), bk. 3, ch. 1, *De affectibus quid sint, et unde oriantur*, pp. 575–6: 'Sane Aristoteles in eis libris quos de rhetorice conscripsit, multos enumerat, et quid sit quisque, quibusque rebus oriatur, extinguaturque rursus, copiosissime prosequitur: ut fuit vir ille ingeniosissimus, omnique rerum copia instructissimus'.

27. See Lawrence D. Green (trans. and ed.), *John Rainolds's Oxford Lectures on Aristotle's 'Rhetoric'* (Newark, London and Toronto, 1986), p. 388: 'Eloquentia duplex est alia vitae, alia linguae: illa sine ista multum prodest; ista sine illa plurimum obest. Istam a Cicerone discimus, illam a Christo discamus.'

28. Green, *Rainolds's Lectures*, pp. 279–99.

29. Rainolds was strongly influenced by the views Vives expressed on these matters in *De causis corruptibus artium*, bk 4; in *Opera*, vol. 6, p. 155ff.

30. Green, *Rainolds's Lectures*, pp. 150–2: 'Quamobrem ut paucis concludamus quod pluribus disservimus, commovendi sunt affectus, non ut noceant sed ut prosint, non ut recta depravent sed ut prava dirigant, ut vitium, iniquitatem, flagitia propulsent; virtutem, iustitiam, probitatem, propugnent.'

31. Francisco Benci (Franciscus Bencius, 1542–94), *In librum secundum rhetoricae Aristotelis*, Laurentian MS Redi. 13 (136); not listed in Lohr's census. In the Vatican there is another manuscript of lectures by Benci, presumably of this same set of lectures on the *Rhetoric* (MS Gregorianae 1170 [xvii]), and the description of the Vatican manuscript might serve just as well for this Laurentian manuscript: *in dimidium secundi libri atque in tertium integrum.*

32. I do not wish to get into the intricacies of Book 3 of the *Rhetoric*, since this represents a different strand in the renaissance effort to make sense of Aristotle, but it is worth pointing out that Benci appears, on the face of things, seriously dissatisfied with what Aristotle offers. Having concluded his lectures on the first two books from the point of view of audience and emotion, he starts his lectures on Book 3 with a long account of tropes and figures, very much in the tradition of the *Ad Herennium* and any number of medieval collections, and follows it with a very basic discussion of metrics, primarily a listing of kinds of rhythms and meters. None of this is Aristotelian, and most of what Aristotle actually does have to say about local features of language and style is simply ignored. The lectures end by returning to Aristotle's comments in Book 3 about the formal parts of an oration, of which Aristotle countenances only four: exordium, narration, confirmation and peroration. In short, Books 1 and 2 of Aristotle's *Rhetoric*, if approached correctly, were of enormous use in understanding how to address the characters and passions of men, about how to manipulate opinion by manipulating the passions and faculties that determine opinion. But Book 3 added nothing to what was not already available through the Ciceronian tradition; that book needed to be augmented by better and later studies, and presumably could even be ignored. And in fact this is borne out by other evidence. Contemporaneously with these lectures, Francisco Benci produced a posthumous octavo edition of Marc-Antoine Muret's translation of the *Rhetoric* (Rome, 1585); the edition includes only Books 1 and 2.

33. Nathan Chytraeus (1543–98), Ἦθη καὶ πάθη, *seu de affectibus movendis, Aristotelis ex II. rhetoricum doctrina, accurate et perspicue explicata in academia Rostochiana* (Herborn, 1586), p. 122.

34. See Bernd Schneider (ed.), *Aristoteles Latinus XXXI.1–2: Rhetorica* (Leiden: E.J. Brill, 1978), *Translatio Guillelmi de Moerbeka*, p. 159.17–18.

35. Giles of Rome (Egidio Colonna, Aegidius Romanus ca. 1243/7–1316), *Expositio super tribus libris rhetoricorum* (Venice, 1515), fol. 2 verso.

36. Antonio Riccobono (Antonius Riccobonus, 1541–99), *Paraphrasis in rhetoricam Aristotelis, interiecta rerum difficiliorum explicatione, & collata ipsius Riccoboni multis in locis conversione, cum Maioragii, Sigonii, Victorii, Mureti conversionibus* (Hanau, 1606), p. 18.

37. Trebizond, *Rhetoricorum libri III* (Venice, 1523), p. 109; see note 7 above.

38. Ermolao Barbaro, in Daniele Barbaro, *Commentarii*, p. 16.

39. Ermolao Barbaro, in Daniele Barbaro, *Commentarii*, p. 16: 'non ad negotium, sed ad vendicandum ac subeundum variis artibus iudicem comparantur'.

40. Barbaro, *Commentarii*, p. 21: 'Dixi, mentem esse, in qua scientia et opinio residet: dixi Oratoris munus esse, opinionem inducere. quibus positis, et concessis, iam videtur opinio ratione induci debere, quoniam ratio sola mentem movet: affectus autem non movent tantum, sed vim quandam etiam adhibent, non ut mens opinetur, quod ratio intendit, sed ut obsequatur, ut perturbetur, ut suo se iudicio privet, alienam libidinem persequatur: quare cum ars ad mentem adhibeatur, sola ratione niti debet.'
41. John Henry Freese (trans.), *Aristotle: The 'Art' of Rhetoric* (Cambridge, MA, and London, 1926; reprinted 1975).
42. William M. A. Grimaldi SJ, *Aristotle, 'Rhetoric' I: A Commentary* (New York, 1980), 1.9.
43. Piero Vettori (Petrus Victorius, 1499–1585), *Commentarii in tres libros Aristotelis de arte dicendi* (Florence, 1548), p. 7.
44. *Rhetoric*, 1354a 16–18.
45. Vettori, *Commentarii*, pp. 7–8: 'Qui naturam perturbationum, quae πάθη Graeci appellant, cognitam non haberet, falli hic posset. Et existimare διαβολὴν commotionem animi esse. quamvis igitur Aristoteles addat, καὶ τὰ τοιαῦτα πάθη τῆς ψυχῆς, criminationem non videtur intellexisse: neque unam ex illis esse voluisse: sed posteriores duas tantum res. idest misericordiam et iracundiam, caeterasque, quae eandem naturam haberent, complexum esse . . . Hanc non malam rationem esse putavi huius loci explicandi. qui autem complecti quoque πάθος criminationem, tueri vellet, illuc confugere (ut arbitror) deberet.'
46. Grimaldi, *Commentary*, 1.10–11.
47. Marco-Antonio Maioragio (Marcantonio Majoragio, Marcus Antonius Maiorgius, Maria Antonio de' Conti, 1514–55), *In tres Aristotelis libros, de arte rhetorica, quos ipse latinos fecit, explicationes* (Venice, 1572), fol. 5 recto-verso.
48. Riccobono, *Paraphrasis*, pp. 19–20.
49. Riccobono, *Paraphrasis*, p. 20: 'In eodem errore versatus est amicus meus, qui in Tabulis Rhetoricis inter πάθη enumeravit criminationem, quae odium gignit'. The offending friend was Raphael Cyllenius, in *Tabulae rhetoricae, quibus omnia, quae ab Aristotele de arte dicendi libris, et a Demetrio Phalereo suo de elocutione libello tradiat sunt, praecepta fidissime, et planissime explicantur* (Venice, 1571), p. 2: 'Extra artem, et quasi additamenta, ut πάθη, idest affectus Criminatio odium, Misericordia, Iracundia.'
50. Riccobono, *Paraphrasis*, p. 196: 'Has inter se tam diversas, discrepantesque sententias idem amicus noster in definitione affectus coniungere conatus est, ut ex doctrina Stoicorum tradiderit, affectum esse commotionem animi, aversam a recta ratione, inimicam menti, eiusque tranquillitati, ex opinione boni aut praesentis, aut futuri, et ex opinione mali similiter aut praesentis, aut futuri: atque ex praeceptione Aristotelis addiderit: per quam cum se immutent, differunt indicationibus: omittens illud, quam sequitur molestia, et voluptas. Nec fortasse animadvertit, allatam ab Aristotele definitionem affectibus tum bonis, tum malis convenire, veramque esse quodam

modo de affectibus etiam bestiarum, quae vim habent irascendi, ac concupiscendi, perinde ac homines: illam vero alteram omnes affectus damnare tamquam malos, et hominibus tantum tribuere. Quod quam recte, aliorum sit iudicium.'

2

Ghosting the Reform of Dialectic: Erasmus and Agricola Again

Lisa Jardine

In an earlier piece of work I have begun to tell the story of how Erasmus master-minded the recovery, editing, commentary and circulation of the text of Rudolph Agricola's key work in dialectic, the *De inventione dialectica*.[1] The charismatic and inspirational nature of Rudolph Agricola's example in the Low Countries, as the first native-born scholar to bring Italian humanism back to northern Europe, is not in doubt. But the model he offered was largely as a living figure: at his death he left few, and relatively inconsequential published works, and little (as it emerged) suitable for publication by those concerned to convince an international readership of the eminence and stature of their greatest home-grown humanist.[2] In the book of which both the present and the previous piece of textual detective work form a part, I show how Erasmus intervened repeatedly in the history of Agricola's works, to generate, and then to consolidate, a reputation in *print* to match the example which the great Frisian humanist had estabished during his lifetime. I also argue that this was no disinterested move on Erasmus's part: that at the height of Erasmus's own publishing career, Agricola's reputation served to provide the institutionally non-aligned Erasmus with a respectable intellectual pedigree as the inheritor of a 'tradition' of northern humanism – as the chosen son on whom Agricola's mantle had fallen.[3]

The present chapter began as an attempt to understand, in the light of Erasmus's respect for Agricola's *De inventione dialectica* and his involvement in its emendation (or possibly rewriting) for publication, how we should read Erasmus's own, equivalently widely read and influential schoolroom textbook, *De copia*. What quickly transpired, however, was that having once proposed that an intellectual milieu is being consciously stage-managed by assiduous intervention in the editing, publishing and dissemination of texts, the traditional intellectual–historical concept of a 'context' for a work is altered: transformed from a fixed frame to an animate and active one. In this case, a work like *De copia* does not simply need to be inserted into a succession of related texts, printed around the same time, by those who read and responded to each others' works. Rather, *De copia* might depend for its 'meaning' on our restoring it to a setting consisting of a collection of disparate texts, all to a greater or lesser extent sponsored by Erasmus, and published with the conscious intention of creating a network of mutually supporting and reinforcing significance. What makes this version of intellectual historical influence distinctive, is that it is quite possible to find that the group of sponsored works which give meaning to a selected work of lasting significance need not lie within a single 'field', in our modern sense – may not all be texts deemed to belong to the 'history of dialectic', for example, in the case of texts giving meaning to Agricola's *De inventione dialectica*. And indeed, what emerged in the case of *De copia*, as the present paper will show, was that the meaning of *De copia* was intimately and inextricably bound up with the publishing history of the prose works of Seneca, rather than that of more obviously 'rhetorical' works.

FINDING A CONTEXT FOR 'COPIA': FOLLOWING THE PUBLISHING TRAIL AGAIN

One of Erasmus's earliest public remarks linking his own enterprise with that of Rudolph Agricola occurs as a pendant closing paragraph – a kind of afterthought as it seems – to a preface to *De copia*. At the end of the new prefatory letter to the 1514 edition, addressed to the printer, Erasmus wrote:

> We are eagerly expecting at any moment the *Lucubrationes* of Rudolph Agricola (a truly inspired man). Whenever I read his writings, I venerate and give fervent praise to that sacred and heavenly spirit.[4]

Erasmus is here drawing the reader's attention to the small volume of Agricola's *Opuscula*, edited by Faber, published in 1508 (the first

volume to make any works of Agricola available other than as
fragmented and isolated items in other people's works). And the
link between Agricola and 'copia' to which Erasmus is referring is
made in a letter – prominently printed there and much reprinted
thereafter – known as 'De formando studio'.[5] At the end of the 'De
formando studio', a passage occurs which includes the Latin term
copia for the assembling and deployment of linguistic material, and
refers the reader in search of further advice on copia to De inventione
dialectica.[6]

If this allusion to Agricola as having been engaged in something
like the same project as himself is implicit rather than explicit,
Erasmus is more direct in a letter to Budé in October 1516, published
in the Epistolae elegantes, edited by Gilles and published by Martens
in 1517. There Erasmus writes:

After [De copia] was published I discovered a certain amount in
Rudolphus Agricola.[7]

Here Erasmus is certainly referring to De inventione dialectica,
published the previous year, with his own support, also by
Martens, at Louvain.[8] And indeed, Dorp's letter to the reader,
which introduces that volume, explicitly links the two projects –
copia and dialectical invention – as part of the same larger
enterprise.[9]

What all this suggests is that we should take a close and serious
look at what might conceivably be considered to be the relationship
between Agricola's De inventione dialectica, which is persistently
characterised in the literature as a revised, humanistic handbook of
dialectic for technical argumentatio, and Erasmus's De copia, which is
equally consistently described as a compilation of 'abundant speech'
– of creative, and above all unstructured, linguistic virtuosity. Both
texts have proved curiously resistant to critical attention. In spite of
the efforts of historians of dialectic (including myself), De inventione
dialectica has continued to appear cryptic and internally incoher-
ent.[10] De copia is a similarly unreadable text, I suggest, for similar
reasons – we can construe it, we can translate it, we can recognise
some of its sources and indebtednesses, but we cannot recognise a
purpose for it, beyond the trite one of simple 'resourcing' –
accumulation of material. Yet Erasmus is insistent that copia is
abundance without redundancy: we therefore need a reading which
allows us to recognise due, apt or appropriate abundance. This

paper sets out to recover a specifically northern renaissance intellectual context, and identifies associated, familiar texts, to enable us to reconstruct the problem towards whose solution both texts were envisaged as contributing.[11]

'ALIUM PRODIDI SENECAM': REVISING SENECA

In the preface to his *Lucubrationes* of Seneca (1515), Erasmus brackets Seneca and Jerome together, as the two great masters of eloquence – pagan and Christian.[12] As Erasmus pointed out, Jerome himself had expressed the highest regard for Seneca, and considered him worthy of respect as quasi-Christian:

> Jerome is the one author in sacred literature whom we can match even against the Greeks; without him I simply do not see whom we could put into the field who really deserves the name of theologian, if we are allowed to speak the truth. And Seneca was so highly valued by St Jerome that alone among Gentiles he was recorded in the *Catalogue of Illustrious Authors*, not so much on account of the letters exchanged between Seneca and Paul (which, being a critic of keen discernment, Jerome well knew were written by neither of them, though he made thorough use of them as a pretext for praising Seneca [*tametsi ad autoris commendationem hoc est abusus praetextu*]), as because he thought him the one writer who, while not a Christian, deserved to be read by Christians.[13]

This prefatory passage supports a Christianised reading of Seneca, and argues for the suitability of Seneca as a guide to Christian morals.[14] Erasmus's *Lucubrationes* of Seneca set out to provide the basis for serious collation of pagan and Christian moral thought, and pagan and Christian *eloquentia*.

But, more than any other work for which he had acted as 'castigator', Erasmus's edition of the prose works of Seneca proved unsatisfactory from the outset. The inadequate nature of the text was already announced on the table of contents;[15] and some extremely shoddy proof-reading had resulted in garbled pageheaders, misnumberings, and other confusions which make the volume difficult to use.[16] In one of his later published letters, Erasmus provided an elaborate story to explain why this had been the case:

the inexperienced junior *castigatores* Nesen and Beatus Rhenanus had been left in charge of the volume in Basle while Erasmus was unavoidably elsewhere. As a result, he claimed, the published volume was hopelessly botched.[17] But Nesen acted as proof-corrector for the 1517 Froben *De copia*, which carried a dedicatory letter to him, and Beatus Rhenanus remained closely involved with Erasmus's publications for many years. It was, moreover, Erasmus's standard practice to produce major editions at speed in collaboration with more junior editors and *castigatores*.[18] This arrangement could, however, conveniently provide grounds on which publicly to announce a change of heart over a published text.[19] Between 1515 and 1529 (when he published a revised Seneca edition) Erasmus had decisively rejected many of the '*spuria*' which had traditionally formed a significant part of the composite 'Seneca's' *oeuvre*, and had considerably modified his representation of the textual significance of Seneca, by clarifying the standard text.[20] There was every reason for him to disclaim the hastily issued 1515 edition, and to replace it with something more authoritative.

The 1529 edition was so substantially revised, according to Erasmus, that it was 'an entirely new Seneca'.[21] The features of this volume which distinguish it most strikingly from the first edition are the decisive separation of authentic from spurious texts, and a considerable amount of additional editorial material.[22] Whereas the 1515 *Lucubrationes* were 'a' Seneca, this volume is definitively 'Erasmus's' Seneca. But it is more than that, as we shall shortly see.

In a number of places in this volume Erasmus's own magisterial voice directs the reader's attention. In addition to a new preface, he added introductions to a number of the individual works, including the 'Seneca/St Paul' letters. In that introduction he rejects the authenticity of the correspondence vigorously and explicitly, specifying some of the textual grounds on which he does so.[23] To illustrate the glaring anomalies which betray these letters as forgeries, Erasmus singles out for especially contemptuous comment a passage in the ninth letter, from Seneca to Paul. 'It is a sign of monumental stupidity', writes Erasmus, 'when [the forger] makes Seneca send Paul a book *De copia verborum* so that he will be able to write better Latin. If Paul did not know Latin he could have written in Greek. Seneca did know Greek. Why should it be that when Seneca teaches that philosophical discourse ought to consist of serious *sententiae* rather than ornate diction, he now requires *copia* of Roman speech in Paul?'[24]

The letter to which Erasmus here refers is extremely brief, and
may be quoted in full, so that we can imagine its full impact, if one
believed (as both Jerome and Augustine appeared to, and as
renaissance readers continued to do) that it was genuinely by
Seneca:

> I know that it was not so much for your own sake that you were
> disturbed when I wrote to you that I had read [your] letters to
> Caesar as because of the nature of things, which summons the
> minds of men away from all upright pursuits and practices, – so
> that I am not astonished in the present instance, particularly
> because I have learned this well from many sure proofs. Therefore
> let us begin anew, and if in the past I have been negligent in any
> way, you will grant pardon. I have sent you a book on facility in
> using words [*De verborum copia*]. Farewell, dearest Paul.[25]

Here, apparently, Seneca indicates his approval *qua* pagan
rhetorician and moralist for Paul's *Epistles*, which has led him
supposedly to show them to Nero. And he offers some kind of
collaboration with Paul, based on a text of his on the '*ars bene
dicendi*'. However clumsy the letter, its sentiments were such as to
make it attractive to a Christian humanist. When, in both editions of
the Seneca, Erasmus explains that he includes the spurious works
because of their historical importance for the formation of 'Seneca's'
reputation in the Christian world, it is these letters which are
crucially at issue.

The forcefulness of Erasmus's denunciation of the authenticity of
the letters in the 1529 Seneca may be connected in part with his
embarrassment that, in spite of his prefatory remarks about *spuria*,
authentic and spurious texts were not satisfactorily distinguished in
the earlier edition.[26] After all this vehemence, then, it is intriguing to
find that in the list which Erasmus provides of works of Seneca
'which are no longer extant' (*quae non extant*), below the table of
contents of the 1529 *Opera* of Seneca, a *Liber De copia* nevertheless
features prominently.[27] The only evidence for Seneca's having ever
written a *Liber de copia* is the supposed reference to it in one of
'Seneca's' letters to St Paul. So in spite of his insistence that he has
always had grounds for regarding the Seneca/St Paul correspondence as a forgery, it appears that the tantalising suggestion found
there that Seneca might have written a pedagogic work on
eloquentia specifically for a Christian writer, captured and held
Erasmus's attention.[28]

AGRICOLA'S ANNOTATED SENECA:
'TANTUM OBVOLVAS ILLUM TUNICIS CHARTACEIS,
UT SUMMUM OPERCULUM SIT LINTEUM CERATUM'

The new preface to the 1529 Seneca is in fact a full introduction, lavishly furnished with instructions on how the reader is to treat the work. It speaks out with the clear voice of Erasmian authority (as the 1515 edition, to Erasmus's own chagrin, did not). Immediately following the careful rededication – emphasising how entirely new the work is (hence entitled to a new dedicatee to match), Erasmus specifies his sources for this *renovatio*. Among those sources, Erasmus tells his reader, was a printed Seneca which once belonged to Rudolph Agricola, and carries marginal corrections in his own hand:

> I have produced another Seneca . . . The efforts of Matthaeus Fortunatus of Pannonia helped us a great deal with this labour (a man, as you may see, of precise learning, diligence, and of sober and sound judgement). For he accurately revised and corrected [the text] of the *Quaestiones naturales*: if only he had executed all the other works as well! Although we followed him freely in many places, we disagreed with him in not a few, above all where the exemplars supported our sense. A codex printed fifty years ago at Treviso, and which belonged to Rudolph Agricola was of great use to us, which he seemed to have read over with great vigilance. This is clear from the annotations in his own hand, where in innumerable places he had corrected the text. In many places he had done so, apparently, by following his own intuitions, rather than by basing his decision on an ancient exemplar. Indeed, it is amazing how much this obviously superhuman man [*vir plane diuinus*] arrived at by guesswork. For I am not able to sum up Rudolphus's many and extraordinary talents more conveniently. Haio Hermann the Frisian made the riches of Agricola's codex available to us – a young man born with such a wealth of native qualities that he seems the only one suitable to succeed Agricola's fame, and to maintain the glorious reputation of such a man.

(Alium [prodidi] Senecam: . . . Adiuuit in hoc labore nonnihil industria Matthaei Fortunati Pannonii, hominis, vt res indicat, exacte docti, diligentis, sobrii sanique iudicii. Is enim Naturalium

Quaestionum [librum] accuratissime recognouit: quod operae vtinam et in caeteris omnibus praestitisset! Quem vt in plerisque libenter sequuti sumus, ita in nonnullis ab eo dissentimus, praesertim vbi nostro sensui suffragabantur exemplaria. Profuit et Rodolphi Agricolae codex typis excusus Taruisii, ante annos quinquaginta: quem is vigilantissime videtur euoluisse. Arguebant hoc notulae manus ipsius, quibus innumera loca correxerat, sed in multis, vt apparebat, diuinationem ingenii sequutus magis quam exemplaris vetusti fidem. Incredibile vero quam multa diuinarit vir ille plane diuinus; non enim possum Rodolphi dotes et plurimas et eximias complecti breuius. Eius codicis nobis copiam fecit Hayo Hermannus Phrysius, iuuenis tam felici natus indole vt vnus videatur idoneus qui Rodolphicae laudis successionem capessat, tantique viri gloriam sustineat.)[29]

Haio Hermann's connection with the retrieval of the works of Rudolph Agricola is comparatively well-documented.[30] Haio Hermann was at the Lily in Louvain with Erasmus in 1519 (and acted as a trusted courier for him between Paris and Louvain). He went to Italy to study, and obtained a doctorate in civil and canon law. On his return north, he married Anna, daughter of Pompeius Occo. Occo, it will be recalled, had inherited Rudolph Agricola's papers from his uncle Adolph Occo, who had attended Agricola during his last illness. In a letter of March 1528, published shortly afterwards in the *Opus epistolarum,* Erasmus congratulated Hermann on his marriage, and urged him to edit the extant works of Agricola.[31]

Hermann published one small translation of Agricola's in 1530[32] but, in spite of Erasmus's flattery, he did not in the end edit his countryman's works.[33] In October 1528, however, Erasmus wrote to Hermann to finalise arrangements for the transport of the precious Treviso Seneca, copiously annotated by Agricola. So Erasmus's flattery had evidently been successful in establishing access to hitherto inaccessible Agricola texts. The letter (also published in the 1529 *Opus epistolarum* volume) is strikingly explicit about the care with which the book is to be transported, and the way in which access to it will be withheld conscientiously from anyone except its intended recipient:

They have begun the Seneca. For we were fully prepared as far as the *De Beneficiis.* Meanwhile we have sent this courier at our own cost, for no other purpose except to bring back to us your codex. Concerning which you need have no fears whatsoever: apart from myself no-one else will touch it. You should wrap it up in numerous coatings made of paper, in such a way that the topmost covering is of linen coated with wax. I will return it with the same care. I will have the opportunity in the preface of commemorating your name with honour, if you will allow. I do not know what codices Vives has seen, unless perhaps yours, or that which a certain friend spent some time collating at the house of Thomas More. In truth, I have accumulated such a collection of annotations that I fear neither that codex nor your own.

(Senecam exorsi sunt; nam ad libros De Beneficiis eramus abunde instructi. Interim hunc veredarium emisimus nostro sumptu, non ob aliud nisi vt nobis adferat tuum codicem: cui nihil est quod metuas; praeter vnum me nullus illum contiget. Tantum obuoluas illum tunicis chartaceis, ita vt summum operculum sit linteum ceratum; remittetur eadem diligentia. In praefatione dabitur oportunitas honorifice commemorandi tui nominis, si modo id pateris. Quos codices viderit Viues nescio, nisi forte tuum, aut eum qui per amicum quendam collatus aliquamdiu fuit apud Thomam Morum. Verum mihi tanta sylua annotationum congesta est vt nec illius nec tuum codicem metuam.)[34]

A letter to Haio Hermann when the volume was returned to him, also published in the 1529 collection, *Opus epistolarum Erasmi*, once again emphasises the importance Erasmus attached to the loaned Agricola Seneca:

I am sending back your codex – than which, as you wrote, nothing is more beautiful – together with two printed copies. My contract entitled me to three; I have given you the greater part. If your codex was worth fifty florins, the printed one is worth a thousand [!]. I do not deny that I profited from yours in many places. Nor have we deprived Rudolphus of his due praise, as I can testify. We have mentioned you in the preface, and we have added your name to the *Ciceronianus*. If however this does not seem sufficient to you, what we have begun will be completed out of my own stock. For since the death of Ioannes Frobenius the printing house is in disorder.

(Remitto codicem tuum – quo nihil, vt scribis, pulchrius – vna cum duobus excusis. Ex pacto mihi dabantur tres; maiorem portionem tibi cedo. Si tuus codex valebat quinquaginta florenis, excusus valet mille: nec tamen inficias eo tuum alicubi profuisse. Non fraudauimus Rodolphum sua laude, vt arbitror. Tui quoque mentionem fecimus in praefatione; et Ciceroniano nomen tuum adiecimus. Si nondum videor animo tuo satisfecisse, quod coepimus implebitur de meo. Nam defuncto Ioanne Frobenio tota off icinae ratio mutata est.)[35]

Evidently Erasmus set enough store by the access given to the annotated Agricola Seneca to pay handsome tribute to Hermann, both with the gift of two of his three publisher's copies of the Seneca *Opera*, and with a commendation in the preface (he also added Hermann to the second edition of his *Ciceronianus*, as one of the *'eruditi'*).[36] Furthermore, he chose to advertise this fact by arranging for the publication of this expression of emphatic indebtedness, to Agricola and to Hermann, almost simultaneously with the issue of the 'new Seneca' itself. The reader is likely to conclude from the two uncharacteristically generous and enthusiastic letters together that Erasmus regarded Agricola's annotations and corrections as the 1529 Seneca's crowning glory.[37] The posthumous involvement of Agricola clinches the preeminence of the edition.

Agricola's annotated copy of the Treviso Seneca is no longer extant. It is, however, illuminating for the present story to consult a Treviso Seneca.[38] This handsome slim folio volume opens with the spurious *'De moribus'*, followed by the spurious *'De quattuor virtutibus cardinalibus'*, then by Seneca's *Declamationes*, Seneca's *De Ira*, *De Clementia* etc., the spurious *Apophthegmata*, the spurious Seneca/St Paul correspondence, and finally the Seneca *Epistulae morales* to Lucilius. It does not contain the *Quaestiones naturales*.[39] We might reasonably expect that Agricola's annotated text would have provided Erasmus with emendations and annotations to the central rhetorical work of Seneca's contained in the volume – the *Declamationes*.

The text of the 1529 Seneca documents punctiliously the use Erasmus has made of the Agricola annotations.[40] At the end of the second work, the *Epistolae* to Lucilius, Erasmus writes:

When the *Epistolae* to Lucilius were already partially printed, the exemplar arrived from Brabant. By collating this we have restored whatever had previously deceived us. Since they could not be inserted into their proper place, we have supplied them in an appendix.

(Quum epistolarum opus iam aliqua ex parte esset excusum, allatum est exemplar e Brabantia, ex cuius collatione si qua prius fefellera[n]t restituimus. Ea quoniam in contextu[m] inseri non potera[n]t, hac appe[n]dice subiecimus.)⁴¹

In case there should be any doubt, Agricola is explicitly and repeatedly named as the annotator whose emendations and annotations to the Treviso text Erasmus gratefully and enthusiastically acknowledges.⁴² The *Epistolae* are the second work in Erasmus's volume, preceded by *De Beneficiis*. So the published letter to Hermann accurately specifies the state of affairs: Erasmus received the Agricola Seneca when the printing of the volume was already underway. Having inserted the six-page appendix of Agricola emendations after the letters, each subsequent work is followed by its own section detailing Agricola's comments. As we expect, there are no annotations for the *Quaestiones naturales* (not contained in the Treviso Seneca) – here Erasmus inserts the Fortunatus emendations, from the published edition whose use he had also publicly ackowledged. Nor does Erasmus include any annotations to the *spuria*, now relegated to a section at the very end of the volume. Surprisingly, however, no Agricola comments are printed for the *Declamationes* and *Suasoriae*. Since these are texts on the *ars disserendi*, we might well expect that Agricola had had something to say about them in his personal copy of Seneca.

But if we turn our attention to the larger publishing milieu at Basle, within which Erasmus was producing editions and commentaries, we find the missing text in an exactly contemporary Basle volume, which irresistibly invites the claim that it was 'ghosted' into published existence by Erasmus himself. The volume is published by Ioannes Bebelius, and contains three of Seneca's *Declamationes*, with an introduction and commentary by Agricola, and a prefatory letter by himself: *L. Annaei Senecae . . . Declamationes . . . cum R. Agricolae commentariolis.*⁴³ According to the Agricola literature, the provenance of this 'commentary' is entirely unknown.⁴⁴ The most likely source for this volume now seems to be the 'heavily annotated' Treviso Seneca, sent with so much care to Basle by Haio Hermann.⁴⁵

As we saw, Erasmus's published expression of gratitude to
Hermann for the loan of the volume elaborately emphasised the care
with which the Agricola Seneca was to be packaged and sent, and
the fact that he alone would handle the volume. Bebelius says in his
introduction that he obtained his Agricolan commentary on Seneca
from 'a certain most learned friend', who, on the parallel evidence of
the 1529 Seneca appears to be Erasmus himself.[46] Bebelius had
originally been a Froben *castigator*, and Erasmus had given works of
his own to him when he set up as an independent printer.[47]
Bebelius's prefatory letter to the Seneca *Declamationes aliquot* stresses
both the importance of the *Declamationes* for the study of *eloquentia*,
and the significance of Agricola, in precisely the terms of Erasmus's
volume.[48] Whether by design or accident, the upshot was that a
further publication saw the light at precisely the right moment to
support Erasmus's claim that the *Declamationes* were an important
and undervalued teaching text, and that Agricola was the
inspirational figure behind the northern European pedagogic
movement of which Erasmus was by now self-appointed leader.
And in any case, the 1529 Seneca *Opera* is a major, substantial piece
of public testimony to Erasmus's commitment to Rudolph
Agricola.[49]

ERASMUS AND DIALECTIC:
STUDIOUS READER OF AGRICOLA

In spite of the absence of recorded Agricola emendations for
Erasmus's texts of the *Declamationes, Controuersiae and Suasoriae* in
the 1529 Seneca, these works carry a strong introduction, in which
Erasmus singles out the *Declamationes* as vital for a practical training
in *eloquentia*.[50] This introduction opens with a clear announcement
of the practical importance of this part of Seneca's oeuvre:

> So far as the needs of scholars are concerned, for none of Seneca's
> works is a pure text more urgently needed than for these
> *Declamations*.

> (Inter omnes Senecae lucubrationes, nullum opus extare integrum
> & inuiolatum magis referebat publica studioru[m] utilitas, quam
> hos declamationum libros.)[51]

It closes with an equally strong endorsement of the classroom usefulness of *declamationes* for a training in 'invention' and 'judgement', and contrasts this with the mere virtuosity (without clear purpose) of 'the dialectic which is currently taught in the schools':

It is incredible how much usefulness these opinions of men excelling in all types of doctrine contribute, not simply to the art of speaking well [*ad bene dicendum*], but also indeed to good judgement, whether in forensic argument [*forensibus causis*], or in popular or military public orations, or in assemblies, or in every activity and function of life, in which in some considerable part the use of language is regulated by prudence. That faculty of invention and judgement, if once it is instilled into young boys, seems to me to yield much more fruit that that dialectic which is currently taught in the schools. Which dialectic, however, I do not estimate to be inferior, nor requiring to be done away with, but simply that, once all frivolous niceties have been done away with, it should be taught for practice and use, rather than childish ostentation. If only in some happy case these books of Seneca's [*Declamationes*] could be restored to us in their entirety.

(Hae censurae hominu[m] in omni doctrinae genere praecellentiu[m], incredibile dictu, quantu[m] utilitas attulissent, non solu[m] ad bene dicendu[m] ueru[m] etia[m] ad iudicandu[m], siue in forensibus causis, siue in concionibus popularibus militaribusue, siue in co[n]sessibus, siue in omni uitae functione, quae maxima ex parte, linguae prudentis officio temperatur. Ea inuenie[n]di iudicandiq[ue] facultas, si statim pueris tradatur, mihi uidetur multo plus fructus allatura, quam quae nunc in scholis traditur dialectica, qua[m] tamen nec improbo, nec submouendam censeo, modo resectis nugalibus argutijs, ad usum potius quam ad puerilem oste[n]tationem tradatur. Atq[ue] utinam felix aliquis casus hos Senecae libros nobis integros restituat.)

These are unusually explicit words on the subject of dialectic for Erasmus. They are also strikingly similar to sentiments expressed by Agricola in the third and final book of *De inventione dialectica*, in which he discusses the practical, and above all the forensic and adversarial use of his revised '*ars ratiocinandi*'. Indeed, editions of

Seneca after 1529, based on the text of the Erasmus *Opera*, take this introduction to be by Agricola. They incorporate it into Agricola's *annotationes* on the *Declamationes*, which they reunite with the other Agricola annotations in the *Opera* text (either from Bebelius's edition, or from Alardus's *Lucubrationes*).[52]

In the terms of a traditional intellectual–historical inquiry, we have come a long way from Erasmus's *De copia*. And yet, the strands which link the Seneca and the Erasmus's handbook for the *ars bene dicendi ac scribendi* are all strong. Our quest for a context which gives meaning back to Erasmus's *De copia* has once again produced a story in which Rudolph Agricola has a starring role, and which identifies a carefully laid trail of published works, grouped around a central text by Erasmus. Here the *Opera* of Seneca provide the ground, as it were, and *De copia* projects the counterpoint. The composite figure, Seneca *rhetor/philosophus*, apparently offers a moral frame compatible with Christian thought, a projected *De copia*, adapting pagan eloquence to a Christian purpose, and a classroom text (the *Declamationes*) which teaches both morals and *eloquentia*. Ironically, however, the period between 1515 and 1529, during which *De copia* evolved in its published form from a skeleton school-text (for Colet's St Paul's school) into the key pedagogic work for the '*ars bene dicendi*', which he placed first in importance in his catalogue of published works, was the period during which he reconsidered and drastically reworked his Seneca.[53]

1515 to 1529 was also the period of growing prominence for Agricola's *De inventione dialectica*, now freely available (thanks to Erasmus's own efforts) in printed (and later, commented) form. Agricola's and Erasmus's rhetorical manuals became increasingly prominent and pivotal in the classroom as the first impetus for reconstructing a Christian–humanist manual of *copia* – the suggestions in Seneca and in Agricola – receded in significance. What remained was the claim that such a work had good classical precedent, and would fill an acknowledged gap in provisions for Christian–humanist *eloquentia*. The Europe-wide availability of both manuals in handy, commented, inexpensive printed form (shrewdly backed as usual by Erasmus and his northern European printers) was the practical impetus for a reform (at least in the north) of taught *eloquentia*. With Erasmus's *De copia* and Agricola's *De inventione dialectica* side by side on the reading desk, flanking a copy of Seneca's and Quintilian's *Declamationes*, *argumentatio* was detached from its formal, technical language-based context in the traditional schools. Freed from the rigid and coercive framework of traditional schools logic, it opened the way to a training in persuasive and effective discourse more appropriate to the civic and forensic context of sixteenth-century education.

Notes and References

1. See Jardine, 'Inventing Rudolph Agricola: Cultural transmission, renaissance dialectic, and the emerging humanities', in A. Grafton and A. Blair (eds), *The Transmission of Culture in Early Modern Europe* (Philadelphia, 1990), pp. 39–86.
2. M. A. Nauwelaerts, *Rudolph Agricola* (The Hague, 1963), p. 157.
3. *Complete Works of Erasmus*, vol. 9 (Toronto, 1989), p. 294.
4. 'Lucubrationes Rodolphi Agricolae, hominis vere diuini, iamdudum expectamus; cuius ego scripta quoties lego, toties pectus illud sacrum ac coeleste mecum adoro atque exosculor' (*De copia*, folio 2E, reprinted in P. S. Allen, *Opus Epistolarum Des. Erasmi Roterodami*, 12 vols. [Oxford, 1906–58], vol. 2, p. 32 [letter 311]). See also *CWE*, vol. 24, p. 289. The preface to the *Parabolae*, published with *De copia* in 1514, addressed to Peter Gilles, explicitly links these works with the Seneca edition on which he was currently working (Allen, *Opus epistolarum* vol. III, p. 33 [letter 312]).
5. See Jardine, art. cit.
6. Alardus, *Lucubrationes* (Cologne, 1539), p. 199. Terence Cave, *The Cornucopian Text: Problems of Writing in the French Renaissance* (Oxford, 1979), pp. 3–7.
7. Allen, *Opus epistolarum*, vol. II, pp. 362–70 (letter 480).
8. We should note as always that Gilles is involved both with publishing Agricola, and with publishing Erasmus.
9. See Jardine, art. cit.
10. Cave, *Cornucopian Text*, pp. 16–17; J. Monfasani, 'Lorenzo Valla and Rudolph Agricola', *Journal of the History of Philosophy* XXVIII (1990), pp. 181–200.
11. For a helpful account of the changing nature of meaningful intellectual questions see N. Jardine, *The Scenes of Inquiry* (Oxford, 1991).
12. Like most of his contemporaries, Erasmus believed 'Seneca' to be author both of the rhetorical and of the moral works (in fact the work of father and son respectively), though he expressed doubt about his authorship of the tragedies. See L. Panizza, 'Biography in Italy from the Middle Ages to the Renaissance: Seneca, pagan or christian?', *Nouvelles de la Republique de Lettres*, vol. II (1984), pp. 47–98, 52–3.
13. *CWE*, vol. 3, p. 66; ep. 325.
14. On Jerome and Seneca see W. Trillitzsch, *Seneca im Literarischen Urteil der Antike: Darstellung und Sammlung der Zeugnisse*, 2 vols (Amsterdam, 1971), vol. I, pp. 143–61.

15. Seneca, *Lucubrationes* (Basle, 1515). On the evolution of Erasmus's Seneca editions see Trillitzsch, *Seneca*, vol. I, pp. 221–50.

16. The copy in the Archives of Speer Library, Princeton Theological Seminary has annotations, dated 1528, which show that the reader was aware of some of the anomalies and mistakes in the volume.

17. This story is in the 1523 'catologus' letter to Botzheim. See L. D. Reynolds, *The Medieval Tradition of Seneca's Letters* (Oxford University Press, 1965), pp. 5–6; Trillitzsch, *Seneca*, vol. I, pp. 225–8.

18. As, for instance, in his description of the 'Herculean labours' which went into the Jerome edition, or the *Adagia*. And, for instance, Bruno Amerbach's letter about that edition (*CWE*, vol. 3, p. 139 [ep 337A]): 'The volume of spurious works is going on even better than it deserves, though the manuscripts are so full of mistakes that it would be less trouble to clean out an Augean cowbyre'. See also Bierlaire, *La familia d'Erasme* (Paris, 1968).

19. See also, for instance, the supposed 'interpolation' by a secretary in the *Adagia*, recounted by M. Mann Phillips in *The Adages of Erasmus: A Study with Translations* (Cambridge, 1964), pp. 162–3.

20. See Reynolds, note 17 above, and Trillitzsch, note 14 above.

21. 'Non hic verbis attollam quantum mihi laboris exhaustum sit. Scio neminem crediturum, nisi priorem aeditionem cum hac contulerit. Id si quis non grauabitur facere, continue fatebitur alium prodisse Seneca.' Allen, *Opus epistolarum*, vol. 8 (Oxford, 1934), p. 28 (ep. 2091). The new edition is a significant improvement.

22. For a concise description of the volume's contents see Trillitzsch, p. 235.

23. See A. Grafton, *Forgers and Critics: Creativity and Duplicity in Western Scholarship* (Princeton, 1990), p. 43. A reference to a *De copia verborum* of Seneca's in Professor Grafton's book started off the train of thinking which is represented in this paper. As always I am immensely grateful to him.

24. Allen, *Opus epistolarum*, vol. VIII, p. 40; cit. Grafton, *Forgers and Critics*, p. 43.

25. 'Scio te non tam tui causa commotum litteris quas ad te de editione epistolarum mearum [tuarum] Caesari feci quam natura rerum, quae ita mentes hominum ab omnibus artibus et moribus rectis revocat, ut non hodie admirer, quippe ut is qui multis documentis hoc iam notissimum habeam. Igitur nove agamus, et si quid facile in praeteritum factum est, veniam inrogabis. Misi tibi librum de verborum copia. Vale[,] Paule carissime', Claude W. Barlow (ed.), *Epistolae Senecae ad Paulum et Pauli ad Senecam <quae vocantur>* (Horn, Austria, 1938), pp. 131–2; translation, p. 144. The alternative readings in square brackets are from L. Bocciolini Palagi, *Il carteggio apocrifo di Seneca e San Paolo: Introduzione, testo, commento* (Florence, 1978), p. 71.

26. The Seneca/Paul correspondence and the *De quattuor virtutibus cardinalibus*, although relegated to the end of the volume, are not explicitly labelled as spurious. By contrast, both the *De moribus* and the *Prouerbia* carried marginal notes declaring them 'non a Seneca fuisse'.

On Martin de Braga and the Seneca *spuria* see Claude W. Barlow, *Martini Episcopi Bracarensis Opera Omnia* (New Haven, 1950), pp. 204–50.

27. Erasmus, *Opera Senecae* (Basle, 1529), sig. a Iv.
28. Barlow, *Epistolae Senecae ad Paulum*, p. 144. We may take it, I think, that Erasmus's own interest in a missing *De copia* by Seneca (contemporary of, if not correspondent with, St Paul) similarly arises out of a concern with a kind of *eloquentia* appropriate to Christianity. In sixteenth-century editions of Quintilian's *Institutio oratoria*, book ten, section one, carries the heading, 'De copia verborum'. And sixteenth-century readers were inclined to link the names of Seneca and Quintilian around the particular rhetorical topic of *Declamationes* and *Suasoriae*. M. Winterbottom (ed.), *The Minor Declamations* ascribed to Quintilian (Berlin, 1984), xxii–xxv; especially xvi–xvii.
29. Allen, *Opus epistolarum*, vol. VIII (Oxford, 1934), p. 28.
30. See *Contemporaries of Erasmus*, 'Haio Herman', 1498/1500–1539/40.
31. Allen, *Opus epistolarum*, VII (Oxford, 1928) p. 368 [Ep 1978]. See also ibid, pp. 533–4 [ep. 2073] (to Haio Cammyngha, a fellow-Frisian, also published in the *Opus Epistolarum*).
32. Translation of Lucian's *De non facile credendis delationibus* (Louvain, 4 July 1530; NK 558). His prefatory letter is reprinted in Agricola, *Lucubrationes*, (note 6 above), pp. 243–5.
33. Allen, 'The Letters of Rudolph Agricola' (note 46 below) suggests that Hermann began as joint editor with Alardus of Agricola's *Opera*, but later dropped out of the project.
34. Allen, *Opus epistolarum*, vol. VII (Oxford, 1928), p. 506 [ep 2056]. Along with the public commendations, Erasmus offered Hermann more practical recompense for his assistance. With this letter he enclosed letters of recommendation to Erard de la Marck and John Carondelet at the Imperial Court at Mechelin (epp. 2054, 2055) (also published in the 1529 *Opus epistolarum*). Hermann's 1530 edition of Agricola's Lucian translation was dedicated to de la Marck.
35. Allen, *Opus epistolarum*, vol. VIII (Oxford, 1934), p. 66 (ep. 2108).
36. Critics have suggested some sort of tension between Erasmus and Hermann after this exchange of codices and compliments. It seems more likely to me that Erasmus had no further use for (and therefore interest in) Hermann hereafter.
37. There is a further letter in the 1529 *Opus epistolarum* volume advertising the extent of Erasmus's search for further 'codices' of Seneca, via Vives and Thomas More. Allen, *Opus epistolarum*, vol. VII (Oxford, 1928), pp. 469–71 (ep 2040). The letter clearly suggests that there are further 'codices' (printed volumes or manuscripts) which Erasmus wished to consult. However, Vives's reply (printed in his own *Opera*, but not amongst Erasmus's letters), declines involvement in the project. On Vives and Seneca see Karl Alfred Blüher, *Seneca en España: Investigaciones sobre la Recepción de Seneca en España desde el siglo XIII hasta el siglo XVII* (Spanish version, expanded and corrected) (Madrid, 1983), pp. 260–84.

38. 'Taruisij per Bernadum de Colonia Anno domini M.cccc.lxxviij'. According to L. D. Reynolds, *The Medieval Tradition of Seneca's Letters*, the Treviso Seneca is a reprinting of the *editio princeps* (Naples, 1475).
39. For a suggestive introduction to the whole question of studying Erasmus as a textual editor see P. Petitmengin, 'Comment étudier l'activité d'Érasme éditeur de textes antiques?', in J. C. Margolin (ed.), *Colloquia Erasmiana Turonensia*, 2 vols (Paris, 1972) vol. I, pp. 217–22.
40. 'In the Copenhagen MS. are two leaves (151–2) of autograph notes by Erasmus, which were printed in this new edition, pp. 348, 333; they give readings from Agricola's volume' (Allen, *Opus epistolarum*, vol. VIII, p. 26).
41. Seneca, *Opera* (Basle, 1529), p. 268.
42. For example, pp. 269, 270.
43. Not yet seen. See M. G. M. van der Poel, *De Declamatio bij de Humanisten* (Nieuwkoop, 1987), p. 9. In 1529 Bebelius also published Quintilian's *Institutio oratoria* and *Declamationes*, with a prefatory letter by Sichardus.
44. See M. A. Nauwelaerts, *Rodolphus Agricola* (The Hague, 1963), p. 166. Huisman, *Rudolph Agricola. A Bibliography* (Nieuwkoop, 1985), does not record editions of this work at all. On Bebelius see *Contemporaries of Erasmus*, 'Ioannes Bebelius' 'documented 1517–38'; the first record of Bebelius is as a *castigator* for Froben in 1517. The text (but not Bebelius's introduction) is reprinted in Alardus's 1539 volume of Agricola's *Lucubrationes* (pp. 91–118). On Agricola's interest in *declamationes* see van der Poel, *De Declamatio*, pp. 9–14.
45. See W. Trillitzsch, 'Erasmus und Seneca', *Philologus* (1965), for further remarks about the impact of the Agricola codex on Erasmus's Seneca edition.
46. Or, more surreptitiously, one of the *castigatores* working with Erasmus on the Seneca was responsible for transmitting the text to Bebelius.
47. For example, *Precatio dominica in septem portiones distributa* (s.d. [1523]); *De libero arbitrio . . .* (s.d. [1524]).
48. The Bebelius volume is extremely rare. I am grateful to I. Sherman for transcribing the prefatory letter from the copy in the Bodleian Library.
49. On the other hand, this testimony is largely symbolic: Agricola's notes, as recorded in the 1529 Seneca, in the main simply record textual variants. There is an occasional indication that Agricola indicated approval for a particular passage.
50. Unlike the Seneca/Paul introduction, this is not included in Allen's *Opus epistolarum Erasmi*, and has therefore largely escaped the notice of critics. The introduction is printed in Trillitzsch, note 14 above. Van der Poel, *De Declamatio*, pp. 13, 14–16.
51. Seneca, *Opera* (Basle, 1529), p. 485.
52. See H. D. L. Vervliet, 'De gedrukte overlevering van Seneca pater', *De Gulder Passer* XXXV (1957), pp. 179–222; 220–01. The first edition listed by Vervliet which includes the Agricola commentary on the *Declamationes* is dated 1537, that is before Alardus's *Lucubrationes* of Agricola were published, but during a period when he had them collected for publication. In the 1540 Basel edition the attribution of

Erasmus's introduction (and indeed all the annotations) is unclear, except for the inclusion on page 268 of the original description of the discovery of Agricola's annotated copy. In the 1573 edition Erasmus's introduction appears on page 502, headed: 'Rodolphi Agricolae in primam Senecae declamationem, commentariolum. AD LECTOREM'. The title page of this volume perfectly exemplifies the influence of the Erasmus/Agricola conjunction on sixteenth-century readers of Seneca: 'L. Annaei Senecae Philosophi Stoicorum omnium acutissimi opera quae extant omnia: Coelii Secundi Curionis vigilantissima cura castigata, et nouam prorsus faciem, nimirum propriam & suam, mutata: Quorum lectio non modo ad bene dicendum, uerumetiam ad bene beateq[ue] uiuendum, prodesse plurimum potest. Post Herculeos insuper C. S. C. labores, Vincentii Pralli H. opera ac studio, innumeris in locis emendata ac restituta. Totius emendationis ratio, quidq[ue] superiori aeditioni accesserit, ex sequentibus statim cognosces. Accessit index Rerum & uerborum copiosus'. Van der Poel reports that the 1557 Basel Seneca (Vervliet, pp. 200–1) also attributes this Erasmian introduction to Rudolph Agricola, *De Declamatio*, p. 13, note 49.

54. The dates of the major authorised, successively revised editions of *De copia* are 1512, 1514, 1526, 1534.

3

The Significance of Philip Melanchthon's Rhetoric in the Renaissance

Kees Meerhoff

Magis affectibus quam argutiis.
Erasmus, *Methodus*

Since I am going to deal with so wide and complex a topic as 'the significance of Philip Melanchthon's rhetoric in the renaissance', I would prefer to begin with an analysis of an example from the huge corpus of Melanchton's writings, and to continue with a description of Melanchthon's teaching practice at the University of Wittenberg (Saxony), where students from all over Europe came to listen to this pale man with his awkward voice.

Philip Melanchthon played a major part in the reformation of the church, as an ally to Martin Luther, as a reformer of Christian education and as a leading humanist scholar. When he came to Wittenberg in 1518, he was already working on his first version of a rhetoric designed along humanist lines, which appeared the next year, very badly printed, in the same small town. Shortly afterwards it was reprinted in a better shape by Erasmus's friend John Froben, in Basel, Switzerland.

After his famous inaugural lecture *On Correcting the Studies of Youth,* he taught Homer and St Paul's *Letter to Titus,* and in the new year he commented on the Hebrew text of the *Psalms,* 'until', he writes, 'a more qualified person can be hired'.[1] We may assume that Reuchlin, his grand-uncle, was of some help to him in his hazardous enterprise. Melanchthon was only twenty-one years old at the time!

Some of the elements I have just mentioned reappear in my first example, his commentary on Cicero's *Topics.* As early as 1524, Melanchthon published in Wittenberg Cicero's text with its traditional companion-piece, the commentary of Boethius. He would have commented orally on the text in his classroom; at least, no written commentary from this period is extant. This was published only in 1533; as so often happened, lack of time prevented him from sending his lecture-notes to the press.[2]

The written commentary starts with some general remarks which are, I believe, very characteristic of his outlook. 'This book', says Melanchthon,

> belongs to that part of rhetoric which describes the method of finding arguments, and the ways in which discourse can be amplified. As such, it clearly parallels the second book of Erasmus's *De Copia*; in fact, the subject-matter of both books is identical, because there is no real difference between arguments and figures of thought. Indeed, one always needs to consider what part of a discipline a given work refers to; otherwise, it is no use studying. So, as I said before, the *Topics* contain precepts about the invention of arguments and a method of amplification. For an example, I might take the first Psalm [*Beatus vir*], which has the following proposition: 'Those who govern themselves according to God's word, are blessed.' The author could have limited himself to this one line. But he has created a whole text in such a way, that it fits in [*consentire*] with this proposition. So, right from the start, the proposition is amplified *a contrario*, and then *ab effectibus*. [Here, Melanchthon summarises the relevant lines.] The same could be said of the Psalm *Ecce quam bonum* [Ps. 133], 'Concord is a good thing'. This proposition is amplified with some very sweet [*amoeniores*] figures [He quotes] . . . . These examples suffice to show of what service this book can be.[3]

Clearly, Melanchthon considers Cicero's *Topics* mainly from a textual, even from a 'literary' point of view. Whereas Cicero presents the *Topics* as technical tools for the lawyer, Melanchthon stresses their use in the process of conceiving and analysing a text. It is for this reason that he refers almost instinctively to Erasmus's *De Copia*, and that he suggests in passing the common basis of arguments and rhetorical figures. In the *Elements of Rhetoric*, published in 1531, Melanchthon presents a scheme in which the figures, especially those which amplify discourse, all derive from the dialectical topics. For example, vivid description, or *hypotyposis*, has its source in the topic of the circumstances, and so on. Since the importance of this chapter of the *Elements* has already been underlined in C. Vasoli's magnificent study of humanist dialectic and rhetoric, I simply point to the absolute identity of point of view in the rhetorical textbook and in the commentary.[4] Indeed, more than once Melanchthon expresses the same ideas in very different contexts; fundamental issues are treated like 'set pieces' which he inserts as vital elements in a variety of texts. These set pieces reflect without any doubt his teaching practice, and show the intimate bond between teaching and writing in Melanchthon's works. Another striking example of this procedure would be his ideas concerning imitation, which he expresses not only in the next chapter of the *Elements of Rhetoric*, but in an almost identical way in some of his major commentaries on Cicero and Quintilian.[5] In short, one can observe an intense circulation in Melanchthon's different texts, especially between textbooks and commentaries. This is the case in his rhetorical and dialectical works, but no less in his theological writings, to which we will return later.

In his introductory remarks to his commentary on Cicero's *Topics*, which remain my first point of reference, Melanchthon quite naturally illustrates the issue of topical invention and amplification with a twofold quotation taken from the Bible. We will see that for Melanchthon, the Scriptures have an essentially rhetorical orientation; and this presentation in the commentary shows that he considers the very lyrical texts of the Psalms to be constructed in exactly the same way as a forensic oration. In both cases, there is a point at issue which has to be developed and put into proper relief; in both cases, there is a rhetorical appeal to a public.[6]

The point I want to stress here is that it is very hard to say whether Melanchthon talks about the actual creation of the Psalm by King David himself, or simply about a convenient method for analysing this kind of text. We may surmise that in his mind, dialectical analysis comes close to the very process of creation.

This conjecture finds further support in Melanchthon's own teaching practice in which, as with so many other humanist scholars, imitation plays a vital part. In the stronghold of the reformation that was Wittenberg University, the study of the Bible and of theology constituted the final goal of the curriculum. Right from the start, Melanchthon was an essential helper to Luther in defending their new theological insights. We have seen that Melanchthon starts his career by lecturing on Paul's *Letter to Titus*. He refers to this analysis in the first version of his rhetoric, which I quoted earlier. Even here, while talking about techniques of interpretation and paraphrase of a biblical text, Melanchthon states that he urged his audience to use their own paraphrases to create a new text by quoting parallel examples, by adducing additional arguments, and so on. He ends his remarks on paraphrase by stating that when used as he suggested, paraphrase can be the source of *mirabilis copia*.[7]

Of course, the very fact that Melanchthon gives so much attention to the techniques of analysing texts in an elementary rhetorical textbook indicates very clearly that for him, analysis and production of texts form an inseparable whole. Indeed, his remarks on paraphrase are only the beginning of a long chapter entirely dedicated to the methodical interpretation of all kinds of texts. The exegesis of the Scriptures features prominently, but by no means exclusively, in these pages, which were read with passion all over Europe by Protestant reformers as well as by anti-Lutheran catholics like Alardus of Amsterdam, the editor of Rudolph Agricola's writings.[8] They are an essential element in the first book of the early *Rhetoric*, which Melanchthon rounds off by presenting his ideas on sermon-writing in a chapter headed '*de sacris concionibus*'. Thus, once again methodical analysis of scriptural texts and the rhetoric of preaching constitute a diptych.[9]

So far I have concentrated mainly on the beginnings of Melanchthon's career, during those crucial years from 1518 to 1524. As we have seen, in this period Melanchthon lectured on both biblical and profane texts, and published his first rhetorical textbook and his commentary on Cicero's *Topics*, among some eighty other texts.

Let us now consider briefly the period around the *Elements of Rhetoric*, the final version of which was published in Wittenberg in 1531. According to the list compiled by Carl Hartfelder one hundred years ago, Melanchthon lectured in 1529 on Paul's *Letter to the Romans*, a few months later on dialectic and the *Organon* of Aristotle, and finally on two Ciceronian orations, *Pro Murena* and *Pro Marcello*. In 1530 he taught Cicero's *De Oratore*, immediately followed by Cicero's *Pro Archia*, and perhaps by another Ciceronian oration. In 1531, he probably lectured on Homer's *Iliad*, and certainly on three Ciceronian orations, *Pro Caelio*, *Pro Sulla*, and the ninth *Philippic*. In 1532, he took up *Romans* again, as he did so many times before and after this period, then the *Ethics* of Aristotle, Book v, and a Ciceronian oration, *Pro Ligario*. Let us stop here, for the same pattern recurs more or less identically.

Evidently, the larger portion of Melanchthon's teaching activities during this period was dedicated to textual analysis, not to dialectical or rhetorical theory. When he taught Cicero's *De Oratore* or Aristotle's *Organon*, more often than not he illustrated his teaching by analysing an oration. The publisher of Melanchthon's famous analysis of the *Pro Archia* was a former student of his. When he issued the text with its commentary in 1533, he wrote a prefatory letter in which he recalls with enthusiasm the huge number of students who had attended the lecture on *De Oratore* some three years earlier, and specifies that Melanchthon added straight away an analysis of the oration, 'in order to confront theory with practice'. This testimony is confirmed by several others.[10] Behind it, we discover a basic principle of humanist education, which explains why most of the humanists' textbooks are relatively slim, and why they repeat so often *reliqua usus docebit*, 'practice will teach you the rest'. *Usus* is *not* doing exercises with formal rules, it is, first and foremost, reading texts.

It is my conviction that the essential aim of humanist dialectic and rhetoric is to be mere tools, first to read texts in a methodical way, and then, once the secrets of composition have been unveiled by textual analysis, to create new, coherent texts on the basis of this methodical reading. I also believe that this is what the humanists themselves considered to be the main difference between their outlook and that of their medieval predecessors. When one finds the rules of the syllogism explained in a humanist textbook in a way very similar to that of medieval manuals, one should bear in mind the very different use that is made of the theory of *iudicium* in both cases. For a humanist, a syllogism is ultimately important only as far as it can be used to test the logical coherence of a text; for a scholastic philosopher, on the other hand, the syllogism will also serve as a testing device, but mainly to test the validity of single propositions, and the formal correctness of the language used, within a theological system.

This very opposition is echoed in an eloquent way in Phrissemius' introductory letter to his commented edition of Agricola's *De Inventione Dialectica*: whereas Peter of Spain teaches you endless rules and pointless distinctions, Agricola will teach you how to deal with a text, either as a whole, or as a significant part of a whole; he will teach you how to read and how to write a Latin that is syntactically sound and logically coherent. Hoping to learn that from Peter of Spain, Phrissemius continues, is like trying to shear a donkey, or to squeeze water from a pumice-stone![11]

It certainly is one of the merits of Dr Peter Mack to have foregrounded this essential feature of Agricola's work. Its historical impact on later generations has been stressed quite correctly in a recent Dutch study and anthology (in translation) of Agricola's writings published by Dr Marc van der Poel.[12]

We know that for Melanchthon, reading Agricola in his student years was quite a shock and also a kind of liberation (*CR*, vol. IV, 716); I would suggest that the sheer quantity of analyses of Ciceronian orations in the Wittenberg curriculum proves, among other things, the correct understanding of Agricola's message by his admirer and biographer.

What, then, is the relationship between these analyses of Cicero and the other highlight of the curriculum, the interpretation of Paul's *Letter to the Romans*? Undoubtedly, the reading of classical orations serves as a model for reading the latter. I think we can speak of a kind of 'moral' priority of Cicero, the method of reading being first practiced on profane speeches in order to avoid a confrontation with the holy texts without proper preparation; 'with unwashed hands', as Erasmus would put it.

Thus, in his earliest analyses of *Romans*, which have come down to us in the form of student's notes, Melanchthon intends to prove the rhetorical skills of Paul by comparing the *exordium* of *Romans* with that of Cicero's *Pro Marcello* and of *Pro Archia*. After all, only the technical abilities of Paul were at stake here, those of Cicero were beyond any possible discussion.[13]

The question of St Paul's rhetorical skills, which had been raised from the time of early Fathers of the church,[14] was of special importance to Melanchthon. Martin Luther proclaimed *Romans* to be the key to the Scriptures as a whole, because in this letter Paul speaks of justification by faith alone, *sola fide*, which soon became one of the cornerstones of the new theology. *Romans* also defines what both Luther and Melanchthon considered to be the basic issues of the biblical message, such as 'sin', 'law', 'mercy' and 'faith'. In their eyes, Paul offers all the definitions and distinctions, especially that between 'law' and 'gospel', which they regarded as essential to the correct interpretation of the entire Bible and called therefore *loci communes*, 'central headings', 'points of reference'. As early as 1520, Melanchthon contends that *Romans* offers *the* final method of interpreting the Scriptures, thus implying that Paul himself is the ultimate interpreter, the Christian Hermes.[15]

In short, Paul is an expert in methodical reading, who explains Christian doctrine *ordine et artificio plane rhetorico*. But he is more than a cold dialectician, as he does more than merely teach. He is a real orator, and as such he moves and seduces his reader with all possible means: *doctissimus est Paulus et facundus!*[16]

These ideas about Paul's rhetorical abilities are voiced in Melanchthon's earliest lectures on *Romans*, and are very eloquently expressed in the oratorical companion-pieces of these lectures, namely the declamations in which he advocates the study of Paul's letters. In these festive speeches, Melanchthon clearly aims at matching Paul's eloquence, at giving a living example of its elegance and effectiveness. Melanchthon thus becomes a kind of reincarnation of Paul, or at least of the Melanchthonian image of Paul. It is quite curious to see that in turn, his own orations came to be considered as 'classical' models of eloquence. In many classrooms in Wittenberg, Strasburg and elsewhere, they were read and analysed, and often provided with dialectical and rhetorical annotations in the margins, in order to reveal their subtle, Pauline *artificium*.[17]

But even in those early days, around the year 1520, Melanchthon's activities and conceptions are echoed with astonishing rapidity. We know, for instance, that John Phrissemius lectured in Cologne, that very year, not only on Erasmus's *De Copia* and Agricola's *De Inventione Dialectica*, but also on *Romans*; we know as well that in the same year, Maarten van Dorp, the other prominent editor of Agricola's writings, pronounced and published in Louvain an oration in which he announces his own lecture on St Paul and praises effusively the Apostle's divine eloquence.[18]

It is in this period that the image of Saint Paul as a fully fledged orator seems to prevail as far as Melanchthon is concerned. He will moderate his views later on, still stressing Paul's remarkable dialectical skills, but playing down the excellence of his style. What remains, is the idea of *Romans* as a *method*, a *compendiaria via* to the Scriptures, and the urgent need to analyse *Romans* in an adequate way, that is, a methodical way.

In fact, what we have here is quite a complex, reflective system, in which the issue of humanism versus scholasticism returns. Melanchthon, indeed, develops two complementary oppositions: on the one hand, that between a persuasive, eloquent mode of expression as against an arid, uninspired and technical machinery; on the other hand, an adequate, rhetorical *analysis* of a text, treating it as a coherent whole as against the scholastic approach, which chops a text into inarticulate little pieces, tearing it apart in order to proceed to a formal interpretation of the fourfold significance of a fragment. This is what Melanchthon calls *de quatuor sensibus in singulis prope syllabis nugari*. Both oppositions occur, for example, in his *Small Declamation concerning the Study of Paul* (1520), which I referred to above. Let us look into this more closely.

The first opposition recurs in many Melanchthonian writings, for instance in the famous *Reply* to Pico della Mirandola (*CR*, vol. IX, pp. 678–703). It can be summarised in a formula like 'persuasive elegance versus cold logic'. The 'pursuit of eloquence' (H. Gray) can be considered as one of the distinctive features of humanist theological thinking. It is already present in Agricola and is paramount in Erasmus's thought. The humanists all want to translate into the field of language their experience of the biblical message as primarily affective, as a direct appeal to a person's emotions. The Pauline concepts of law and gospel, which Melanchthon uses as basic ingredients for his Protestant dogmatics in the *Loci Communes* (1521), both possess a two-way impact, on reason and on the emotions. Law furnishes both the knowledge of sin and the terrifying experience of God's anger; it is this emotional shock which paves the way for the reception of the gospel. Gospel, in turn, implies knowledge about God's will, about Christ and his gifts (*beneficia*) to mankind, about justice, and so on; it is also a promise, a vivifying force, as it dispenses hope and consolation. This twofold system, both rational and affective, also informs Melanchthon's homiletics, in which teaching and appealing to the emotions are the two complementary goals. In this case, Melanchthon tries to build his homiletic theory on Paul's remarks in his first *Letter to Timothy* (1 Tim. 4:13) to which he refers on at least ten different occasions; he even dedicates a formal oration to this very passage in 1546.[19] In this last text, Melanchthon gives an account of what he considers to be Paul's own preaching practice, as shown in his letters; and it goes without saying that Melanchthon again presents his hero as an expert in dialectical procedure while teaching the elements of Christian faith, and as an oratorical magician while stirring up his audience's emotions.[20]

Thus, both in theory – the twofold function of the basic topics of law and gospel – and in practice – preaching as appeal – Melanchthon attributes to non-rational processes a major part in Christian faith. The Bible, a most appealing message in itself, has found an eloquent interpreter in St Paul. As early as 1520,

Melanchthon makes a dramatic contrast between Paul's stirring eloquence and the impurity and ugliness of scholastic quibbling, which offers no satisfaction whatsoever to the heart.[21] Of course, this whole passage in the *Small Declamation* has distinctly Erasmian overtones.

Let us now turn to the parallel opposition that is found in the same declamation of 1520: scholastic versus humanist interpretation of texts. It is concerned with what has been called, in a somewhat different context, 'medieval fragmentation' as opposed to 'renaissance reintegration'.[22] Melanchthon suggests that bad theology, bad preaching and inadequate textual analysis are all results of the same, basically cold and arrogant attitude, characteristic of scholasticism. Scholastic theologians like nothing better than tearing apart texts; they simply refuse to consider any other approach, insensible as they are to the beauty and harmony of a well-wrought text. When they have to analyse *Romans*, for instance, they totally ignore Greek sentence structure with its delicate rhythm and balance; so, firstly they distort the text by superimposing on it a completely non-classical syntax as a consequence of their bad Latin; after that, they pursue the grinding by analysing this already perverted text according to Aristotelian procedures, taking out little fragments in order to insert these in their frivolous systems. These systems are thus built out of scraps taken from many kinds of text, biblical as well as patristic, or even Aristotelian. Melanchthon implies that Protestant theology, on the other hand, is based on the respectful analysis of complete, unaltered texts, and, above all, on the careful interpretation of *Romans*, which offers the key to the Scriptures.[23]

A formal attack on scholasticism based on exactly the same opposition appears some ten years later, in 1529, in the prefatory letter which Melanchthon publishes as an introduction to his rhetorical analysis of *Romans*. In this violent letter Melanchthon compares the scholastics with people whose supreme joy consists in looking at some remnants of antique sculptures, and who do not care at all about the work of art as a whole, about the beauty which results from coherence and symmetry. People like that will never grasp the intention of Paul's letter, which one can understand only by paying close attention to the work as a whole, to its structure, to the skillful connections of its constituent parts.[24]

These two oppositions reveal the core of Melanchthon's rhetorical conception. The second one in particular offers the basic principle behind his own textual analyses. In this respect, his terminology is very revealing. The analysis of *Romans* (1529) that I have just mentioned can serve as an example. It is called *Dispositio*. In this name we discover once again the ambiguity I pointed out at the beginning of this chapter: is Melanchthon referring to the creation of a text or to its methodical analysis? I think we can safely assert now that it is both, in that *dispositio* is meant to reconstruct the actual process of creation and thus to disclose an author's fundamental intention.[25]

In order to re-create the author's intention, we must try to answer some elementary questions, such as: what is the author's basic goal in the broadest possible sense? Does he want to obtain something, or to teach, and so on? Let us stick to *Romans*. According to Melanchthon, Paul intends to teach us something, namely, what is the essence of the gospel. This essence is justification by faith alone, *not* by good works. To make this central issue clear, Paul introduces the opposition between gospel and law, and so on. Melanchthon translates these questions into rhetorical concepts. To ask for the general aim is to ask for the oratorical genre, *genus orationis*, in this case the so-called didactical genre. To ask for the central issue is to determine the *status causae*; in this case it is the *status finitivus*, for Paul wants to defend against those opponents who stress the importance of good works his idea concerning justification by faith. Finally, once these two basic questions have been answered, Melanchthon wants us to examine how Paul has developed this central thesis, how he defends his case. This boils down to asking how he backs up his thesis by argumentation, and how the arguments are connected logically.

In other words, *dispositio* is the uncovering of logical invention as a chain of arguments supporting one basic contention; it is, in fact, *inventio* and *dispositio* intertwined, and considered from the point of view of textual coherence.[26] Indeed, *Romans* can only serve as a key to the Scriptures as long as Paul is proven to be an impeccable logician.[27] And this is precisely Melanchthon's personal aim: to show by a methodical procedure that Paul's method to the Scriptures has been built up in a methodical way.

I have tried to show elsewhere how, with this in his mind, Melanchthon systematised some of Rudolph Agricola's intuitions and suggestions concerning the combination of dialectical and rhetorical concepts. As early as the 1519 *Rhetoric* he contended that the logical 'deep structure' of a text is reducible to an underlying syllogism, the conclusion of which coincides with the rhetorical *status causae*.[28] Reformers of the second generation such as Henry Bullinger, Zwingli's successor, John Calvin, and Martin Bucer, who eventually moved from Sturm's Strasburg to Cambridge, all used this very method for their exegesis of the Scriptures. They were all familiar not only with Erasmus and Melanchthon, but with Agricola as well, this founding father of textual analysis.

Outside the church, the method was widely used in classrooms all over Europe, either in purely Melanchthonian shape or faintly disguised by people such as Latomus and Peter Ramus.

When, in the early 1560s, a student and friend of Melanchthon's, David Chytraeus, delivers a solemn speech *Concerning the Proper Study of Dialectic*, he strongly insists on the importance of textual analysis according to the rules that Melanchthon formulated.[29] He also looks back, offering a kind of genealogy of dialectical studies. By way of conclusion, I will simply report the scholars he quotes, and whom he considers to constitute modern dialectic's golden chain. The first to be quoted is Melanchthon, because his dialectical textbook (the *Erotemata*) is still the most popular in Germany; after that, Chytraeus turns to R. Agricola, J. Willichius, J. Sturm, J. Caesarius, and finally – after mentioning in passing F. Titelmans (from Louvain), Lorenzo Valla and George of Trebizond – Peter Ramus. 'After Philip [Melanchthon], nobody has shown the use one can make of dialectic in analysing the works of eloquent poets and orators more clearly and fully than Peter Ramus'.

It is all the more unfortunate that Peter Ramus only wanted to have followers, and loathed the idea of predecessors. He preferred to come out of the blue, to struggle in single combat with Aristotle, guided only by an invisible Socratic demon. But that is another story; I do not intend to tell it now.[30]

Notes and References

1. On Melanchthon's first *Rhetoric*, see my 'Mélanchthon lecteur d'Agricola: rhétorique et analyse textuelle', in *Réforme–Humanisme–Renaissance*, vol. XVI, no. 30 (1990), pp. 5–22 (p. 8 and note 3). Melanchthon's first lectures in 'Verzeichnis der Vorlesungen Melanchthons' at the end of K. Hartfelder, *Philipp Melanchthon als praeceptor Germaniae* (Berlin, 1889), pp. 555–6. Cf. Melanchthon's correspondence in *Corpus Reformatorum* (hereafter *CR*), vol. I, 76 (3 April 1519) and vol. I, 81 (21 May 1519): 'Ego psalterium praelego, dum doctior aliquis conducitur.'

For more information, see L. C. Green and Ch. D. Froehlich, *Melanchthon in English – New Translations into English with a Registry of Previous Translations*, Sixteenth-Century Bibliography, vol. 22 (Saint Louis, 1982); (P. Melanchthon) *A Melanchthon Reader*. Translated by R. Keen, American University Studies, series VII, vol. 41 (New York, 1988); R. Keen, *A Checklist of Melanchthon Imprints through 1560*, Sixteenth-Century Bibliography, vol. 27 (Saint Louis, 1988).

2. In 1524, Melchior Lotter the Younger prints in fact *two* Ciceronian texts, both preceded by a letter signed P. Melanchthon: the oration *Pro Milone* and the *Topica, cum commentariis Boe(thii)*. See *VD*, 16: C.3319, C.3783; *Index aureliensis*, vol. VIII (1989), 137.739–740; *CR*, vol. I, 700; *CR*, vol. XVI, 805. The combination is highly instructive.

3. *CR*, vol. XVI, 807; cf. *CR*, vol. XIII, 479, *CR*, vol. XVI, 872. See also Melanchthon's commentary on the Psalms, 1553–1555, in *CR*, vol. XIII, 1019, 'Argumentum ac dispositio primi Psalmi' and ibid., *CR*, vol. XIII, 1224–5.

The commentary on the *Topics* has been often republished in combination with others; see for example *Bibliotheca Belgica*, vol. VI, pp. 131 sqq.; *CR*, vol. XVI, 805; Keen, 1988, 147.

4. C. Vasoli, *La dialettica e la retorica dell' Umanesimo* (Milan, 1968), pp. 328–9. *Elementa Rhetorices*, 1531[1], chapt. 'tertius ordo figurarum', *CR*, vol. XIII, 479–80: '. . . Figurae supra traditae, etiam ab indoctis iudicari possunt, sed amplificatio singularem requirit artem atque usum. Ad hanc rem scripti sunt utilissimi libri De Copia Erasmi, quorum prior continet figuras quibus verba variantur, posterior continet figuras quae maiorem rerum copiam suppeditant. Idem nos in hoc tertio figurarum ordine docebimus quomodo crescat oratio, partim verbis, partim etiam rebus aucta. Sed nos breviores erimus, quia omnibus in manu sunt Erasmi libelli . . . . Cum enim res inventae atque dispositae sunt, quae negotii substantiam continent, postea videndum est, ubi pluribus verbis in una re utendum sit, ut verbis tanquam pictae et illuminatae res fiant illustriores. Deinde ubi etiam prosit plus addere rerum . . . . Observet autem studiosus lector figuras omnes, praesertim has quae augent orationem ex locis dialecticis oriri, ad quos si quis prudenter sciet eas referre, plaeraque in causis subtiliter et acute iudicare, et definitas negotii regiones melius videre poterit. Nam iidem loci cum confirmandi aut confutandi causa adhibentur, argumenta sunt ac nervi, ut vocant. Cum adhibentur illuminandi causa, dicuntur ornamenta.' See also R. Agricola, *DID*, III, chs 1–7 (see note 11 below).

5. *CR*, vol. XIII, 492 sqq.; cf. *CR*, vol. XVI, 722 sqq., *CR*, vol. XVI, 858 sqq., *CR*, vol. XVII, 670 sqq. (Comm. Cic. *De orat., Part. Or.*, Quint. *Inst. Or. X*). Another 'set piece' would be the attacks on uncontrolled allegorical interpretation. See also note 28 below.

6. See note 25 below.

7. P. Melanchthon, *De rhetorica libri tres* (Basel, 1519), 30–1, 'cum sacram illam ad Titum epistolam praelegissem . . .'

8. See my article, 'Rhétorique néo-latine et culture vernaculaire', *Etudes littéraires* (Canada, Laval), vol. XXIV/3 (1991–2), pp. 63–85.

9. P. Melanchthon, *De rhetorica* (1519) pp. 29–41, on *enarratio*; ibid., pp. 103–7 (end of Book 1) on sermon writing.

10. K. Hartfelder (note 1 above), pp. 558–9; *CR*, vol. XVI, 895, the letter of the publisher in Haguenau (1533). For other testimonies, see my article referred to in note 1 above.

11. R. Agricola, *De inventione dialectica libri tres, cum scholiis J. M. Phrissemii* (Cologne, 1523) f. 7v. In the last chapter of *DID*, Agricola states explicitly: 'Usum duabus in his rebus fore accipio, scriptis autorum cuiusque generis expendendis, et nostris deinde ad illorum exemplum quantum datur effingendis' (Cologne, 1539), pp. 452–3. Carl Bullemer, *Quellenkritische Untersuchungen zum I Buche der Rhetorik Melanchthons* (Würzburg, 1902), p. 2ff, already stresses Agricola's influence on Melanchthon in this respect. This small thesis is still worth reading.

12. P. Mack, 'Rudolph Agricola's Reading of Literature', *Journal of the Warburg and Courtauld Institutes*, vol. XLVIII (1985), pp. 23–41; M. van der Poel (ed. and trans.), *Rudolf Agricola: Over Dialectica en humanisme* (Baarn, 1991), Introduction , esp. p. 36.

13. E. Bizer (ed.), *Texte aus der Anfangszeit Melanchthons* (Neukirchen-Vluyn, 1966), for example p.50: 'Paulus si ineruditus homo fuisset, non potuisset tam ornatum contexere exordium [*sc. Rom.* 1: 8] in quo magna verborum Emphasi utitur. In oratione aliqua primo aliquid proponitur, postea causa subjicitur, ut Cicero *pro Marcello* in principio: item *pro Archia*'. In his commentaries on these orations, Melanchthon will stress the coherence of their exordia, which results from the logical link between a proposition and what he calls *aetiologia*. See my article (note 8 above), and compare *CR*, vol. XVI, 897, 909, 925, 948.

14. See E. Norden, *Die Antike Kunstprosa*, vol. II (Darmstadt, 1971), pp. 492ff, 516ff on theories about the language of the New Testament.

15. *CR*, vol. I, 276 (1520): 'Porro autem rerum theologicarum summam, nemo certiore *methodo* complexus est, quam Paulus in Epistola, quam ad Romanos scripsit, omnium longe gravissima. In qua communissimos et quos maxime retulit Christianae philosophiae locos excussit . . . quibus cognitis nihil superest quod desideret Theologus'; *CR*, vol. II, 456 (1530): 'Haec [*sc.* Epist ad Rom.] enim propemodum est *methodus* totius scripturae, quia disputat de iustificatione, de usu legis, de discrimine legis et evangelii, qui sunt praecipui loci doctrinae Christianae.' *CR*, vol. II, 944 (1535): 'Talis [*sc.* methodus] est Pauli Epistola ad Romanos; quare decrevi, eam iterum enarrare'. In his preface to Luther's *Operationes in Psalmos* (March 1519), Melanchthon compares the letter to the Romans with 'Atticus Mercurius, ad reliquas iter indicat', *CR*, vol. I, 72.

16. P. Melanchthon, *Annotationes in Epistulam Pauli ad Rhomanos* (Nürnberg, 1521) folio A3r; cf. Bizer (note 13 above), pp. 45, 48.

17. The first editions of both speeches were printed by Melchior Lotter: *Declamatiuncula in D. Pauli doctrinam* (Wittenberg, 1520, see note 21 below) and *Adhortatio ad Paulinae doctrinae studium* (Wittenberg, 1520; *CR*, vol. XI, 34–41) published as an appendix to Erasmus's Latin translation of *Romans*. Lotter's address to the reader (*CR*, vol. I, 276) was written by Melanchthon and is quoted in note 15 above. See the

important bibliography of Melanchthon's orations by H. Koehn, 'Philipp Melanchthons Reden. Verzeichnis der im 16. Jahrhundert erschenenen Drucke', *Archiv für Geschichte des Buchwesens*, vol. xxv (1984), col. 1323, no. 51 and col. 1325, no. 54.
As examples of orations with a rhetorical *artificium* in the margins I may quote the 1529 R. Estienne edition of *Encomium eloquentiae* (1523) Koehn, col. 1331, no. 71, and the *Adhortatio* (1520) as reprinted in *Liber selectarum declamationum* (Strasburg, 1541), pp. 1–11 (cf. also the introduction, ff iii–iv) which constitutes the start of an impressive series of collected orations, mainly printed in Strasburg. See Koehn, col. 1302, no. 1 (1541), and nos 2–39.

18. On Phrissemius and Dorp, see my article (note 1 above), pp. 7, 9n, 14n. Dorp's orations have been edited by J. IJsewijn (Leipzig, 1986). The same pattern recurs ten years later, when John Sturm, at the request of a progressive Sorbonne Doctor writes in Paris a rhetorical analysis of *Romans*, which unfortunately is lost. See J. Sturm, *Epistola apologetica contra J. Andream alterum flagrum Aegyptium* (Strasburg, 1581) p. 3, quoted by Ch. Schmidt in *La vie et les travaux de Jean Sturm* (Strasburg, 1855; reprinted Nieuwkoop, 1970), p. 11. On the relationship between Melanchthon and Sturm see my article, 'Logic and Eloquence?', *Argumentation*, v (1991), pp. 357–74.

19. See the account of this in S. Wiedenhofer's outstanding study *Formalstrukturen humanisticher und reformatorischer Theologie bei Philipp Melancthon*, Regensburger Studien zur Theologie, vol. ii (Berne, 1976) pp. 195 ff., 326 ff., Ibid., p. 66 ff., on Erasmus's 'affective theology', which inspired Melanchthon's.

20. P. Melanchthon, *Oratio de dicto Pauli 1 Timoth. IV*, in *CR*, vol. xi, p. 757: 'Cumque de totis libris primum dixit [sc Paulus], postea dividit partes materiarum, quas continent. Partim enim continent doctrinam, id est, dogmata seu articulos [fidei], quos ostendunt qualis sit Deus, et quomodo se patefecit, . . . quomodo et quo tempore filius Dei missus, crucifixus et resuscitatus sit, quae beneficia nobis donet; partim vero conciones divinae sunt adhortationes, traducentes animos ad adfectum aliquem . . .' 'Admonere tantum volui, ut cogitetis, prudentissime significari Pauli verbis, ad quos fines dirigendae sint studia, videlicet ad agnitionem veram Dei, deinde ad accendendos pios adfectus.' Cf. *CR*, vol. vi, 694–5 and *De modo et arte concionandi* (ca. 1538) where Tim. 4:13 is combined with 1 Cor. 14:3. Text in *Supplementa Melanchthoniana*, vol. V/2, P. Drews and F. Cohrs (eds), (Leipzig, 1929, reprinted Frankfurt, 1968), pp. 33–55. Ibid., p. 33: '(Nam) cuiuslibet concionis finis est proprie, ut vel doceat auditores de dogmatibus, vel ut traducat animos ad aliquem affectum.' For further details, see U. Schnell, *Die homiletische Theorie Philipp Melanchthons*, Arbeiten zur Geschichte und Theologie des Luthertums, vol. xx (Berlin, 1968).

21. P. Melanchthon, *Declamatiuncula in D. Pauli doctrinam* (1520), in *Melanchthons Werke in Auswahl*, ed. R. Stupperich, vol. i (Gütersloh, 1951), pp. 28–43 (also called 'Studienausgabe', abridged SA or MSA), and as an appendix to *Die Loci Communes Philipp Melanchthons in ihrer Uhrgestalt*, G. L. Plitt and Th. Kolde (eds) (Erlangen, 1890), pp. 262–77.

Ibid., p. 273: 'scholae, quae miseris modis excarnificant afflictas conscientias per summas suas, quae adfectibus vitiorum adeo non medentur, frivolis et nugacibus disputationibus, ut et morbo morbum addant'; 'inter scholas et sacram Pauli doctrinam quantum intersit, facile cernent, qui vel hunc a limine salutaverint. Neque iam ago, quale sit in scholis sermonis genus, quam impura et sordidata docendi disserendique ratio . . . Ita nec in scholastica theologia animo satisfecerit pius quispiam, tot hominum argutiis, nugis, technis et traditiunculis conspurcata.'

22.   B. Vickers, *In Defence of Rhetoric* (Oxford, 1988), chapters 4 and 5. Unfortunately, I cannot agree with Vickers's interpretation of Melanchthon, who in his Reply to Pico would have 'no taste for mock-encomium or irony', would have 'missed' Pico's irony, and so forth (ibid., pp. 192, 193). On the contrary, Melanchthon very well understood the passage quoted by Vickers, *l.c.*, p. 189. As early as 1523, Melanchthon states that he believes Pico was only playing: 'ludens, credo, in ἀδόξῳ argumento', that is, using the tricks of a mock encomium: *Encomium eloquentiae*, one of the most frequently reprinted orations (see Koehn, 1984), available in *CR*, vol. XI, 50 ff, and in *SA*, vol. III, pp. 43–62) as well as in other modern editions; passage quoted: *SA*, vol. III, p. 47. In a forthcoming article in *Archiv für Reformationsgeschichte* (1992), E. Rümmel shows that the *Reply* to Pico was written by one of Melanchthon's pupils. I should like to thank Judith Rice Henderson for drawing my attention to this article.

23.   P. Melanchthon, *Declamatiuncula* (1520) *l.c.*, 1890, p. 274: 'Quod Paulina minus intelliguntur, debemus eximiis istis Magistris nostris, qui cum omnis veteris literaturae rectaeque eruditionis imperiti essent, divinam Pauli orationem et rhetoricis vinctam membris, et suis compactam articulis, primum novis interpunctionibus dissecuerunt, deinde suo more secundum Aristotelem enarraverunt: ita ut nusquam ne versus quidem cum versu conveniret. Ad haec non erat vulgaris hominis officium, de quatuor sensibus in singulis prope syllabis nugari. Nec puduit audaces homines in re tam seria ludos agere . . . etc.' Immediately afterwards, Melanchthon quotes Erasmus's *Methodus* (1516).

24.   P. Melanchthon, Letter to Count Herman of Neuenahr (a pupil of Caesarius and a friend of Erasmus), Spring 1529, in *CR*, vol. I, 1043–5.

25.   Ultimately rhetorical analysis reveals the principles of God's own rhetoric, especially in the Scriptures. See for example *CR*, vol. XIII, 1224–5, already referred to above: 'Cogitemus Psalmos sapientiam, et vocem Dei esse, et Deum fontem eloquentiae, sapienter, recte et ordine loqui. Ideo in singulis Psalmis quaeratur unum aliquod principale argumentum, ut in aliis carminibus erudite scriptis, et consideretur quomodo membra cohaereant . . .; it et hic quaerimus propositionem, seriem partium, et accomodamus Psalmos, alios ad alia genera causarum, videlicet, ut iuxta puerilia praecepta diligentius consideretis, quis sit finis, quid velit efficere scriptum, an doceat, aut petat aliquid' (Comm. on Ps. 51). See also R. Schäfer, 'Melanchthons Hermeneutik im Römerbrief-Kommentar von 1532', in *Zeitschrift für*

Theologie und Kirche, LX (1963), pp. 216–35 (p. 217): 'Melanchthon geht von dem fruchtbaren Grundsatz aus, dass man ein literarisches Werk allein dann richtig versteht, wenn man es nach denselben Gesichtspunkten interpretiert, mit deren Hilfe es erzeugt worden ist.'

26. P. Melanchthon, *Dispositio orationis in Epistola Pauli ad Romanos* (1529) in *CR*, vol. XV, 445, 450–1: 'Nunc demum pervenit ad principalem propositionem, quae est huius totius Epistolae status. Ut autem architectus totam aedificii formam in animo inclusam habet, et videt quomodo omnes inter se partes consentiant, ita nos in legendis gravibus disputationibus, omnium propositionum atque argumentorum seriem oportet animo complecti. In primis autem meminisse statum necesse est, qui continet negotii summam, ad quem omnia argumenta tanquam ad caput referentur.' *CR*, vol. XV, 482: 'Porro ut architectus totius formam aedificii in animo complecti solet, ita nos totius scripti tanquam ideam quandam in animam includere debemus, ut Apostoli sententiam penitus perspiciamus . . . . Semper autem in hanc Epistolam intueri nos oportet, semper oportet habere positam ob oculos hanc sententiam, quod fide in Christum iustificemur coram patre . . . Quoties orabimus, primum in hanc Epistolam intuendum est, ut erigamus nos ac sciamus nos exaudiri, si credimus in Christum non propter merita nostra.'

27. P. Melanchthon, in *CR*, vol. I, 1044 (see note 24 above): 'Cum autem epistola ad Romanos . . . veluti methodum universae Scripturae contineat, non satis est, unum atque alterum ex illa versiculum decerpere. Tota legenda est, et considerandum, quomodo omnes inter se partes, omnia membra cohaereant atque consentiant, et venanda certa, perpetua et simplex sententia Apostoli . . . . Ego igitur in hac epistola totius seriem disputationis breviter ostendi . . . . Sed me fortasse nonnulli ridebunt, quod orationem Pauli ad vulgaria dicendi praecepta exigam. Verum res loquitur ipsa, non sine certa ratione disputasse Apostolum.'

28. See my articles cited above (notes 1, 8 and 18). The final remarks of the *Topics* commentary summarise this procedure (*ad* Cic. *Top.* 25, 29): 'Unaquaeque causa habet unum aliquem principalem statum, ut 'Milo occidit Clodium iure.' Habet quoque unaquaeque causa firmum aliquod argumentum prae reliquis, ut hoc: 'Vim vi repellere licet' [=major], Milo vim vi repulit [=minor]: ergo iure occidit Clodium. Conclusio est status . . .': *CR*, vol. XVI, 832. This example is also a 'set piece'. See for example *CR*, vol. XIII, 430, 597, 643; *CR*, vol. XVI, 975, 982–3, 989–91, 1005–6, 1017–19 (*Dispositio* of the *Pro Milone*), etc. Compare with Agricola, *DID*, ed. 1539, pp. 242, 268, 280, 'tota pro Milone oratio in ratiocinationem coniecta est'.

29. J. Willichius, *Erotematum Dialectices libri III. Quibus accessit D. Chytraei De studio dialectices recte instituendo libellus* (Basel, 1568). The prefatory letter of the latter is dated from Rostock, March 1563. Chytraeus summarises with the following dialectical analysis: 'hoc modo, ut in omni autore bono . . . primum Quaestionem, seu Propositionem, totius scripti summam continentem, excerpamus. Deinde praecipua membra et argumenta, et ex quibus locis ea ducta sint, consideremus. Tertio

nuda argumenta formis syllogismorum inclusa, et ad leges syllogismi accommodata iudicemus . . . Ornamenta vero quae accesserunt . . . praeceptis et legibus artis rhetoricae et grammaticae examinantur. Habent autem Adolescentes illustria huius . . . generis exercitationum Dialecticae exempla, in omnibus disputationibus orationum Ciceronis, et epistolarum Pauli, et enarrationibus autorum, quos in scholis explicari quotidie audiunt': pp. 272–3. Ibid., p. 274, Agricola, *DID*, II, chs 19–21 in particular; p. 275, J. Willichius, *Erot. dial. lib. III*; pp. 275–6, J. Sturm, *Part. dial lib. IV*; p. 276, J. Caesarius, *Dial. lib. X*; pp. 276–7, cf. pp. 280–1, P. Ramus: 'Nemo autem post Philippum . . . usum artis Dialecticae, in disertorum poetarum et oratorum scriptis recte intelligendis et explicandis, facilius et uberius ostendit, quam Petrus Ramus'. At the beginning and the end of this genealogy figures Philip Melanchthon, 'reverendus praeceptor noster' (p. 280). *VD.* 16, C.2759.

30. See my article in *Argumentation*, vol. V (note 18 above). In a hitherto unknown letter to P. Ramus, dated from Rostock, 22 April 1570, Chytraeus expresses his admiration: 'Etsi igitur nulla inter nos consuetudo familiaris hactenus intercessit: tamen multos iam annos, lectione librorum a te . . . editorum, in quibus velut Hercules, divinitus nostrae aetati donatus, totum orbem artium, a monstris inutilium et peregrinarum praeceptionum liberas, et suas cuique arti regiones ac fines certos attribuens, rectissimam singulis docendi et discendi viam demonstras: mirifico me tui amore et desiderio, et virtutis ac sapientiae admiratione accensum esse fateor', D. Chytraeus, *Epistolae . . . editae a D. Chytraeo authoris filio* (Hanau, 1614), pp. 547–8. Ramus was travelling in Germany at the time.

4

Order, Reason and Oratory: Rhetoric in Protestant Latin Schools

Dilwyn Knox

During the sixteenth and early seventeenth centuries rhetoric was a standard subject in Latin schools of German-speaking Protestant Europe.[1] We can chart its development in these schools through two types of source: first, school textbooks[2] and, second, school regulations and curricula.[3] The former, obviously enough, covered rhetorical theory, the latter established how rhetoric was to be taught, to whom, when and why. In this paper I would like to put the two together and outline how instruction in rhetoric at these schools responded to contemporary paedagogical exigencies.

To begin, let us look at a typical Protestant curriculum.[4] The syllabus for the Latin or 'particular' school in Krems was laid down in regulations completed in 1580 by Johannes Matthaeus, a leading Wittenberg theologian.[5] It is very much a showpiece, part of a programme, an unsuccessful one as it proved, to stamp Krems definitively Lutheran. In the most elementary class, the fifth, a boy aged about six or seven learned to write, recited the catechism and began learning Latin at the traditional rate of two words a day.[6] Some time after his seventh birthday he might be promoted to the next class, the fourth, where he would continue a very similar syllabus at a moderately more advanced level. To practice his Latin he would study, for example, a collection of elementary Latin dialogues, Sebald Heyden's *Formula puerilium colloquiorum pro primis tyronibus*, on Mondays, Tuesdays, Thursdays and Fridays from one to two o'clock and Joachim Camerarius' *Praecepta morum puerilium* on Thursdays and Fridays from two to three o'clock. The latter also introduced him to *civilitas*, or good comportment, an accomplishment much emphasised in Protestant curricula.[7] In the next class, the middle of five, when nine or more years old, he would continue

religious instruction, begin arithmetic and Greek, and improve his
Latin and moral fibre with Aesop's *Fables*, the *Disticha Catonis* and
Erasmus' *De civilitate*, a text on good comportment like Camerarius's. Some time after his eleventh birthday a schoolboy would
move up to the second class. He continued religious instruction,
Erasmus's *De civilitate* and arithmetic, and studied Latin and Greek
grammar and comprehension at a more advanced level. He began
studying theology and music. Finally, if he passed his examinations
and was more than thirteen years old, he was promoted to the first
class. His syllabus remained similar to that of the previous class,
apart from two additions, dialectic and rhetoric.

Why did Matthaeus reserve rhetoric and dialectic for the end of
the curriculum? Certainly not because the required primers of
rhetoric and dialectic, those of Lucas Lossius, were difficult. They
were considerably more straightforward than, say, the intermediary
Latin and Greek grammar taught in the second and first class. The
explanation lies instead in what was by Matthaeus's day accepted
policy. Students were to study subjects in a fixed order and
according to age and ability.[8] At Krems they could be promoted to
the fourth, third, second and first classes only after, respectively,
their seventh, ninth, eleventh and thirteenth birthdays. This rule,
Matthaeus insisted, applied to all boys, however quick and retentive.
A sound education required more than that a boy should acquire
knowledge and pass examinations. To profit fully from each subject
a boy needed a commensurate psychological and moral maturity.[9]

For rhetoric the requisite maturity was rationality. Until the age of
seven a boy was only potentially a rational being. The formative
stage was the next seven years, from the age of seven to fourteen or
fifteen, the years during which he was at Latin school. During these
years parents and teachers had to direct the growth of a boy's
reason, his capacity to reflect on information from the senses and to
control impulses like hunger, fear and anger. A Latin school
promoted this variously. It taught a boy to check instinctive,
unreflective verbal expression by making him learn Latin and speak
it in and out of the classroom. It taught him to check instinctive
bodily movement according to the rules of *civilitas*. And it taught
him ethical and theological imperatives that censured improper
thoughts provoked by a disordered will inherited from Adam.
These controls had to be in place before a boy could be entrusted
with rhetoric and dialectic. Only when he had acquired *ratio*, only
when he was more than thirteen years old and was just or was about

to become an *adolescens*, should a boy begin to learn *oratio*, that is, the rhetorical and dialectical techniques that would permit him to express rather than suppress his thoughts. To rephrase Cato's influential definition of an orator,[10] first, the *puer bonus*, then the *adolescens bonus dicendi peritus*.

Matthaeus's curriculum and objective are typical. Like the Latin school at Krems, Protestant Latin schools and gymnasia throughout German-speaking Europe taught rhetoric and dialectic in conjunction. They assigned these subjects with remarkably few exceptions[11] only to boys in the most advanced class of standard five-class Latin schools or a corresponding class in other schools, that is to say, to students who were, ideally, more than thirteen years old, who had already a good grounding in Latin grammar and who had begun Greek and other advanced subjects, including possibly Hebrew.[12] For instance, in regulations published in 1570 for the Latin school at Breslau, the newly appointed rector, Petrus Vincentius, assigned Melanchthon's rhetoric and dialectic to, and only to, the most advanced of five classes.[13] Even highly selective schools reserved rhetoric for the end of the curriculum. Regulations drawn up for the *Gymnasium* to accompany its move from Nuremberg to nearby Altdorf in 1575 mandated only three classes, since the school enrolled boys who had already studied Latin grammar at ordinary Latin schools. Rhetoric remained confined to the most advanced class.[14] Again, *Fürstenschulen* at Meissen, Grimma and Pforta in Electoral Saxony enrolled students who had already excelled in standard Latin or 'particular' schools. They too assigned rhetoric and dialectic only in the most advanced class, that is, the equivalent of the class, the first, in which these subjects were introduced in standard five-class Latin schools of Electoral Saxony.[15]

Some curricula, admittedly, recommended that students learn elementary rhetorical ideas and terminology earlier in the curriculum. At Krems, Matthaeus suggested that teachers of the second as well as the first class should explain 'metaphors and other tropes and figures' when going through Virgil and Terence.[16] Occasionally, too, curricula assigned books or sections of books on the figures and tropes in the second most advanced class.[17] Again, students in classes other than the most advanced sometimes practised rhetorical style from Erasmus' *De copia*[18] or wrote prose and verse compositions that must have required some rhetorical instruction.[19] Nevertheless only in the most advanced class did boys begin rhetoric and dialectic in earnest and learn them as instruments of articulation rather than analysis. This eliminated dialectic and rhetoric from the many Latin schools where resources or population warranted fewer than five elementary classes. Nor, obviously, did vernacular schools or schools for girls ever teach rhetoric or dialectic.

The allocation of rhetoric and dialectic at the end of the curriculum limited what could be taught. Students had only one or possibly two years to acquire a good grounding in subjects that they would need immediately at university[20] and eventually in their intended positions in church and state.[21] Clearly they could not be expected to do more than learn the essentials. School regulations geared their remarks accordingly. Teachers had to finish prescribed rhetorical primers within a set period, usually one[22] or at the most two[23] semesters. They were forbidden to introduce material on their own initiative.[24] They were not to encumber students with unnecessary theoretical subtleties.[25] And so on.

Two further considerations limited rhetoric and dialectic to essentials. First, Protestant school regulations and authors emphasised practice rather than theory. Secular and religious authorities wanted Latin schools to supply orators of the spoken and written word, not rhetoricians. The rules taught at Latin schools should, therefore, be ones that students could apply in written and oral exercises.[26] With this in mind, school regulations sometimes even braved the vernacular and recommended that boys should practice rhetoric by writing letters, supplications, legal defences and the like in German as well as Latin.[27] As exercises for oratory they suggested that boys should perform plays to practice their delivery of voice and gesture.[28] The most important rhetorical exercises, however, were declamations and similar compositions.[29] These exercised the full range of written and spoken rhetorical techniques. When writing them, students practised the invention of arguments (*inventio*), arrangement of argument (*dispositio*) and style (*elocutio*). When reciting them aloud, they practised memory (*memoria*) and delivery of voice and gesture (*pronuntiatio*).[30] For delivery, indeed, such exercises in oratory provided the only means of practising and assessing a skill that successful students would eventually need as lawyers, councillors, preachers and in other secular and ecclesiastical professions.[31] Not by chance, therefore, declamations and similar oratory featured prominently in the public calendars of Latin schools. They were occasions on which students marshalled a full array of rhetorical techniques and displayed them to public scrutiny. At Krems, for example, on feast days and at examinations held twice a year students would recite from memory compositions appropriate to the occasion. Less advanced students would, say, deliver declamations composed by their teachers. More advanced students, including perhaps some from classes other than the first, could deliver their own.[32]

Second, teaching methods encouraged this drive to simplicity. The governing principle for rhetoric and dialectic, as for other subjects, was that students should thoroughly learn a little each lesson and gradually accumulate overall proficiency. For instance, regulations of 1583 for the gymnasium in Nordhausen required teachers to cover half a page of a primer (about eighty words) in each of the two weekly lessons on rhetoric.[33] Practical considerations necessitated this approach. Since most students could not be expected to buy books, schools often resorted to dictation. This restricted how much could be covered within an hour, as regulations implicitly acknowledged. Rhetoric teachers were told, for instance, to keep dictations short and simple, repeat dictated material several times and check that boys had copied correctly.[34] This prepared the ground for what was to follow. A teacher had two obligations. First, he had to explain what he had dictated. He could do this best through examples, especially classical and Scriptural ones; he should avoid abstract theoretical analysis. This was a point on which school regulations insisted.[35] At Krems, for instance, during rhetoric classes the rector had to complete within two semesters not only the prescribed rhetoric primer but also an oration by Cicero to flesh out the theory.[36] Second, a teacher had to help students begin memorising the dictation. The preferred method at this point, for rhetoric as for other subjects, was the catechism.[37] After the lesson students would continue memorising the dictation both at home and in school hours reserved for preparation.[38] Finally, during the first fifteen or so minutes of the next hour devoted to rhetoric a teacher might repeat the previous hour's material and test students on what they had memorised.[39]

Procedures often differed in detail, sometimes in substance.[40] For instance, contemporaries recognised the shortcomings of dictation. It wasted time and, if not carefully monitored, left boys with inaccurate copies from which to memorise. When possible, therefore, they recommended that dictation should be dispensed with.[41] If so, they presumably knew or believed that students could use school copies for memorising rhetorical material. At least one rector published a textbook of rhetoric so as to eliminate dictation.[42] But whatever the methods, the goal remained the same. The object was to implant into a student's memory a complete, if schematic, rhetoric and dialectic[43] together perhaps with illustrative passages and perhaps an entire oration. Teachers could reinforce this cumulative memorisation by regular tests. Some regulations, for instance, required that once every three or four weeks teachers should at random ask students to recite from memory a half or full section of their primer.[44] More imposing were the examinations held in the presence of school inspectors.[45] At Krems, for instance, examinations were held twice a year, once in March and then in September just before the vintage. On these occasions, all students in the first class, except those from outside Krems and older students who decided of their own accord that they were insufficiently prepared, were examined by the rector in the presence of the four school inspectors – the town preacher supported by three well-educated townsmen. For rhetoric and dialectic, as for other subjects, students had to recite passages of their primer from memory.[46] These may seem daunting expectations today. To memorise the whole of, say, Lossius's abbreviated version of Melanchthon's rhetoric and dialectic within a year would require learning about a page of a typical octavo school edition or 140 words each week. But contemporaries, even highly experienced ones like Petrus Vincentius, thought this or similar expectations realistic, even too modest.[47] Certainly they were no more demanding than those for other subjects on the syllabus.

The pedagogical and practical constraints outlined above determined the type of rhetorical textbook used in Protestant Latin schools. Classical rhetorics like Cicero's *De oratore*, *Orator*, *De inventione*, *Partitiones oratoriae*, Quintilian's *Institutiones oratoriae* and the pseudo-Ciceronian *Rhetorica ad Herennium* were deemed unsuitable primers.[48] They were assigned, if at all, as supplementary rather than required texts, and usually at gymnasia rather than ordinary Latin schools.[49] They were appropriate instead for university or special schools where curricula overlapped with those of universities. This held true also for popular Renaissance works like Agricola's *De inventione dialectica*.[50] Ambitious syllabi, notably those of Sturm and others for the gymnasium at Strasburg, that assigned classical Latin and Greek works on rhetoric and dialectic as the main texts and sometimes at early stages of the curriculum,[51] were very rare.[52] Presumably contemporaries thought them impracticable and pointless. Even gymnasia, like those at Hornbach and Lauingen, for which Sturm drew up curricula,[53] later diluted his syllabus for rhetoric.[54] Nor did former pupils of Sturm or other Latin school rectors fully conversant with his programme at Strasburg implement his rhetorical syllabus in their own schools.[55]

What Latin schools needed instead was a concise textbook stripped of all impractical details.[56] Such a rhetoric was to hand, that of Melanchthon, the chief architect of the Protestant school programme. During the early years of the Reformation it had appeared in three versions: the *De rhetorica libri tres*, first published at Wittenberg in 1519; the *Institutiones rhetoricae*, first published at Hagen in 1521; and the *Elementorum rhetorices libri duo*, first published at Wittenberg in 1531.[57] In these various redactions Melanchthon's rhetoric immediately became standard in Protestant Latin schools.[58] Melanchthon had done more than trim classical rhetoric. To rid rhetoric of all impracticalities Melanchthon completely eliminated two of the five departments into which rhetoric had been divided since Roman antiquity:

> The art of rhetoric is almost wholly incorporated in three subjects, the devising of subject matter, arrangement of subject matter and expression. Therefore I shall not propound rules for the other two subjects of memory and delivery. The former is helped very little by theoretical rules, while delivery nowadays is quite different from what it was in antiquity. The most appropriate manner of delivery should be learned by imitating public speakers.[59]

Protestant authors and school regulations[60] built on Melanchthon's foundation. Like Melanchthon they limited instruction in rhetorical theory to *inventio, dispositio* and *elocutio*. This is not to say that they thought memory and delivery unimportant. On the contrary, both were essential in oratory. The appeal of declamations and other spoken compositions, as mentioned above, was precisely that they did exercise the full range of rhetorical techniques, not least memory and delivery. But rules for the last two, contemporaries agreed with Melanchthon, would serve little. Students should memorise declamations and other oratory just as they memorised everything else at Latin school, that is, by building up a stock of perfectly memorised short passages, rather than through mnemonic tricks and tags of the kind described in classical rhetoric. Nor could boys usefully learn delivery of voice and gesture from fixed rules, especially antiquated classical ones. Instead they should observe contemporary standards of good delivery and learn them by practice rather than theory.[61]

Good though it was, Melanchthon's rhetoric had two drawbacks. First, it was, as school regulations pointed out, a guide to the *methodus* of rhetoric, that is, it taught through *'definitiones*, regel unnd andern *praecepta'*. In the classroom it had to be supplemented with readings from Terence, Cicero, Aesop, Virgil and others.[62] In short, Melanchthon's rhetoric did not, on its own, present rhetoric through examples rather than rules, as contemporaries preferred. Second, Melanchthon's textbooks of rhetoric and dialectic were not catechetical. To remedy these shortcomings Protestant authors such as Georg Meier,[63] Lucas Lossius,[64] Martin Crusius,[65] Michael Neander,[66] Johannes Rivius,[67] Johann Mercklin[68] and other authors rewrote Melanchthon's rhetoric and dialectic, sometimes with the latter's blessing, as a catechism and supplied more and longer examples.[69] These 'Melanchthonian' rhetorics, rather than Melanchthon's originals, were the ones that best corresponded with the needs of sixteenth-century Protestant classrooms. To quote the regulations of 1559 for Latin schools in Württemberg:

> In the second hour from nine to ten o'clock Melanchthon's *Rhetorica* should be studied in the most advanced of the five classes. This should be used and kept at hand together with Georg Meier's *Quaestiones rhetoricae*, since this is a fine abridgement of Melanchthon's work in the form of a catechism and since it also includes a selection of good passages from orations in which rhetorical skills are well applied by Latin authors. One or two rules should be explained clearly and thoroughly. At the same time on the next day the class should repeat and recite these rules from memory before continuing onto the next rule. Since rhetorical rules are bare and useless unless they are illustrated by examples, and so that students can see how the rules should be used, a passage from an oration by Cicero or from Livy, as quoted in the above mentioned work by Meier, should be studied to illustrate each *status* or *genus causae*. Then the teacher should carefully point out the *argumentum*, the *partes orationis*, the *status*, the *argumenta confirmationis* and how they are embellished and developed in each part of the speech. The teachers should concentrate first on *inventio*, then *dispositio* and finally *elocutio*, and thereby demonstrate the rules of rhetoric in the above mentioned way.[70]

During the early years of the Reformation, then, instruction in rhetoric in Protestant Latin schools assumed a distinctive pattern. It promoted a simple, complete introduction to essential rhetorical ideas that adolescent students could apply in analysis and oratory. Its pedagogical methods were not in themselves new or peculiarly Protestant. During the fifteenth and early sixteenth centuries Northern European school regulations and authors, spurred by what they saw as the success of Italian humanist pedagogy, had insisted that teachers complete texts within an allotted time, teach the *trivium* or parts of it simply and eliminate theoretical intricacies. Like their Protestant counterparts, too, they recommended the catechism, repetition, a steady, incremental memorisation, and instruction by examples and reading texts rather than theoretical analysis.[71]

What was, however, new was the application of these methods to rhetoric. It was new because before the end of the fifteenth century rhetoric had been the Cinderella of the *trivium* in Latin schools. Curricula in Northern Europe – at least as far as school regulations and teaching contracts tell – had emphasised grammar and dialectic[72] rather than rhetoric, and disputations rather than declamations.[73] From the late fifteenth century onwards, however, rhetoric features more conspicuously.[74] During this period, too, Northern humanists wrote primers of rhetoric and recommended oratory, notably the declamation, as the best way to acquire eloquence.[75] These were reforms inspired by Italian and subsequently Northern humanists' insistence that schools teach rhetoric alongside dialectic.[76] When taught at schools without rhetoric, wrote Melanchthon, dialectic became a poor and useless thing.[77] Scholastic quibbles, particularly those of boys and adolescents, were proof enough.

With Melanchthon's rhetoric, in its original and adapted versions, Protestant Latin schools found an appropriate means for realising their objectives. It lasted well. In the first quarter of the seventeenth century it was still the standard rhetoric. This is contrary to what is, I believe, the accepted opinion that Ramist rhetoric supplanted Melanchthon's by the turn of the century. Certainly Ramist rhetoric did achieve some popularity during the last decade of the sixteenth century and the first two or so of the seventeenth.[78] For instance, the Latin schools of the town of Braunschweig used a version of Melanchthon's rhetoric from the 1530s to about 1600.[79] From the 1590s onwards they began adopting

Ramist rhetoric, at first in conjunction with Melanchthon's,[80] and later on its own.[81]

And, on paper at least, Ramist rhetoric certainly suited the purposes of Protestant schools well. It was simple, easily memorisable, and integrated into a curriculum that promised to teach all subjects to students between the ages of seven to fifteen.[82] Every branch of philosophy and every part of each branch could be defined by a process of definition and dichotomy. Rhetoric and dialectic were the two arts of speaking and writing coherently and elegantly. Rhetoric could be divided into the two subjects of *elocutio* and *pronuntiatio*.[83] These in turn could be divided into two. *Pronuntiatio*, for instance, could be divided into delivery of voice and gesture. And so on. By this simple process or 'method' students could easily understand and memorise all parts of rhetoric. Ramist tables further facilitated comprehension and memorisation. Furthermore, Ramist rhetoric, unlike Melanchthon's, had a further advantage in that it laid down rules even for delivery of voice and gesture. For a pedagogy that emphasised *civilitas*, that is, the control of bodily movement and discourse according to rational standards, this was an advantage indeed. Even in the early years of the Reformation Protestant authors had objected that Melanchthon's comments on rhetorical delivery were too sweeping. In detail classical rules were anachronistic, but nevertheless decorum and *civilitas* provided absolute standards that obtained at all times and places.[84]

Despite these advantages, however, Protestant Latin schools did not adopt Ramist rhetoric wholesale. Printed sources that I have seen suggest instead that most schools still used an original or revised version of Melanchthon's rhetoric in the first quarter of the seventeenth century and that when they did adopt Ramist rhetoric they often taught it, as at Braunschweig, together with Melanchthon's.[85] Furthermore Ramist works on rhetoric, for reasons and in ways that I have not explored adequately, were rapidly superseded in Protestant Latin schools in German-speaking Europe by new primers of rhetoric primers like those of Vossius.[86] Perhaps the most that can be said for Ramist rhetoric is that it loosened the hold of Melanchthon's rhetoric in Protestant Latin schools and thereby prepared the way for new primers that drew eclectically on many sources, including Melanchthon, Ramus and their followers.

*   *   *

Regulations and textbooks tell us only what should have happened. How successfully Protestant Latin schools taught rhetoric is quite another matter and not one I can address here. But to conclude I would like to suggest what sources might help us gauge the success of their programme. Orations, letters, pamphlets and other texts tell us, unfortunately, very little. We cannot determine whether their authors perfected their rhetoric, if any, at a Latin school or whether they did so at university. For the same reason comments on contemporary oratory, for instance assessments of pastors' preaching in visitation records, are irrelevant. Nor do representative school exercise books survive. Those that do survive were written by German princes or other noble-born pupils with private tutors.[87]

We do, however, have at least some records of Latin school examinations held in the presence of school inspectors.[88] Furthermore, records of visitations to Latin schools and of visitations of other kinds that included school inspections survive in abundance.[89] Most remain unpublished. But those that have been published suggest that unpublished archival material of this kind might provide, if not answers, at least clarification. For instance, published visitation records suggest that Latin schools were on the whole tolerably competent, particularly Latin schools which taught rhetoric and dialectic.[90] Perhaps, then, students and teachers were more or less fulfilling their requirements for rhetoric. Comments specifically on rhetoric and dialectic in printed sources, however, are too few and varied to permit general conclusions. Sometimes visitors found all as it should be.[91] At other times they found instruction of rhetoric so unsatisfactory that they had to remedy matters immediately. A visitation to Speyer in 1595, for instance, found the rector so incompetent at rhetoric, amongst other things, that the visitors ordered that the teacher of the second class, whom they judged to have a good knowledge of rhetoric, should take over rhetoric in the most advanced class.[92] But even unfavourable assessments reveal something. They tell us that instruction in rhetoric and dialectic at Latin schools was taken seriously and that secular and religious authorities took whatever measures they could to ensure that it was taught according to the guidelines laid down in contemporary school regulations.

74   *Order, Reason and Oratory*

Notes and References

In the notes I have used the following abbreviations:

CR   *Corpus reformatorum.*
ES   *Evangelische Schulordnungen,* 3 vols, ed. by Reinhold Vormbaum (Gütersloh, 1860–4).
IL   *Institutionis literatae sive de discendi atque docendi ratione tomus primus[-tertius],* 3 vols in 4 pts, ed. by the Schola Torunensis (Toruń, 1586–8).
MGdESG   *Mitteilungen der Gesellschaft für deutsche Erziehungs- und Schulgeschichte.*
MGP   *Monumenta Germaniae Paedagogica.*
MP   Karl Hartfelder, *Melanchthoniana paedagogica* (Leipzig, 1892).
SPUF   *Les statuts et privilèges des universités françaises depuis leur fondation jusqu'en 1789,* 4 vols, ed. by Marcel Fournier (vol. 4 with Charles Engel) (Paris, 1890–4).
SWSG   *Sammlung der württembergischen Schulgesetze,* ed. by Theodor Eisenlofir and Carl Hirzel, 3 pts (Tübingen, 1839, 1847, 1843).
VfSO   *Vor- und frühreformatorische Schulordnungen und Schulverträge in deutscher und niederländischer Sprache* (2 vols), with continuous pagination, ed. by Johannes Müller (Sammlung selten gewordener pädagogischer Schriften früherer Zeiten, 12, 13) (Zschopau, 1885, 1886).

1. For sixteenth-century Protestant education, see Gerald Strauss, *Luther's House of Learning. Indoctrination of the Young in the German Reformation* (Baltimore, 1978). For more recent literature, see Susan C. Karant-Nunn, 'The Reality of Early Lutheran Education. The Electoral District of Saxony – A Case Study': *Lutherjahrbuch,* vol. LVII (1990), pp. 128–46, idem in *Renaissance Quarterly,* vol. XLIII (1991), pp. 788–98.
2. J.J. Murphy, *Renaissance rhetoric. A Short Title Catalogue* (New York, 1981) includes many titles, though incompletely.
3. For convenient collections of original and paraphrased regulations, see *ES,* vols 1–2; Georg Mertz, *Das Schulwesen der deutschen Reformation im 16. Jahrhundert* (Heidelberg, 1902).
4. For the Latin school at Krems, see Anton Baran, *Geschichte der alten lateinischen Stadtschule und des Gymnasiums in Krems* (Krems, 1895); Franz Schönfellner, *Krems zwischen Reformation und Gegenreformation* (Horn, 1985), pp. 111–20.
5. Johannes Matthaeus, *Scholae Cremsensis in Austria descripta formula. Nunc demum in novorum paedagogorum gratiam, qui ad scholas aperiendas vel regendas vocantur, edita* . . . (Wittenberg, 1581), sig. b7ᵛ–c4ʳ. Matthaeus's preface is dated 1580 on sig. a4ᵛ. Matthaeus discusses his timetable: ibid., sig. a8ʳ–b7ʳ. This and Mattheus' German version of about 1576 are reprinted in Baran, *Geschichte,* pp. 16–18, 21–7, 28–45, together with Moses Neumann's 1567 regulations.

6. Pre-Reformation regulations stipulated the same rate; see for example *VfSO*, vol. 2, pp. 147 (Nuremberg, ca 1505), p. 171 (Nördlingen, 1512).
7. Dilwyn Knox, 'Erasmus' *De civilitate* and the Religious Origins of Protestant Civility', in *The Renaissance Revisited*, ed. by Alison Brown and Pat Rubin (Oxford, forthcoming).
8. Cf. for example Melanchthon, *Ratio scholae Norembergae nuper institutae* (a. 1526) in *MP*, p. 9; *IL*, 3: 321–22 (Görlitz, 1586).
9. Matthaeus, *Scholae Cremsensis formula*, sig. c7^v-c8^r.
10. Quintilian, *Institutio oratoria*, 12.1.1.
11. For example note 77 below; and *ES*, vol. 1, pp. 494–8 (Stralsund, 1591), vol. 2, p.76 (Joachimsthal, Gymnasium, 1607).
12. See references in notes 13, 58, 63, 79, 80 and 81 below; and for example *MP*, p. 4 (Eisleben, 1525), p. 9 (Nuremberg, 1526), *ES*, vol. 1, p. 20 (Hamburg, 1529), p. 65 (Mecklenburg, 1552), pp. 73n, 89n, 99 (Württemberg, 1559), pp. 73n, 87n (Württemberg, 1582), *MGP*, vol. 38, p. 161 (Rostock, 1544); vol. 60, p. 333 (Augsburg, 1557).
13. *ES*, vol. 1, pp. 200–1, 203–5, 216, 217 (Breslau, 1570).
14. *IL*, vol. 2-2, pp. 195, 197, 211.
15. *ES*, vol. 1, pp. 244, 282, 283, 285 (Electoral Saxony, 1580).
16. Matthaeus, *Scholae Cremsensis formula*, sig. b5^{r-v}.
17. Curricula assigned works or sections of works such as (i) Mosellanus' *Tabulae de schematibus et tropis*; see for example *MGP*, vol. 38, p. 287 (Wismar 1566); *IL*, vol. 2-2, pp. 195, 197, 212 (Altdorf, 1575) and (ii) sections from one of Melanchthon's rhetorical textbooks, which boys would study completely in the most advanced class; see *MGP*, vol. 42, pp. 492–5 (Regensburg, 1615); vol. 55, pp. 165–6 (Graz, 1594).
18. See *ES*, vol. 2, pp. 30, 43 (Gotha, Gymnasium, 1605); *MGP*, vol. 1, p. 57 (Braunschweig, 1535), p. 112 (Braunschweig, Martineum, 1562); *MGP*, vol. 42, pp. 492, 494, 495 (Regensburg, Gymnasium poeticum, 1615).
19. Of the kind described in Aphthonius's *Progymnasmata* and Joachim Camerarius (the elder), *Elementa rhetoricae*.
20. Melanchthon in *CR*, vol. 10, 86; *ES* vol. 1, pp. 70–1, 73 (Württemberg 1559, 1582), 200 (Breslau, 1570).
21. See for example *Loßdorffische Schůlordnung. Auff befelch deß Wolgeborn Herren, Herrn Hanns Wilhelmen, Herrn zü Losenstein vnnd Schallenburg etc. gestelt, imm Jar . . . 1574* (with *Leges Scholae Losdorfianae & Argentinensibus*) (Augsburg, 1574), sig. C7^{r-v} (Loosdorf, 1574).
22. For example *MGP*, vol. 1, p. 177 (Town of Braunschweig, Latin schools, 1621); *Loßdorffische Schůlordnung*, sig. D2^v–D3^v (Loosdorf, 1574).
23. For example Matthaeus, *Scholae Cremsensis formula*, sig. b1^{r-v}, b4^v; *ES*, vol. 1, p.87 (Württemberg, 1582).
24. For example *ES*, vol. 1, p. 232 (Electoral Saxony, 1580); *Loßdorffische Schůlordnung*, sig. D4^r-D5^r (Loosdorf, 1574).
25. For example *ES*, vol. 1, p. 112 (Württemberg, cloister schools, 1582), pp. 460–1 (Augsburg, 1558); *Loßdorffische Schůlordnung*, sig. D2^v–D3^v , E3^r (Loosdorf, 1574); Matthaeus, *Scholae Cremsensis formula*, sig. b4^v.
26. For example Joannes Rivius, *De puerorum institutione*, published with his *De rhetorica libri II* and other works (Louvain, 1550), sig. i5^v.

27. For example *Loßdorffische Schülordnung*, sig. C7^{r-v} (Loosdorf, 1574); *MGP*, vol. 38, pp. 479–83 (Güstrow, 1602, 1662).

28. For example Petrus Vincentius in *ES*, vol. 1, pp. 198–9 (Breslau, 1570); *IL*, vol. 3, p. 265 (Görlitz, 1566). On plays as an important part of Protestant and Catholic education, see Strauss, *Luther's House of Learning*, p. 143 and references there.

29. For example Bebel in note 75 below; and *ES*, vol. 1, pp. 174–5 (Pomerania, 1563), p. 204 (Breslau, 1570); *MGP*, vol. 42, pp. 495, 497 (Regensburg, 1615).

30. For delivery in oral exercises, see for example *ES*, vol. 1, p. 317 (Brieg [Brzeg], 1581), p. 497 (Stralsund, 1591); vol. 2, p. 47 (Gotha, Gymnasium, 1605); Sturm, *De exercitationibus rhetoricis liber academicus* in *IL*, vol. 1, pp. 389, 392, 397.

31. See for example David Chytraeus, *De ratione discendi et ordine studiorum in singulis artibus recte instituendo* (Wittenberg, 1564), sig. D5^{r-v}, pt 2, ch. 6. Church ordinances gave guidelines for examining pastors and sextons on their delivery; see *Churfürstlicher Pfaltz Kirchen-Raths Ordnung de Anno 1564* (S.l., s.d.), pp. 15–16 (Electoral Palatinate, 1564).

32. Matthaeus, *Scholae Cremsensis formula*, sig. b6^v–b7^r. Similarly students sometimes practised disputations before they studied dialectic in the first class; ibid., sig. b7^r, c2^v.

33. See *MGdESG*, vol. 2, pp. 123, 127.

34. For example *MGP*, vol. 1, pp. 128 (Town of Braunschweig, 1596); *MGdESG*, vol. 2, p. 89 (Nordhausen, 1583).

35. See for example *ES*, vol. 1, p. 89 (Württemberg, 1559), p. 245 (Electoral Saxony, 1580); vol. 2, p. 98 (Görlitz, 1609).

36. Matthaeus, *Scholae Cremsensis formula*, sig. b1^{r-v}, b4^v–b5^v.

37. For the catechism in Protestant education, see Strauss, *Luther's House of Learning*, pp. 155–75.

38. For example Matthaeus, *Scholae Cremsensis formula*, sig. b8^v–c3^v, c8^v, d3^v–d4^r.

39. For example *ES*, vol. 1, p. 87 (Württemberg, 1582), p. 89 (Württemberg, 1559), pp. 244–5 (Electoral Saxony, 1580).

40. For methods of teaching rhetoric see for example *ES*, vol. 1, pp. 87, 112–13 (Württemberg, 1582), pp. 202–3 (Breslau, 1570) , pp. 244–5 (Electoral Saxony, 1580), *MGdESG*, vol. 2, pp. 91–2, 125, 127 (Nordhausen, 1583); Matthaeus, *Scholae Cremsensis formula*, sig. b4^v–b6^r, d3^v–d4^r; *Loßdorffische Schülordnung*, sig. D2^v–D3^r, E2^v–E3^v (Loosdorf, 1574).

41. For example Matthaeus, *Scholae Cremsensis formula*, sig. b4^r, b5^r, b5^v; *Loßdorffische Schülordnung*, sig. D2^v–D3^v, E3^v (Loosdorf, 1574).

42. Georg Meier (Maier), *Quaestiones rhetoricae ex libris M. Ciceronis, Quintiliani, et Philippi Melanchthonis* (Magdeburg, 1535), sig. A3^r.

43. For example *ES*, vol. 1, pp. 202–3 (Breslau, 1570), p. 283 (Electoral Saxony, Fürstenschulen, 1580); *MGP*, vol. 38, p. 212 (Mecklenburg, 1552).

44. *ES*, vol. 1, pp. 112–13 (Württemberg, cloister schools, 1582).

45. For rhetoric in such examinations, see for example *ES*, vol. 1, p. 99 (Württemberg, 1559), pp. 246, 262, 265–6, 286–7 (Electoral Saxony, 1580), p. 378 (Nordhausen, 1583); *MGP*, vol. 27, p. 46 (Darmstadt, 1629).

For records of examinations that included rhetoric, see for example MGdESG, vol. 6, pp. 218–22, (Laubach, 1584–1602); vol. 8, p. 36 (Weimar, 1610).

46. Matthaeus, *Scholae Cremsensis formula*, sig. a5^r-a7^v, c4^v, c6^v.

47. *ES*, vol. 1, p. 203 (Breslau, 1570).

48. By contrast classical rhetorical texts are prominent in Jesuit curricula for schools in German-speaking Europe and elsewhere; see *MGP*, vol. 2, pp. 151, 195, 209; vol. 5, pp. 193–4, 196–9, 398–425, 474–9; vol. 16, pp. 6–14; and so on. On Jesuit rhetoric manuals, see Andrea Battistini, 'I manuali di retorica dei Gesuiti', in *La 'Ratio studiorum'*, ed. Gian Paolo Brizzi (Roma, 1981) pp. 77–120. Despite their preference for classical works (ibid., pp. 83–4) Jesuits too recognized that school students needed a primer (ibid., p. 84ff.).

49. For example *ES*, vol. 1, pp. 201, 203, 217 (Breslau, 1570), p. 464 (Augsburg, 1558); vol. 2, pp. 762–3 (Melanchthon, *Ratio scholae Norembergae nuper institutae*, a. 1526); *IL*, part 2, vol. 2, pp. 195, 197 (Altdorf, Gymnasium, 1575); *SWSG*, vol. 2, p. 22 (Tübingen, Gymnasium, 1557).

50. Latin schools and gymnasia only rarely assigned Agricola's *De inventione*; see for example *ES*, vol. 1, p. 464 (Augsburg 1558); *IL*, vol. 2-2, p. 195 (Altdorf 1575); *VfSO*, vol. 2, p. 257 (Zwickau 1523); *SWSG*, vol. 2, p. 22 (Tübingen, Gymnasium, 1557).

51. For documents and curricula, see *SPUF*, vol. 4, part 1, pp. 19–21, 31–2, 51, 53–4, 60–1, 67–9; *ES*, vol. 1, pp. 653–745.

52. I have found only three curricula emulating, at least in part, Sturm's specifications for rhetoric; see *ES*, vol. 2, pp. 30, 43, 44, 47 (Gotha, Gymnasium, 1605); *GSB*, vol. 1, pp. 96–7 (Basel, 1589); *IL*, vol. 3, pp. 658–9 (Gandersheim, Paedagogium, 1571).

53. *ES*, vol. 1, pp. 723–45 or *MGP*, vol. 49, pp. 51–96 (Lauingen, 1565); *MGP*, vol. 49, pp. 97–9 (Hornbach, 1573) and *SPUF*, vol. 4, part 1, pp. 78–88 (Lauingen, 1564-65).

54. Curricula for these gymnasia record for example (i) 'Rhetorica Philippi Melanthonis'; see *MGP*, vol. 49, p. 131 (Hornbach 1575); (ii) Nicolaus Reussner's *Elementa artis rhetoricae*, first edn Strasburg, 1571; see for example *MGP*, vol. 49, p. 100 (Lauingen, 1573), p. 102 (Hornbach, 1574); (iii) an unspecified 'rhetorica'; see *MGP*, vol. 49, p. 99 (Hornbach, 1573) and (iv) 'Rhetorices Crusii lib. secundus de tropis et schematibus'; see *MGP* vol. 49, p. 98 (Hornbach, 1573). Regulations for Latin schools elsewhere cited Sturm approvingly but ignored his curricula for rhetoric; see for example *Loßdorffische Schülordnung*, sig. C5^r, C7^v, D2^v–D5^r, E3^r, F1^v (Loosdorf, 1574).

55. See for example (i) Georgius Fabricius, *Rerum misnicarum libri VII* (Leipzig, 1569), pp. 195–7 for the 1546 curriculum for the Fürstenschule at Meissen and (ii) *GSB*, vol. 1, pp. 66–9, for the 1541 curriculum for the Latin school at Basel drawn up by Thomas Platter; when planning his curriculum, Platter visited Sturm's gymnasium (ibid., p. 63).

56. Cf. *IL*, vol. 2-2, pp. 195, 211 (Altdorf, 1575).

57. For these works, see *MGP*, vol. 7, pp. 580, 581, 589; *CR*, vol. I, pp. 62–6, *MP*, pp. 211–17; and Meerhoff's article in this volume.

58. For example see notes 79, 80, 85 below; and *VfSO*, vol. 2, p. 257
     (Zwickau, 1523); *ES*, vol. 1, pp. 36, 42 (Schleswig-Holstein, 1542),
     46 (Braunschweig-Wolfenbüttel, 1543), pp. 74n (Württemberg, 1559);
     vol. 2, pp. 75, 76 (Joachimsthal, Gymnasium, 1607); *MGP*, vol. 24,
     pp. 437, 438 (Baden-Baden, 1541); vol. 38, p. 270 (Rostock, 1561);
     GSB, vol. 1, pp. 67–9 (Basel, 1541); *IL*, vol. 2-2, pp. 195, 211 (Altdorf,
     1575).
59. Melanchthon, *Rhetorices elementa*, p. 11: 'Et in his tribus partibus [that
     is, *inventio, dispositio* and *elocutio*] fere tota ars consumitur. Itaque nos
     de aliis duabus partibus nihil praecipiemus, quia memoria parum
     admodum ab arte adiuvatur. Actio vero longe alia nunc est, quam
     qualis apud veteres fuit. Et quid maxime in agendo deceat, in foro
     discendum est imitatione.'
60. *ES*, vol. 1, p. 89 (Württemberg, 1559), p. 112 (Württemberg, cloister
     schools, 1582), pp. 245, 246 (Electoral Saxony, 1580), p. 314 (Brieg
     [Brzeg], 1581).
61. See further D. Knox, 'Ideas on Gesture and Universal Languages
     c. 1550–1650', in *New Perspectives on Renaissance Thought. Essays in
     Memory of Charles B. Schmitt*, ed. by J. Henry and S. Hutton (London,
     1990), pp. 101–36.
62. For example *ES*, vol. 1, p. 74 (Württemberg 1559); Georg Meier, *Tabulae
     . . . in Rhetorica Philippi Melanchthonis. In Erasmi Rotero. libellum de duplici
     copia*, with a work by Mosellanus ([Antwerp], 1529), sig. B7ᵛ.
63. Georg Meier, *Quaestiones rhetoricae* (1535). Meier wrote this while rector
     of the Latin school at Magdeburg. For curricula assigning it, see for
     example *ES*, vol. 1, pp. 88–9 (Württemberg, 1559), pp. 244–5 (Electoral
     Saxony, 1580).
64. *Erotemata dialecticae et rhetoricae Philippi Melanthonis . . .* (1552); and id.,
     Elementa dialecticae et rhetoricae, ex Erotematis Lucae Loßij . . . (1556). For
     curricula assigning these works, see for example *ES*, vol. 1, pp. 174
     (Pomerania 1563), p. 552 (Walkenried 1570); *Loßdorffische Schůlordnung*,
     sig. D2ᵛ (Loosdorf 1574); Matthaeus, *Scholae Cremsensis formula*, sig.
     b1ʳ⁻ᵛ.
65. Crusius published a catechetical and heavily annotated version of
     Melanchthon's *Elementa rhetorices* (1563) for students at Tübingen
     University. He published a version without notes in 1581 for use in
     Latin schools. Gymnasia or cloister schools occasionally assigned one
     or other of Crusius' works or part of them; see *ES* vol. 1, pp. 111–12
     (Württemberg, cloister schools, 1582); *MGP*, vol. 49, p. 98 (Hornbach,
     1573).
66. *Compendium dialecticae ac rhetoricae Philippi Melanchthonis . . . collectum e
     praelectionibus Michaëlis Neandri* (1580). See Neander in *ES*, vol. 1,
     p. 760.
67. *De rhetorica libri II.*
68. Johann Mercklin, *Quaestionum rhetoricarum . . . libri II. Quibus adiecta
     sunt in aliquot M.T. Ciceronis & T. Livij Orationes argumenta* (Basel, 1577).
     For a curriculum assigning this work, see *ES*, vol. 2, pp. 150, 156–8, 160,
     164, 167–8, 169 (Electoral Palatinate, 1615).
69. For example Meier, *Quaestiones rhetoricae*, sig. A2ᵛ.

70. *ES*, vol. 1, pp. 88–9: 'Zu der andern Stund von neun biß zehen Uhr, soll *Rhetorica Philippi Melanthonis* gelesen werden. Weil aber *Georgius Maior per quaestiones*, dieselb nicht allein in ein fein *Epitomen* verfaßt, sondern auch schöne *Orationes* darzugesetzt, aus wölchen der *usus artis* fein auff die *latinos authores* appliciert würdt, Soll demnach solches *Epitome*, ausser den *Rhetoricis Philippi* gebraucht, und für die Hand genommen, und ein *Praeceptum* oder zwey, deutlich und wol expliciert, und den nächsten tag hernach zu diser stund, ehe man wider lißt, repetiert, und *memoriter* recitiert werden. Und dieweil die *Praecepta*, für sich selbs bloß seind, unnd keinen nutz schaffen, wo sie mit *Exemplis* illustriert werden, Und aber die Knaben den *usum* auch sehen mögen, soll auff ein jeden *Statum* oder *genus Causae* ein *Oratio Ciceronis* oder *Liuij*, wie in gemelten *quaestionibus Georgij Maioris* sie getruckt, gelesen werden, Dann der *Praeceptor* fleissig das *Argumentum*, die *partes Orationis*, den *Statum*, die *Argumenta Confirmationis*, darnach *in singulis partibus Orationis*, wie sie orniert und tractiert werden, anzeigen. Und soll der *Preceptor* erstlich auff die *inventionem*, nachmals *dispositionem* und letstlich *elocutionem* acht haben, und also die *praecepta* auff gehörte weiß demonstriern.'

71. Anon., *Exercitium puerorum grammaticale* (Deventer, 1489), sig. a2ʳ, a4ᵛ– a5ᵛ, n4ᵛ, n5ʳ⁻ᵛ, F7ᵛ; Bebel, *Opusculum*, sig. Aa6ᵛ-Aa7ʳ; *VfSO*, vol. 1, p. 82 (Bayreuth, ca 1464), p. 132 (Stuttgart, 1501); vol. 2, p. 145 (Nuremberg, ca 1505), pp. 181–5 (Memmingen, ca 1513) pp. 216, 218–19 (Nördlingen, 1521).

72. For Latin grammar, see *VfSO*, passim. For dialectic, see for example *VfSO*, vol. 1, p. 119 (Nördlingen, 1499), pp. 126–7 (Ulm, ca 1500); vol. 2, p. 150 (Nuremberg, ca 1505).

73. For example *VfSO*, vol. 1, p. 57 (Vienna, St Stephan, 1446), p. 119 (Nördlingen, 1499); pp. 127–8 (Ulm, ca 1500); vol. 2, p. 173 (Nördlingen, 1512).

74. *VfSO*, vol. 1, p. 119 (Nördlingen, 1499); vol. 2, pp. 183, 184 (Memmingen, ca 1513), p. 216 (Nördlingen, 1521), p. 329 (Lüneburg, 1500). Rhetoric features prominently in what may conveniently be called the first Protestant school regulation, that of Leonhard Natther for the Latin school at Zwickau published in 1523; see ibid., pp. 251–2, 255, 257.

75. Jakob Wimpfeling, *Elegantiae maiores. Rhetorica . . . pueris utilissima* (Tübingen, 1513). Wimpfeling's prefaces are dated 1493 and 1499 respectively. Heinrich Bebel, *Opusculum de institutione puerorum*, with other works by Bebel (Strasbourg, 1513), sig. Aa8ʳ. The *Opusculum* is dated Tübingen 1506.

76. For example Johannes Murmellius, *De ratione instituendi pueros in schola triviali epistola*, with works by other authors (Deventer, 1515), sig. D1ᵛ–D2ᵛ.

77. For example Melanchthon, *De rhetorica libri tres*, sig. A2ʳ, A3ʳ. See also Melanchthon, *Rhetorices elementa*, pp. 5, 6–7, 10, 11–13.

78. For example notes 80, 81 below, and *ES*, vol. 2, p. 205 (Soest, Gymnasium, 1618), p. 263 (Emden, 1621); *MGdESG*, vol. 6, p. 119 (Laubach, before 1581).

79. *MGP*, vol. 1, p. 51 (Martineum, 1535), pp. 102, 103 (Katharineum, 1548), p. 161 (Katharineum, 1599), p. 164 (Aegidianum, ca 1600).

80. For example *MGP*, vol. 1, p. 127 (Latin schools, 1596), p. 154 (Martineum, ca 1604/5), p. 157 (Katharineum, 1598), p. 174 (Aegidianum, ca 1600).

81. *MGP*, vol. 1, p. 146 (Martineum, ca 1600), p. 152 (Martineum, before Easter 1604), p. 177 (Latin schools, 1621).

82. See Neander, *Bedenken, wie ein Knabe zu leiten und zu unterweisen*, in *ES*, vol. 1, p. 746.

83. Melanchthon, on the other hand, had reduced rhetoric to *inventio*, *dispositio* and *elocutio*. The differences between the two rhetorics, however, are not as great as they appear at first sight. Both included *elocutio* and eliminated *memoria*. Ramus shifted *inventio* and *dispositio* to dialectic.

84. Jodocus Willich, *Libellus de pronunciatione rhetorica* (Frankfurt, 1550), fol. 17^r, 19^v–20^v, 22^v, 24^v; Sturm, *De exercitationibus rhetoricis*, in *IL*, vol. 1, p. 397 and the Calvinist Clemens Timpler, *Rhetoricae systema methodicum libris V comprehensum* (Hannover, 1613), pp. 463, 474, 475.

85. See also for example *ES*, vol. 2, pp. 75, 76 (Joachimsthal, Gymnasium, 1607); *MGP*, vol. 42, pp. 494–6 (Regensburg, 1615).

86. See for example *ES*, vol. 2, pp. 273–5, 280–1 (Moers, 1635), p. 421 (Braunschweig-Wolfenbüttel, 1651); *MGP*, vol. 42, p. 460 (Regensburg, 1654); vol. 49, p. 428 (Speyer, 1617).

87. See *MGP*, vol. 14, pp. 401–34.

88. See note 45 above.

89. Strauss, *Luther's House of Learning*, passim.

90. For example *MGP*, vol. 47, pp. 97–8 (Hornbach, 1561); vol. 49, p. 47 (Hornbach, 1559); *MGdESG*, vol. 7, pp. 209–45 (Electoral Saxony, Grimma, Meissen, Pforta, Rossleben, 1554–75).

91. For example *MGdESG*, vol. 7, p. 213 (Grimma, 11 Sept. 1554).

92. For example *MGP*, vol. 49, pp. 402–3 (Speyer, 1595).

5

Some Reflections on the Rhetoric Textbook

Brian Vickers

The great success of rhetoric in Greco–Roman culture ensured its place as an essential element in education, as historians of classical rhetoric have abundantly demonstrated.[1] Its place in the *trivium*, and the transmission of inherited knowledge through the encyclopedia tradition, preserved rhetoric through the Middle Ages, while the energetic revival and assimilation of the classical heritage in the Renaissance firmly established rhetoric as an indispensable acquisition for all properly educated men (and gradually, women) down to the nineteenth century and beyond. Historians of this enormously fertile tradition can draw on documents of primary rhetoric, as we might call it: the speeches of Demosthenes or Cicero, the more elaborate declamations and panegyrics of the empire, the poetry, the speeches, sermons and other genres that have continued this primary rhetorical tradition down to our time.

But of much greater significance to historians of rhetoric are the secondary works, the preparatory, propaedeutic handbooks which have communicated rhetoric as a *technè* or *ars*, a practical discipline to be mastered. As one of the most influential rhetoric books ever written – the anonymous *Rhetorica ad Caius Herennium*, ca 80 BC – puts it, rhetorical skills are acquired in the triple process of *ars*, *imitatio*, *exercitatio*:

> By theory [*ars*] is meant a set of rules that provide a definite method and system of speaking. Imitation stimulates us to attain, in accordance with a studied method, the effectiveness of certain models in speaking. Practice is assiduous exercise and experience in speaking.[2]

The role of the schoolmaster, whether he used extant textbooks or made up his own, was to apply that triad over a period of several years' intensive work until the pupils had absorbed the whole discipline and could use it, in their professional careers, writings, or in everyday life, effortlessly and effectively. The teachings of the rhetoric book, properly absorbed, leave no sign other than the students' eloquence.

Historians working from such textbooks are, however, as I have observed elsewhere,[3] in an anomalous position. They are trying to reconstruct a system of enormous cultural significance over two millennia from manuals that are essentially practical, 'how-to-do-it' handbooks whose effectiveness can only be measured by observing their users in performance, or by evaluating the end-product, whatever literary form it should take. The alpha and omega of rhetoric teaching is to instil the ability to speak or write eloquently. Some historians are at times unwilling to accept the implications of this practical pedagogy. Thus Professor Lisa Jardine, to take an instance close at hand, observes of Rudolph Agricola's *De inventione dialectica* and Erasmus's *De copia* that both texts have proved 'resistant' to discussion in the light of recent critical theory, and seem 'unreadable' since 'we cannot recognize a purpose beyond the trite one of accumulating material abundance', that is, ample resources of eloquence.[4] But trite though it may seem to us, '*copia*' was the be-all and end-all of most rhetorical training at any time between 150 BC and 1850 AD. Whatever else we do with these texts, as historians we must respect their primary goal. A handbook is only a means to an end, a *gradus ad Parnassum*.

In this essay I shall make some 'dispersed meditations' – to use a seventeenth-century phrase which describes my modest goal, with no pretence at a complete or definite treatment of this immense topic – on the role of the rhetoric textbook in its primary context as a teaching tool, whether in schools and universities or for the private reader, the autodidact aspiring to eloquence. My examples will be taken mostly from the European Renaissance, although arguably the same factors apply to rhetoric books at any point in time.

I

In the Renaissance textbooks in rhetoric, as in other subjects, acquired new importance.[5] There were several different kinds of rhetoric textbook, reflecting differences of emphasis within the subject. Some rhetoric books emphasise *inventio*, and easily link up with dialectic: this is the case with Agricola and the Ramist tradition. Others adopt the classical *progymnasmata* approach of Aphthonius, elaborating models for practice in composition: such are the many renaissance editions and commentaries on Aphthonius, and the anglicised version by Richard Rainolde (1563). Others, probably the majority, concentrate on *elocutio*, devoting their energies to enumerating and illustrating the range of figures and tropes. In England such are the treatises by Richard Sherry (1550, 1555), George Puttenham (1589), Henry Peacham (1577, 1593), Angel Day (1586, 1592), John Hoskins (ca 1599), and many more.

The rhetoric books were, as I have emphasised, nothing if not practical, but as that practice changed, so did the handbooks. In quattrocento Florentine humanism, with its influential revival of the civic notion of rhetoric as propagated by Isocrates and Cicero, the main justification for the study of eloquence was its power in a democracy to apply free speech to the democratic goals of justice and liberty.[6] Some European rhetoric books of the later sixteenth century still draw on this tradition with anecdotes and exempla of rhetoric's efficacy in the *vita activa*. So Thomas Wilson, dedicating his *Arte of Rhetorique* (1553, 1560) to John Dudley, Earl of Warwick and Master of the Horse, opened his epistle with the deeds of Cineas, 'a noble Orator, and sometimes Scholer to Demosthenes'. In his campaigns against the Romans Pyrrhus sent Cineas to besieged towns, where 'through the pithie eloquence of this noble Orator, divers strong Castelles and Fortresses were peacably given up', saving many lives.[7] Wilson's wide-ranging claims for the power of rhetoric put him in a direct line of descent from Isocrates, but they also show how far he is from addressing the actual situation of sixteenth-century Europe. Not many of his contemporaries were ever in the position of being able to raise a siege with their eloquence! His work belongs to that rosy picture of rhetoric as an unqualified benefit to man derived from Quintilian and soon to be sharply challenged by the Elizabethan dramatists, above all Shakespeare.[8]

Wilson at least recognises contemporary social reality by granting rhetoric a smaller place in the political arena, and a larger one in the professions of law and theology. Other writers are more humble, presenting their digests of the rhetorical tradition as of purely educational relevance. Melanchthon writes in the 1542 version of his *Elementorum Rhetorices Libri Duo* that his account of rhetoric is intended 'to prepare young people, not so much for speaking correctly, but for prudently evaluating and understanding the writings of others'.[9] Rhetoric will help the young 'in their reading of good authors, who indeed without this method can in no way be understood' (p. 77). Joannes Susenbrotus, who modestly describes himself on the title-page as 'Compilator and Schoolmaster of Ravensburg', recommends his *Epitome Troporum ac Schematum* (1541) as 'No less useful than necessary for understanding authors both sacred and profane', and in his preface pays respectful homage to Melanchthon.[10] The title page of Richard Sherry's handbook (London, 1550), which derives from the Melanchthon tradition, is equally modest: *A Treatise of Schemes & Tropes very profytable for the better understanding of good authors, gathered out of the best Grammarians & Oratours* . . .

This tacit recognition that the rhetoric books could no longer prepare students for the career of orator in a democracy, where major political decisions hinged on one effective speech in an open assembly, was widely shared. As Christine Roaf has noted, by the sixteenth century 'the oration itself had already become a literary genre rather than a means of political persuasion', and many of those published were specimens of epideictic rhetoric, intended for a reader, not for a live audience.[11] The decreasing relevance of spoken oratory can also be seen in Erasmus's rhetorical works, which give very little space to *actio* (or *pronuntiatio*, gesture), and virtually dismiss *memoria*.[12] The practicality of rhetoric, then, survived at a lower level, in teaching students to understand classical (and, in some of the Ramist treatises, contemporary vernacular) authors, and in the preparation of private or personal written genres: the theme at school, the letter in later life (the renaissance witnessing an extraordinary boom in epistolary rhetoric treatises),[13] and for the clergy, the sermon.[14]

II

In the educational world, then as now, the publication of textbooks is conditioned by a mixture of economic and ideological factors. The prefaces to rhetoric textbooks observe the established *topoi* for excusing the 'stigma of print'[15] and justifying their presence in the marketplace. Sherry and Wilson both attribute publication to the initiative of their patrons.[16] Ian Maclean's recent study of Frankfurt editions of Ramus[17] has shown that much of the publication, and many of the claimed 'revisions' or 'new editions' had more to do with the publisher's attempt to establish a monopoly than with student demand or textual change.[18] Towards the end of the sixteenth century, as the Lutherans took over schools and universities where 'previously there had been Calvinists sympathetic to Ramus', a new desire to reconcile the dialectics of Aristotle and Melanchthon with Ramism led to such a phenomenon as Beurhaus's edition of Ramus's *Dialectica* in 1596, where the 80 pages of Ramist text are smothered by '764 pages of commentary and parallel passages' (p. 261). This factor, too, would not have appeared from a purely 'internal' approach. Many assumptions in the history of rhetoric may have to be corrected in the light of a proper study of publishing contexts, and more research of this kind is urgently needed.

III

One of the declarations of purpose made by compilers of rhetoric books which can be taken at face value concerns the need for introductory treatises, handbooks that would bridge the gap between the grammar-school lower forms and the first-year university course. In his *De Arte Rhetorica Libri Tres*,[19] explicitly identified as *Ex Aristotele, Cicerone, & Quintiliano praecipue deprompti* (1562), Cyprian Soarez, SJ, informs the 'Christian reader' that he has produced his textbook in response to the disappointment of teachers in the Society of Jesus that 'there was no book of ancient writers which opened the first door to eloquence for eager youth'. Cicero and Quintilian are the outstanding authorities, of course, but their writings are 'less suited for initial instructions to beginners' (p. 105). Soarez reviews the main documents of classical rhetoric in turn, describing their unsuitability as elementary texts: Cicero's *Partitiones Oratoriae* are too short and concise; *De Oratore* 'quickly passes over techniques of lesser moment, but especially essential for learners' (p. 106); Cicero's *Orator* summarises 'or almost omits very many of the ordinary rules which are particularly useful for learned students eager to speak' (p. 107). For this reason he has acted to supply the need felt by his Jesuit superiors, namely

to collect all the elements of eloquence in some book, method, and plan; to explain these with definitions and to illustrate them with examples from the teaching of Aristotle; in the case of Cicero and Quintilian to include not only their teaching but usually their very words (pp. 107–8).

His goal is preparatory, only: 'to assist young men to read the learned books of Aristotle, Cicero, and Quintilian wherein lie the well-springs of eloquence' (p. 108).

Soarez was not the only compiler of a rhetoric book to emphasise its propaedeutic usefulness,[20] but he was surely the most successful. First published in 1562, a second edition of his manual (revised by his Jesuit colleague and teacher Perpinian) appeared in 1565, and was frequently reprinted. The first formal curriculum of the Jesuit order, the *Ratio Studiorum*[21] of 1586 (at which time it had jurisdiction over 162 schools), did not specify any particular rhetoric textbook, but the 1599 *Ratio* adopted Soarez's manual, guaranteeing it an astonishing dissemination. Dr Flynn has counted at least 134 printings in 45 different European cities over a period of 173 years, and a total of 207 reprints in all forms (p. 37). The Order controlled 245 schools in 1599, 444 by 1626, and by 1739 some 669 colleges and 176 seminaries (p. 45). If an average school had 1000 pupils (p. 44), then by 1599 (when the Order had about 10 000 members, most of whom were either teaching or training to teach), something like a quarter of a million students across Europe (and reaching South America) were exposed to Soarez's manual each year. By the end of the seventeenth century, then, some five million pupils had absorbed this well-organised digest of classical rhetoric, a lucid and detailed synthesis which can still be recommended to any intermediate student (or teacher). Like so many rhetoric books, it suffered both condensations and expansions, reappearing as a *Compendium*, a *Summa*, and as *Tabulae*, all frequently reprinted (p. 38). Its enlargement by Worpitz as *Manuale Rhetorum* or *Methodus* (1688) was itself expanded further, the 1711 edition being more than twice the size of the 1562 text, and going through another ten printings over the next fifty years (p. 39). Although never printed in England, given the official hostility to Jesuits, it was drawn on by English compilers of rhetoric books (pp. 51–2), from Thomas Vicars, *Manuductio ad Artem Rhetoricam* (1621) and Thomas Farnaby, *Index Rhetoricus* (1625, 1633 enlarged), down to John Holmes, *Art of Rhetoric Made Easy* (1739).

The case of Soarez exemplifies another characteristic of the rhetoric textbook which can be disconcerting to modern readers, the fact that it lacks any definite form or size. The smallest, most nakedly pragmatic form is a table or list of rhetorical processes, intended (like everything else in the renaissance school) to be learned by heart. The best known tabular text was produced by Petrus Mosellanus or Peter Schade (1493?–1524), his *Tabulae de schematibus et tropis* (Antwerp and Strasbourg, 1529). Only 26 pages long, it treated 98 rhetorical figures and tropes, running through at least eight editions by 1553. In his preface Mosellanus expatiates on the excellence and usefulness of knowing the classical figures and tropes, and advises his readers that if they 'affix' his table 'in some spot to which you frequently turn, it will come to pass that even when it is no longer observed by the eyes, it will be preserved beyond damage in the treasury of memory' [22] – an early recognition of subliminal perception. Vives, in his *De Tradendis Disciplinis* (1531), takes up the point:

> Peter Mosellanus has also prepared for use a table of figures of speech, which can be hung up on the wall so that it will catch the attention of the pupil as he walks past it, and force itself upon his eyes.[23]

Other renaissance educationalists shared Vives's opinion, and Mosellanus appeared in the Eton timetable by 1530.[24]

Mosellanus represents the small end of a continuum which stretches in the other direction to the *Thesaurus Rhetoricae* of Giovanni Baptista Bernardo (Venice, 1599), with over five thousand entries, alphabetically arranged.[25] In the next century, what Robert Bolgar called 'the natural fanaticism of expertise',[26] led to ever more-inclusive treatises, such as the wrist-breaking or shoulder-dislocating tomes of Louis Cressolles, *Vacationes autumnales; sive, de perfecta oratoris actione et pronunctiatione, libri iii* (Paris, 1620), which runs to 706 pages, and Nicholas Caussin, SJ, *Eloquentiae sacrae et humanae parallela libri XVI* (Paris, 1619), which weighs in at 1010 pages.[27] Such treatises become self-defeating in their completeness, for rhetoric handled at such length is no longer an art to be mastered for practical purposes but a field where knowledge can celebrate its own thoroughness. Who needs to know everything about a topic?

Most rhetoric-book compilers had the more modest aim of issuing a revised edition which would make their text more complete, or easier to use. Henry Peacham ends the dedicatory epistle to *The Garden of Eloquence* (1577) beseeching his patron, John Elmer, Bishop of London, to accept 'this little treatise, the fruite of my travayles, as a token of my good will; which at the nexte edition I trust shall come forth more perfect and trimly pulished, which now lack of leysure hath left undone' (Sig. Aiii^v). The work duly reappeared in 1593, 'corrected and augmented', when Peacham not only substantially enlarged it but added new sections at the end of each figure, listing 'the use' and 'the caution' to be observed in its application, important evidence for the growing renaissance awareness (especially in England, it would seem) of the proper functionality of rhetoric.[28]

IV

The very existence of Peacham's rhetoric book, however, poses a slight problem for historians, that is the fact of its being in English. As he explains in the 1577 Epistle, being convinced of the Ciceronian principle of a necessary link between wisdom and eloquence, he was disappointed to find

> many good bookes of Philosophy and precepts of wysedome, set forth in english, and very few of Eloquence: I was of a sodaine mooved to take this little Garden in hande, and to set therein such Fyguratyve Flowers, both of Grammer and Rhetorick, as doe yeelde the sweate savour of Eloquence, & present to the eyes the goodly and bewtiful coulors of Eloqution: such as shyne in our speech like the glorious stars in Firmament . . . (Sig. A$_{ii}$^{v}–A$_{iii}$^{r}).

His predecessor, Richard Sherry, some twenty years earlier, felt obliged to defend his use of such strange words as 'scheme' and 'trope'.[29] Sherry and Peacham are evidently part of the movement which defended the vernacular as of equal value to the classical languages.[30]

But what readership were they aiming at? All education in English schools and universities was meant to be in Latin, diligent schoolmasters even employing spies among the schoolboys to peach on any of their fellows who spoke English in the classroom, or even in the break. The textbooks used for rhetoric instruction, from elementary to advanced, were overwhelmingly in Latin. The fact that Latin was the normal language of instruction in rhetoric makes English abnormal, indeed there is some evidence that rhetoric books in English were not much sought after. Richard Rainolde's *The*

Foundacion of Rhetorike (1563) is an adaptation of the ubiquitous *Progymnasmata*, or 'preliminary exercises', of the sophist Aphthonius (fourth century), which attracted editions and commentaries from many famous scholars in the Renaissance, such as Rudolph Agricola, J.Camerarius, J.M.Cataneo, Natalis Comes. The most popular edition was that by Reinhard Lorich, professor of rhetoric at Marburg University in the 1530s and 1540s, whose commentary (1537, typically expanded in 1542 and again in 1546 to six times its original size) was reprinted hundreds of times across Europe. As F. R. Johnson observed, in his edition of this text, Rainolde's English version (like, indeed, the majority of English rhetoric books in the sixteenth century) was never reprinted, and 'the lack of any continued demand for an English adaptation of Aphthonius . . . was probably due to the widespread popularity in the grammar schools of Lorich's Latin text', which had established itself as the basic model in English grammar schools 'for the student learning to write Latin themes'.[31] Similarly, Thomas Derrick points out that 'there were only four English editions of Erasmus's *De Duplici Copia* (1528, 1556, 1569, 1573) although the continental editions in Latin and the digests of them numbered in the hundreds during the sixteenth century'.[32] Sherry's second edition (1555) was expanded into alternating (or parallel) sequences of Latin and English, as if he were having second thoughts, trying to catch the scholastic market after all.

The existence of English rhetoric books is something of an anomaly:[33] Who bought them? Who read them? One category of reader was certainly never officially envisaged, namely university students, possibly unsure in Latin, who evidently used them as 'cribs' to the more demanding classical treatises. For there is evidence, among the surviving lists of books owned by Cambridge University graduates, and sometimes donated to college libraries, of the resort to easier English texts.[34] Another class of readers may have been lawyers, who worked primarily with English (but also law French). Although they had had a thorough grammar-school or even university education before going to the Inns of Court, Latin may have come to seem too remote, while English was of daily relevance. This was evidently the readership that Abraham Fraunce was trying to reach with his Ramist treatise, *The Lawiers Logike* (1588), which is addressed to 'the Learned Lawyers of England, especially the Gentlemen of Grays Inn', where Fraunce had enrolled after Cambridge. The market for a lawyer's rhetoric had probably been cornered by Thomas Wilson's *Arte*, which, with its eight editions, was the most popular English handbook of the period, and clearly appealed to preachers, lawyers, and statesmen. One of its most diligent readers was Gabriel Harvey, who acquired the 1567 edition in 1570, some years before he himself turned toward a legal career (entering Trinity Hall in 1578 to that end). Harvey frequently wrote in his copy of Wilson the abbreviation 'J.C.', standing for 'Juris consultus' or lawyer, and in his Quintilian, appropriately enough, Harvey recorded that

> Wilsons Rhetorique and Logique, the dailie bread of owr common pleaders, and discoursers.

In his copy of Wilson Harvey singled him out, with Quintilian, as 'necessarie, and important . . . in every parlie, and discourse, private, or publique'.[35] Although anomalous, then, in some areas the English rhetoric books had an important role, which calls for further study.

V

The final point I wish to touch on is the extent to which textbook authors tried to make their work palatable. Many, understandably, claim that their works are useful, more thorough than their predecessors', but few attempt to produce anything other than a handbook. The two exceptions I shall mention (not that I claim them to be unique) go beyond the handbook towards established literary genres, the letter and the colloquy. Angel Day's *English Secretorie* offers instruction in how to write a letter, the necessary qualities it should have ('comeliness in deliverance', 'aptness of words', and 'brevity'), compositional processes (description, praise, blame), and the main categories of epistle: laudatory and vituperative, hortatory and dehortatory, suasory and dissuasory, conciliatory, reconciliatory, petitory, commendatory, consolatory, monitory, giving in each case a 'responsary' or model reply. The types are profusely illustrated with model letters, and Day declares at the end of the table of contents that 'almost all of which Epistles before set downe were nowe sodenly by the Author ordered and invented to their severall examples' (Sig.n 4ᵛ). Indeed, although drawing on some continental models, Day deserves credit for the imagination shown in these invented epistles.

The concluding section deals with 'Partes Amatorie or of love: The discourse whereof including letters framed upon divers sondrie effectes, continueth to the end of the book' (ibid.). As Day explains, the 'humours of all sortes' possessed by love 'are so infinite', and 'so innumerable are the supposes [deceits] wherewith the raynes of love are conducted', that he will not attempt any strict order or method (p. 232). But in order to give the reader the necessary insight into 'the conveiance of their particular meanings', he has decided to annex 'the severall occasions', that is, the circumstances of composition. These are, of course, fictitious!

> You shall therefore understand for the first of these examples, that the writer thereof loving a Gentlewoman, whose inward vertues surmounted far the parts of her outward favour, and having sondry times receaved of her hands both allowance and libertye to declare his mind, whereunto she nevertheless gave a modest & courteous refusal, he thereupon devised to convay the residue of his imaginations, into the melancholy form of this letter following (p. 232).

Here Day's imagination transforms the invented epistle from a pedagogic help into a creation in its own right. We are in the familiar late renaissance version of courtly love, with the deferential suitor and the kind but virtuous mistress. This suitor, like so many more, continues to solicit his mistress's favours, 'sometimes by gratifying her with divers sonettes, otherwise in admiring her prayses . . .' (p. 238). In effect, the rhetoric book is being transformed into an epistolary novel. Day adds to the fictitious letters an interspersed commentary-cum-narrative of his own, inventing a triangular situation and then whipping up misunderstanding, jealousy and envy. Finally he brings the whole affair to the typical conclusion of so many Elizabethan love stories, frustration leading to an angry separation (pp. 232–51). In this mixture of rhetoric, love doings and letters, Day is using the same ingredients as Lyly in *Euphues* (1578, 1580), or other romance writers in verse or prose. The notional line between the categories of rhetoric book and romantic fiction begins to dissolve. Day's involvement with his love story becomes so great that he neglects his pedagogy, forgetting to print in the margin the names of the rhetorical schemes, tropes, and structural divisions (*narratio, partitio, confirmatio*) that his invented epistles were meant to demonstrate.

The last rhetoric textbook I shall discuss also gets carried away, but not to the point of forgetting the rhetorical figures, indeed they take the centre of the stage here. Samuel Shaw (1635–96), Headmaster of Ashby-de-la-Zouch school, published in 1679 an original little book, *Words Made Visible: or Grammar and Rhetorick Accommodated to the Lives and Manners of Men*[36] (reprinted in 1680 and 1683 with the title *Minerva's Triumph*). As R. C. Alston observes in the prefatory note to his facsimile edition, 'the presentation of grammar and rhetoric by means of a dramatic entertainment, which incidentally provides the author with splendid opportunities for satire, is without antecedent in English linguistic history'. In his preface Shaw affirms of his book that "tis *no Translation* . . . nay let me tell you, the matter and *Fancy* as well as *stile* is fresh, and never before sullied with any others Ink, a grand rarity!' Both parts, he explains, 'were composed for private diversion, and *Acted* by the Lads of a Country School'.

The first part (pp. 1–92) concerns Grammar,[37] and presents a court in which '*Gymnasiarches*, the Lord Lieutenant', together with four judges, '*Amo, Doceo, Lego*, and *Audio*, the Lords Commissioners of *Syntaxis*' assemble to 'hear, and finally determine all manner of grievances amongst *the eight Parts of Speech*' (p. 4). These are arranged in a witty social hierarchy, 'Nobles or Verbs; Knights or Nouns; Gentlemen or Pronouns; Yeomen or Participles; Husbandmen or Adverbs; Tradesmen or Conjunctions; Labourers or Prepositions; Beggars or Interjections'. Each is examined in turn, their abuses or excesses rebuked (nouns might be 'abridged of some of their *Genders*': p. 35; pronouns are charged to '*rehearse* no more than you must needs, and never any more than what was in the Antecedent': p. 44), the colloquy ending with a 'happy civil union amongst them' being restored (p. 91).

The second part, on Rhetoric (pp. 93–187), is considerably closer to us. Indeed, one of Shaw's main goals, as he states in the *Prologue*, is to show that

there is a certain Vein of Rhetorick running through the Humane Nature . . . which infects all their Sentiments, and modifies all their Actions. So that indeed there is no such thing as Philosophy, or Divinity; but *Rhetorick* governs all the World; and *Tropes* and *Figures* (with a little *Grammar* to teach them to speak) carry all before them. They talk of plain, simple, literal, ingenious, cordial, real and I know not what; but the plain truth is, there is nothing plain nor true amongst men; but the whole life of man is a *Tropical Figurative* Converse, and a continual Rhetorication (p. 98).

These seemingly modern ideas (rediscovered with great and largely disillusioned emphasis in our own time by such writers as Hayden White and Paul de Man) belong to one of the oldest arguments justifying rhetoric, that it is but the codification of linguistic resources common to humanity at large, and used naturally in emotional states.[38] As Shaw puts it, if all the authors of rhetoric books were to perish, 'there would be no dearth of Rhetorick: for every individual man is a system of it. That the most illiterate people, in their most ordinary communication, do Rhetoricate by *Instinct*, as well as others do by Art, is very obvious': 'an ingenious and well practis'd Scold' will 'give Examples of half the Tropes and Figures in *Butler* at one heat' (pp. 98–9). 'But that's not all', he goes on, coming to his main point: 'for men live *Tropes* and *Figures* as well as speak them: and this is the thing . . . principally design'd to be represented to you' (p. 99). That men live out in their life and thought some particular rhetorical device is all too familiar in our time. In the work of Lévi-Strauss, the systematic use of inversion in such figures as *antithesis* and *antimetabole* has been called 'a true forma mentis', much of his methodology deriving from 'the dynamics of inversion'.[39] As for Derrida, we could hesitate between hyperbole and *aporia*, alternately exceeding all norms of argument and then plunging himself and all his followers into doubt and uncertainty.

The plot of Shaw's little play concerns 'King *Eulogus* (by some call'd Rhetorick)', who had two sons, '*Ellogus* and *Eclogus* (sometime call'd *Elocution* and *Pronunciation*)', between whom 'he divided his Kingdom, giving them each in charge to be very industrious to propagate the Rhetorical Dominions' (ibid.). This reflects the Ramist system, in which rhetoric is primarily concerned with *elocutio* and *pronuntiatio*. Another sign of Ramist influence is that Shaw recognises only four tropes: metonymy, irony, metaphor and synecdoche.[40] But in the Ramist system, as in all others, the parts of rhetoric are interdependent, and the dispute between *elocutio* and *pronuntiatio* turns out to be inconclusive. 'Prince *Elocution* with all his *Tropes* and *Figures* signifies nothing without *Pronunciation*' (p. 187).

The plot is a device which allows Shaw to achieve several goals at once. First, he has each of the figures and tropes appear as individual speaking characters. Just as in Ravel's *L'Enfant et les*

Sortilèges, where the inhabitants of the nursery come to life at night, from the dolls to the tea-pot, so Shaw can bring on various rhetorical devices with a self-identification:

> *Prolepsis:* I am that *Figure,* Sir, by whom Men warily foresee, and foreseeing baffle the Arguments of their Adversaries (pp. 130–1).
> *Etiologie:* I am he, who have taught men to subjoyn a reason, and assign a cause of their words and actions . . . (p. 142).
> *Prosopope:* I am that *Figure,* Sir, whereby men act some other person living or dead (p. 171).

But Shaw is too witty to give only such plain definitions, making some figures demonstrate their own nature in the process of self-definition. Thus Ecphonesis (in Latin *exclamatio*) says: 'I am that *Figure* whereby men insert *Interjections* (and oh! the vast number and several kinds of them!) into their discourse' (p. 163). Similarly Epanorthosis (Latin: *correctio*) enacts his functioning:

> By me, Sir, it is that all men correct themselves, and retract any thing that they have done or said; so that all the honest penitents in the World are my Votaries. My Votaries! Pardon me that Phrase, Sir, I mean . . . (p. 165).

The wittiest of these definition demonstrations leads on to dialogue, as Eclogus (*pronuntiatio*) questions these servants of his rival *elocutio*.

> My name, Sir, is *Aposiopesis,* my office to conceal some part of a Sentence; but as to my Successes, what tongue—
> *Eclogus:* Alas, Sir, does the very view of your conquests, put you into an *Aposiopetick* fit?
> *Aposiopesis:* And well it may, for I have obtain'd more by concealing a part, than any of my Brothers by speaking all. Oh the rare feats that *mental reservations* have done, dextrously manag'd by the ingenious Sons of *Loyola!* (p. 168).

It is hardly surprising that Shaw, who was also a non-conformist divine, should have a dig against the Jesuits, as he does elsewhere against the Pope. But that example brings out the second main aim of his work, to show how certain rhetorical processes are frequently used in everyday life, not always for the noblest ends. Ecphonesis points out that 'sometimes an inarticulate far-fetch'd sigh shall by my authority, be thought to confute the most sinewy argument of an opponent . . . . I have . . . everywhere made *Exclamation* to pass for the most ingenious way of *Argumentation'* (p. 163). This is a shrewd comment on the opportunistic use of inarticulacy. *Epanorthosis*, recalling a phrase in order to substitute one more suitable, can have ulterior intentions, as that figure explains:

> By me mens actions are ratified and words recanted . . . . By the same skill differently imploy'd, men retract their retractations, and repent of their repentings. I can dispence with bargains, promises, vows and good words as well as bad ones; and indeed, to speak the truth, the better words are, the fitter they are to be eaten. By me all retrograde and dissembling *Temporizers* shift their Religions . . . swear Allegiances to their Princes, und unswear it again (p. 166).

That satire is keener, mocking human disloyalty and evasiveness, together with the verbal form it takes. *Etiologie*, the giving of a reason or cause, admits that this figure is frequently used by people who cannot in fact explain what they pretend to. Natural philosophers at a loss tend to invoke an *'Occult Quality'*, that all-purpose category to conceal their ignorance; the female sex can now, thanks to this rhetorical figure, 'pass for rational creatures' by using 'that most ingenious reason of, *Because it is'* (p. 143).

At this point Eclogus objects: 'I perceive there is nothing sincere amongst you all, when even your *plainness* is *figurative*, and *rightness* itself is *wrong'* (p. 145). Here Shaw uses this proto-dramatic form to underline the third main goal of his work, a defence of rhetoric along Aristotelian lines against Plato's charge that rhetoric was by its very nature immoral. In effect Shaw revives the argument of Aristotle's *Rhetoric*:

> if it be objected that one who uses such power of speech unjustly might do great harm, *that* is a charge which may be made in common against all good things except virtue.[41]

At the beginning of this 'dramatic entertainment' Trope, one of the two 'Ministers of State' to Ellogus, affirms that 'all the World is turn'd *Tropical* (save only what's become *Figurative*) and that not only in those babbling things call'd words . . . but in manners and minds, in practices and principles too' (p. 109). Yet Trope's *apologia*

pro vita sua is not without its faults, as he is made to glory in the way
that he and Figure have gained dominion over the world. They have
'refin'd [it] from its ancient rudeness and roughness', he claims,
which some morose philosophers 'call'd *Simplicity* and *Plainness* . . . . Plain Speech was indeed an adjunct of the illiterate Ages
of the World, and so was plain dealing (which some old fashioned
People call the ornament of those antique times) . . . .' But now, he
proudly affirms, the 'imperfections' belonging to 'those unbred
Ages' have vanished under the 'benign influence' of *elocutio*, and
now

> men not onely speak ingeniously and artificially, but live and act,
> love and hate, buy and sell, nay eat and drink, sleep and wake, as
> artificially as they speak, which his Excellency is pleas'd to call
> *Tropically* and *Figuratively*.
>   *Eclogus*: Come, come, *call a spade a spade*, dissemblingly and
> deceitfully you mean (p. 108 *bis*).[42]

Here the laugh is against rhetoric, indeed the prospect of the whole
of human affairs being conducted 'ingeniously and artificially' is
appalling. Shaw has pushed *elocutio* over the top in order to satirise
the excessive claims made for it, and to suggest that eloquence is
worth little without wisdom and ethics. Yet his ability to present
two sides of the case takes a further twist, from an attack on rhetoric
to a defence of it. Figure now enters the debate, warning Eclogus
against

> either by slighting honesty to court us into a neglect of it with
> your self, or else by pretending that you can serve the interest of
> it, invidiously to intimate to the World that we do not. For *Tropes*
> and *Figures* do indifferently serve the designs of vertue and
> honesty, as well as their contraries, as we hope to make evident to
> you before you go hence (p. 109 *bis*).

Figure then turns the tables on *pronuntiatio*, asking Eclogus

> to *pronounce* it to that part of the World, that depends wholly
> upon your *Oral Tradition*, that *Tropes* and *Figures* are not in their
> own nature calculated for the Meridian of Vice and Wickedness,
> but are sometimes unhappily against their wills abused to evil
> ends; an ill luck that sometimes attends your dear *Voice* and
> *Gesture* as well as us (p. 112).

The moral relativism of rhetoric, as described by Aristotle, must apply to all its parts and processes. Shaw's realistic awareness that a tool can be abused is a considerable advance, it seems to me, on such rhetoricians as Quintilian or Thomas Wilson, who urge that the orator is by definition a good man.[43] Yet Shaw adds the optimistic rider that

> *Tropes* and *Figures* are more useful (I wish I could say more us'd) for the instructing and informing of men, than for the seducing and debauching of them (ibid.).

Samuel Shaw's purpose, we can now see, is more complex than it first appeared. He wants to explain the main tropes and figures with a definition, and examples where suitable; he wants to show how they are used in life, for what social and individual purposes, good or evil. These are standard pedagogic goals. But, more original, he wants to defend rhetoric while at the same time warning his students against its misuse. His satire, then, can work in several directions. Metonymy, first of the tropes, defines itself as 'the great *Nomenclator* of the world: if I please to put the *cause* for the *effect*, or . . . the *Adjunct* for the *Subject*, so they must stand' (p. 114). The satirical application quickly follows: 'It is by a real Metonimy that men of devout and refin'd minds discern the *Creator*, where others see nothing but the *Creature*; . . . that all *Hypocrites* present us with the *sign* instead of the *thing signifi'd* . . .' (p. 115). With the next trope satire becomes more complex, for *Irony* carries the war into the enemy's camp, urging that voice and gesture constantly use his resources, 'for certainly there can be no Oratory without dissimulation'. Eclogus rises to the bait as Irony concludes his claim that, where '*Honesty, Plain dealing*' has only one, he has 'an hundred subjects':

> All that write not as they speak, all that speak not as they think, all that think not according to truth, all that intend not as they pretend, all that practise not as they profess, all that look one way and row another, are my Subjects.
> *Eclogus*: I perceive then that all the knaves in the World are yours, Sir.
> *Irony*: Aye Sir, and so would all the rest be too, if they were not Fools: For dissimulation and deceit are as necessary to the practice of *Virtue* as to the propagation of *Vice* (pp. 117–18).

The wisest king, captain, or master, Irony argues, must sometimes pretend a displeasure, assume a severity that they do not really feel, for the good effect it will have on those under them. This is too much for the critic of *elocutio*:

> *Eclogus*: Well, I perceive, there is nothing but deceit in the World.
> *Irony*: Nothing, Sir.
> *Eclogus*: Then I conclude that you have spoke deceitfully whatever you have spoke all this while.
> *Irony*: And I, that yours is a deceitful conclusion.

'Touché!', as the fencer in the James Thurber cartoon says, having just removed his opponent's head.

The best praise of Samuel Shaw's work would be the familiar tag from Horace,

> *omne punctum tulit, qui miscuit utile dulci.*

As he says in his preface, 'Schoolboys cannot but be hugely pleas'd . . . to find *Rhetorick*, that was their Toil become their *pastime*, all the most usefull *Tropes* and *Figures*, first, properly explained, and then aptly Illustrated in facetious reflections on the Lives and Practices of men'. But beyond the pedagogical level, of teaching pupils to recognise the individual devices, is the deeper ethical intent of warning his students against their frequent misuse. How far *elocutio* and *pronuntiatio* have prevailed in the world, the prologue tells us,

> you will see when you hear them speak for themselves. But be sure you hear them cautiously, or else they may cheat you: for they'l Rhetoricate if their lives lay on't, and I dare lay my life on't you'l say so (p. 99).

We do, and are all the more grateful to a textbook writer who can offer at the same time an exposition of rhetoric and a critique of it, so drawing our attention to that darker side of eloquence that too many historians of rhetoric still prefer to avoid.

Notes and References

1. On rhetorical education in antiquity and after see R. R. Bolgar, *The Classical Heritage and its Beneficiaries* (Cambridge, 1954); S. F. Bonner, *Education in Ancient Rome. From the elder Cato to the younger Pliny* (London, 1977); M.Fuhrmann, *Die antike Rhetorik. Eine Einführung* (Munich, 1984); G. Kennedy, *The Art of Persuasion in Greece* (London,

1963), and *The Art of Persuasion in the Roman World (300 BC–AD 300)* (Princeton, NJ, 1972); J. Monfasani, 'Humanism and Rhetoric', in A. Rabil, Jr (ed.), *Renaissance Humanism: Foundations, Form and Legacy* (Philadelphia, 1988), vol. 3, pp. 171–235.

2. *Ad C. Herennium De Ratione Dicendi*, I.ii.3, ed. and tr. by H. Caplan (London, 1954) pp. 6–8.

3. Brian Vickers, *In Defence of Rhetoric* (Oxford, 1988, 1989), pp. 13–14.

4. Lisa Jardine, 'Ghosting the reform of dialectic: Erasmus and Agricola', in this volume, pp. 27–45.

5. 'The Textbook Tradition in Natural Philosophy, 1600–1650', *Journal of the History of Ideas*, vol. XXX (1969); 17–32, at pp. 18–19.

6. See for example E. Garin, *Italian Humanism: Philosophy and Civic Life in the Renaissance*, tr. by P. Munz (Oxford, 1965) and *Portraits from the Quattrocento*, tr. by V. and E. Velen (New York, 1972); H.H. Gray, 'Renaissance Humanism: The Pursuit of Eloquence', in *Renaissance Essays*, ed. by P.O. Kristeller and P.P. Wiener (New York, 1968), pp. 199–216; N.S. Struever, *The Language of History in the Renaissance. Rhetoric and Historical Consciousness in Florentine Humanism* (Princeton, NJ, 1970); B. Vickers, *In Defence of Rhetoric*, p. 275, note 73.

7. *The Arte of Rhetorique* (1560), ed. by G.H. Mair (Oxford, 1909), Sig. A$_{ii}$^{r}. See also the old-spelling edition meticulously prepared by Thomas J. Derrick (New York, 1982), which notes (p. 555) Wilson's source, Plutarch's *Pyrrhus*, xiv.1–2.

8. See B. Vickers, '"The Power of Persuasion": Images of the Orator, Elyot to Shakespeare', in *Renaissance Eloquence. Studies in the Theory and Practice of Renaissance Rhetoric*, ed. by J.J. Murphy (Berkeley and Los Angeles, 1983), pp. 411–35.

9. See Philip Melanchthon: *Elementorum Rhetorices libri duo* (Wittenberg, 1531), ed. and tr. by Sister J.M. La Fontaine (PhD Diss., University of Michigan, 1968), p. 76.

10. I quote from the outstanding doctoral dissertation of Joseph Xavier Brennan, which sets the highest standard for editions of rhetoric books, 'The *Epitome Troporum ac Schematum* of Joannes Susenbrotus: Text, Translation, and Commentary' (PhD Diss., University of Illinois, 1953; University Microfilms Order No. 53–6921).

11. E.C. Roaf, 'Bartolomeo Cavalcanti, 1503–62: A Critical and Biographical Study' (D.Phil. Diss., Oxford University, 1959).

12. See for example his preaching manual, *Ecclesiastes* (1535), in the Leyden *Opera Omnia*, 10 vols (1703–6), vol. 5, pp. 955–6, and Jacques Chomarat, *Grammaire et Rhétorique chez Erasme*, 2 vols (Paris, 1981), pp. 514–18, 1066.

13. See for example J. Monfasani (cited in note 1); J.R. Henderson, 'Erasmus on the Art of Letter-Writing', in *Renaissance Eloquence. Studies in the Theory and Practice of Renaissance Rhetoric*, ed. by J.J. Murphy (Berkeley, 1983), pp. 331–55; F.J. Worstbrock, *Der Brief im Zeitalter der Renaissance* (Weinheim, 1983).

14. See J.W. O'Malley, *Praise and Blame in Renaissance Rome: Rhetoric, Doctrine, and Reform in the Sacred Orators of the Papal Court, c.1450–1521* (Durham, NC, 1979), and 'Content and Rhetorical Form in Sixteenth-

Century Treatises on Preaching', in *Renaissance Eloquence*, ed. by J.J. Murphy (cited in note 8), pp. 238–52; K. Dockhorn, 'Rhetorica movet. Protestantischer Humanismus und Karolingische Renaissance', in *Rhetorik. Beiträge zu ihrer Geschichte in Deutschland vom 16.–20. Jahrhundert*, ed. by H. Schanze (Frankfurt, 1974), pp. 17–42; B. Stolt, *Wortkampf: Frühneuhochdeutsche Beispiele zur rhetorischen Praxis* (Frankfurt, 1974); W. Fraser Mitchell, *English Pulpit Oratory from Andrewes to Tillotson* (London, 1932); J.W. Blench, *Preaching in England in the late Fifteenth and Sixteenth Centuries* (Oxford, 1964); P. Bayley, *French Pulpit Oratory 1598–1650* (Cambridge, 1980).

15. 'The Stigma of Print', *Essays in Criticism*, vol. I (1951).

16. Richard Sherry, *A Treatise of Schemes and Tropes* (London, 1550) pp. 4–7; Thomas Wilson, cited in note 7 above, Aiii^r; Angel Day, *The English Secretorie* (London, 1586), sig. n.1^r-3. J.J. Murphy, in *Renaissance Rhetoric. A Short-Title Catalogue* (New York, 1981), pp. 108–9, lists 17 editions between 1586 and 1635.

17. See Walter Ong, SJ, *A Ramus and Talon Inventory* (Cambridge, Mass., 1958), and *Rhetoric, Romance, and Technology* (Ithaca, NY, 1971) p. 166. Students of Ramus have been prolific of late. In addition to the substantial monographs by Nelly Bruyère, *Méthode et dialectique dans l'oeuvre de La Ramée* (Paris, 1984), and Kees Meerhoff, *Rhétorique et poétique au XVIe siècle en France* (Leiden, 1986), Jean-Claude Moisan has published a detailed set of 'Commentaires sur les *Rhetoricae Praeceptiones*, Epitomé Ramiste Anonyme de 1572', *Humanistica Lovaniensia*, vol. XXXIX (1990) pp. 246–304 (see p. 249, note 17 for other recent studies), and has added an 'Edition d'un épitomé ramiste anonyme de 1572, les *Rhetoricae praeceptiones*' in *Cahiers des Etudes anciennes*, vol. XXIII (1990), pp. 145–58.

18. 'Philosophical books in European markets, 1570–1630: the case of Ramus', in *New Perspectives on Renaissance Thought*, ed. by J. Henry and S. Hutton (London, 1990), pp. 253–63.

19. I quote from the very useful translation and commentary by Lawrence J.Flynn, SJ: 'The *De Arte Rhetorica* (1568) by Cyprian Soarez, SJ: A Translation with Introduction and Notes' (PhD Diss., University of Florida, 1955; University Microfilms Order No. HUJ 100–16926).

20. See, in this volume, the chapter by Dilwyn Knox, 'Order, Reason and Oratory: Rhetoric in Protestant Latin Schools' for German parallels.

21. See Allan P. Farrell, SJ, *The Jesuit Code of Liberal Education. Development and Scope of the Ratio Studiorum* (Milwaukee, Wis., 1938), and E.J. Lynch, SJ, 'The Origin and Development of Rhetoric in the Plan of Studies of 1599 of the Society of Jesus' (PhD Diss., Northwestern University, Evanston, Ill., 1968; University Microfilms Order No. 69–6958).

22. Cit. and tr. by T.W. Baldwin, *William Shakspere's Small Latine & Lesse Greeke*, 2 vols (Urbana, Ill., 1944), vol. 2, pp. 138–9. Baldwin notes that early copies of Mosellanus' *Tabulae* are frequently bound up with similar tabulations of Melanchthon's *Rhetoric* and Erasmus' *De Copia* (ibid., note). For a list of early editions see J.J. Murphy, *Renaissance Rhetoric* (cited in note 16), pp. 209–11.

23. *Vives: On Education*, tr. by Foster Watson (Cambridge, 1913), p. 134 (reprinted Totowa, NJ, 1971).
24. A. F. Leach, *Educational Charters and Documents 598 to 1909* (Cambridge, 1911), p. 451. On the vogue for Mosellanus' *Tabulae* in the grammar-schools during the first half of the sixteenth century (subsequently he was replaced by the better-organised collection of Susenbrotus) see the still unequalled study of renaissance literary education, T. W. Baldwin, *William Shakspere's Small Latine & Lesse Greeke* (cited in note 22), vol. 1, pp. 82, 101, 157, 161, 232, 405, 508; vol. 2, pp. 13, 25, 32, 36–9, 40, 43, 138–40, 176, 215, 252, 266, 697–8.
25. See J. J. Murphy, *Renaissance Rhetoric*, p. 47.
26. 'Humanism as a Value System with Reference to Budé and Vives', in A. H. T. Levi (ed.), *Humanism in France at the end of the Middle Ages and in the early Renaissance* (Manchester, 1970), pp. 199–215, at p. 208.
27. See J. J. Murphy, *Renaissance Rhetoric*, pp. 104, 67, and Marc Fumaroli, *L'Age de l'éloquence. Rhétorique et 'res literaria' de la Renaissance au seuil de l'époque classique* (Paris, 1980), pp. 279–98, 299–326, 362–70, and the index s.v. Caussin, Cressolles.
28. B. Vickers, *In Defence of Rhetoric*, pp. 294–339, especially 300–01, 322–35.
29. Sherry (see note 16 above), Aii^v–Aiii^v.
30. See R. F. Jones, *The Triumph of the English Language* (Stanford, CA, 1953) especially chapter 6, 'The Eloquent Language', pp. 168–213. Similarly George Puttenham, in his *Arte of English Poesie* (1589) has an early chapter entitled 'That there may be an Art of our English Poesie, aswell as there is of the Latine and Greeke'; ed. by G. D. Willcock and A. Walker (Cambridge, 1936, 1970), pp. 5–6.
31. *The Foundacion of Rhetoricke*, facs. ed. with introduction by F. R. Johnson (New York, 1945), p. xix.
32. Thomas Wilson, *Arte of Rhetorique*, ed. by Thomas Derrick (New York, 1982), pp. lxviii–ix.
33. The only historian so far to attempt a full survey, W. S. Howell, *Logic and Rhetoric in England, 1500–1700* (Princeton, NJ, 1956) seems never to have noticed this.
34. I owe this point to Peter Mack. The booklists have now been published as *Books in Cambridge Inventories*, ed. by S. E. Leedham-Green, 2 vols (Cambridge, 1987).
35. Quoted by Derrick, op. cit., pp. lxxxviii–xc.
36. I quote from the facsimile edition by R. C. Alston (Menston, 1972) in his pioneering Scolar Press series, 'English Linguistics 1500–1800', of which this is no. 317. In quoting from the prefaces I have reversed Roman and italic type.
37. Professor G. K. Hunter suggests to me that Shaw may have been inspired by Leonard Hutten or Hutton's(?) *Bellum Grammaticale sive Nominum Verborumque Discordia Civilis*, a Latin allegory referred to in 1591 and performed at Christ Church, Oxford, in 1592. A later English imitation, *The War of Grammar* (BM Add. MS 22725), was performed at Cranebrook School in 1666, but not printed. See E. K. Chambers, *The Elizabethan Stage*, 4 vols (Oxford, 1925), vol. IV, pp. 373–4; A. Harbage and S. Schoenbaum, *Annals of English Drama 975–1700*, rev.ed. (London,

1964), pp. 48–9, 164–5; and J. Bolte, *Andrea Guarnas, Bellum Grammaticale und seine Nachahmungen* (Berlin, 1908).

38. See B. Vickers, *In Defence of Rhetoric*, pp. 1–3, 295–305.

39. J. G. Merquior, *From Prague to Paris. A Critique of Structuralist and Post-Structuralist Thought* (London, 1986), pp. 50, 61.

40. See J.-C. Moisan's essay in *Humanistica Lovaniensia* (cited in note 17 above), pp. 257–75, also B. Vickers, *In Defence of Rhetoric*, p. 439 note 10, and B. Vickers, 'The Dangers of Dichotomy', *Journal of the History of Ideas*, vol. LI (1990), pp. 148–59, p. 158, note 16.

41. *Rhetoric* 1355b, tr. by W. Rhys Roberts, in *The Works of Aristotle*, ed. by W. D. Ross, vol. XI (Oxford, 1924).

42. Due to a printer's error, the pagination here runs 105, 108, 109, 108, 109, 112, 111, 112 . . .

43. *Institutes of Oratory*, 12.1.1–44; *Arte*, ed. by Mair, p. 222; ed. by Derrick, p. 438.

6

Rhetoric and Renaissance Drama

George K. Hunter

The recent interest in the rhetoric of the renaissance shares many features with other recent forms of historicism. Its appeal derives, of course, from its capacity to create an impression of oneness with the thought processes of the past; yet, like other historicisms, it is obliged to focus that past through the lens of modernity, inside the framework of modern values, assumptions and preferences. It is no accident that the conference on renaissance rhetoric held in July 1991 was supported by a Department of English Literature or that most of those attending should earn their living as teachers of literature. But the homology between these modern institutional and personal positions and the presence of rhetoric in the past (the renaissance or any other time when it was a dominant interest) is by no means to be relied on. For those who spend their lives explicating literary texts, rhetoric does indeed seem to have an appropriate function as a means of clarifying or explaining the meaning or effect of what is written on the page. But this is in fact a strange departure from the function of rhetoric as understood in its heyday, from the classical period to the Enlightenment. In this period there was a general agreement that rhetoric was a science (or art or *techne*) of persuasion, an art, that is, of public activity, a science of *doing* rather than knowing, a means to power over others, a process whose practical fulfilment lay in victory rather than understanding. This is as unlike the institution of literary criticism, as that is understood in the later twentieth century, as can be imagined, for this latter is institutionally conceived as requiring a personal relationship with texts so as to bring meaning into focus and so understanding and even 'truth' (that touchstone of academic discourse). So far only Professor Stanley Fish has had the courage (or impudence) to bring criticism into line with traditional rhetoric and argue that the aim of literary criticism is not truth but victory.[1] I assume that he is not the last who will make this point, but I must leave that future to those with a more robust imagination than I possess.

Those who would bridge the gap I have described between modern literary criticism and renaissance rhetoric often allege a convergence between rhetoric and something called poetics (recipes for writing poems).[2] If this refers to generalised *defences* of poetry (as in Sidney, Puttenham or Lodge and their contintental precursors) then it is certainly true that the argument that literature has a public function and is justified by its public effects, can draw on an assumption that it operates in this like rhetoric. But this defence has little to do with criticism or indeed with renaissance literature considered as a literary phenomenon, described then as a vehicle for universal truths and enjoyed today inside the standard modern assumption that literature is powerful as a disinterested aesthetic activity and that literary criticism should therefore respect its aesthetic autonomy or transcendence. Those modernist (or perhaps post-modernist) critics who argue that literature should not be considered transcendental but should be read primarily as a response to historical events in its own time are not, of course, however strongly they object to literary autonomy, arguing for literature's efficacy as a vehicle for public virtue and are as far from bringing the two disciplines into line as anyone else.

Another way in which the lack of homology between standard literary criticism and the practice of rhetoric shows itself is in the modern concentration on *elocutio*, the third part of rhetoric (see the handbooks of Lanham and Sonnino and the larger study of Sister Miriam Joseph), together with the comparative neglect of the first two parts, *inventio* and *dispositio*.[3] Sister Miriam tells us in the preface to the third edition of her much-used book that 'to recognise . . . to name the devices that enriched the great works of the Renaissance and of Shakespeare in particular can be a valuable and rewarding experience'. It is no doubt historically appropriate knowledge to understand that Shakespeare used anaphora, epizeuxis, polyptoton and so on, and probably knew he was doing so. But is such 'enrichment' inevitably good in itself or is it only good if it is germane to the experience it presents? Sister Miriam's viewpoint seems to separate style from the matter it deals with and from the affect that the context demands. My esteemed colleague, Professor Brian Vickers, has mounted a spirited defence of concentration on *elocutio*, on the rhetorical figures, as a procedure entirely appropriate to the renaissance period. I easily allow the historical truth he points to – that there are many renaissance rhetorics that did just this. What I do question is whether the figures can be seen truly when cut off from the modes and structures of argument and speaking that seemed natural or even inevitable then. Can they be responded to now without a complementary appreciation of the situations and larger literary structures and arguments that they were able to 'enrich'? The florid and copious (or bombastic) style of Elizabethan drama cannot be satisfactorily explained as the self-indulgence of authors affected by logorrhea, nor by the naive taste of a semi-barbaric, or Gothic, culture. Its use is purposive and rationed; it appears regularly in certain contexts and is absent from others. The authors are self-aware about both presence and absence and apply this linguistic enrichment only where the underlying structure makes it appropriate.

Take the case of Dekker and Webster's *Westward Ho!*, a run-of-the-mill and mainly prosaic comedy about the sexual escapades of free-living citizens' wives and their London gallants. Unusual in this kind of play is the presence in *Westward Ho!* of an outsider, an Italian merchant (Justiniano) whose wife is pursued not simply by a local gallant but by an unidentified 'Earl', whose methods of seduction belong to high melodrama and therefore demand high poetic rhetoric in response. In Act IV, scene ii, a scene unique in style in the play, the Earl awaits the arrival of Mrs Justiniano. But instead of the lady, her husband appears, masked and wearing his wife's apparel. He unmasks, to the horror of the Earl, and (taken for a succubus) demands the fulfilment of the contract. Next he reads a letter from his wife stating her Lucrece-like determination to die rather than yield, and unveils a tableau in which the corpse of Mrs Justiniano is presented, dead from poison she required her husband to administer.

Dekker (the scene is probably his) is able to supply a rhetoric that matches these high audacious deeds. It is impossible to quote the whole scene but a few samples may indicate the quality of the verbal equivalents. Here is the high-born (and therefore conscience-stricken) sensualist anticipating the lady's arrival:

This night shall my desires be amply crowned,
And all those powers that taste of man in us
Shall now aspire that point of happiness
Beyond which sensual eyes never look (sweet pleasure!).
Delicious pleasure! Earth's supremest good,
The spring of blood, though it dry up our blood!

We feed, wear rich attires, and strive to cleave
The stars with marble towers, fight battles, spend
Our blood to buy us names; and in iron hold
Will we eat roots to imprison fugitive gold.
But to do thus, what spell can us excite?
This the strong magic of our appetite,
To feast which richly life itself undoes.
Who'd not die thus? To see and then to choose?
                         . . . A woman! O the spirit
And extract of creation! This, this night
The sun shall envy. What cold checks our blood?
Her body is the chariot of my soul,
Her eyes my body's light, which if I want,
Life wants.[4]

Now hear Justiniano when he reveals that his wife is not dead after all and converts the Earl from lust to virtue:

Justiniano   See, Lucrece is not slain,
  Her eyes which lust called suns have their first beams,
And all these frightments are but idle dreams.
Yet, afore Jove, she had her knife prepared
To let her blood forth ere it should run black.
Do not these open cuts now cool your back?
Methinks they should. When vice sees with broad eyes
Her ugly form, she does herself despise.
Earl   Mirror of dames, I look upon thee now
As men long blind having recovered sight,
Amazed, scarce able to endure the light.
Mine own shame strikes me dumb; henceforth the book
I'll read shall be thy mind and not thy look.

The jewels which I gave you wear; your fortunes
I'll raise on golden pillars. Fare you well:
Lust in old age like burnt straw does even choke
The kindlers, and consumes in stinking smoke.
                              (lines 154–73)

The Earl exits at this point and the play's language immediately collapses back into colloquial prose:

Justiniano Come, Moll. The book of the siege of Ostend writ by one that dropped in the action will never sell so well as a report of the siege between this *Grave*, this wicked elder, and thyself . . . if all the great Turk's concubines were but like thee, the ten-penny infidel should never need keep so many geldings to neigh over them (pp. 186–194).

I am not claiming that this scene gives us 'great' poetry. But it does offer a rhetoric capable of projecting as emotional and intellectual excitement the extreme situations that the action sets up, and so is able to translate the melodrama of what is seen into ideas and generalisations that help redeem it from mere sensationalism. And it is this power of relating action to thought that separates rhetoric from the judgments that attach to literary critical connoisseurship. A standard renaissance school text such as the *Progymnasmata* of Aphthonius of Antioch, worked on by several of the most enlightened pedagogues of the period and in use across Europe, may look like an anthology of elaborate writing, exemplary to the aspiring pupil, and in this parallel to the modern school anthology of verse or prose. The parallel is however quite misleading: the latter exists to exemplify good taste, to present examples of aesthetic power that the pupil will learn to cherish as touchstones; the former offers models for deconstruction into a set of rules and conventions that can be internalized and regurgitated whenever a particular social opportunity arises, when powerful, witty or appealing discourse can be applied and made appropriate to the argument needed.[5] The distinction between a brilliant and a bombastic style depends not only on the knowledge and use of the figures but on a grasp of the mental and social preconditions that make it appropriate to invent and dispose the arguments that can carry them.

When we read of pupils in humanist grammar schools and even universities studying Ovid and Virgil and Cicero we are liable to think of them as undergoing a 'literary education' in some way comparable to that available in a modern department of English. Once again I think the parallel misleading. The children who slaved from dawn to dusk marking the figures in these classical texts, extracting *sententiae* and noting metaphors, were not engaged in anything the modern world would accept as literary study. They were breaking these classical models into their parts so as to become facile and copious in their own writing and so their own public speaking. Then they would be capable of exerting power over audiences whenever the social conditions allowed that – whether the conditions were those of real life or those of simulated reality in drama or other kinds of performative fiction.

It will be evident that much of what I have been saying here marches in a somewhat uneasy lockstep with post-modernist criticism of what I have called modernity – the institutional structures and basic assumptions of the universities that we have grown up in. Post-modern critics[6] tell us that the category of 'literature' is a romantic invention which can only be justified if we imagine things that are not – private or 'essential' soul states independent of external pressure from the political environment. My argument that modern literariness and renaissance rhetoric are at odds obviously relates to this. The interest in rhetoric in recent times, not only in literary circles but in economics, historiography, in the history of science, in anthropology, is clearly associated with a general revulsion against essentialism (so called), against the assumption that these subjects can be handled by a language of 'truth', free of personal bias and political preconditions.[7]

It is tempting to hail all this as a return to the rhetorical culture of the renaissance. But the analogy cannot be pushed very far. Renaissance rhetoric was in the main a system of using stylistic freedom to find a new way to say the same old thing, and remained firmly associated with the notion of an acknowledged absolute truth. But post-modernist rhetoric is attached rather to a sense of the world as simply 'playful' and resistant to order not only on the surface but at every level. It is the advertising industry that is best placed to exploit this total relativism and it provides today's armature of rhetorical invention and power. Power to change the complexion of the language, and so (to some extent) the complexions of the minds that use it, no longer grows out of literature but out of sound bytes. It is curious but it should not escape our notice that there is an interesting paradox here. Academic revulsion against commercialised society supports the purism of critics such as my former colleagues Paul de Man and J. Hillis Miller, who claim as moral high ground the knowledge that language pursued through philosophically rigorous 'rhetorical analysis' cannot escape contradiction or contamination. But the main effect of such exercises is to hand over all real communication to the impure rhetoric of PR and hype.

The difficulty of defining a true relationship between ethical probity and persuasiveness is not simply a modern issue of course, but, as the history of the subject makes evident, a central problem in the history of rhetoric. Is the power to persuade that Aristotle used as his basic definition an ethical power and is this then an answer to the charge in Plato's *Gorgias* that the skill of the rhetorician is like that of the cook or the cosmetician, a skill in fakery? Greek theory dissolved in Roman practice, of course, and Roman republican attitudes could hardly allow (even to Socrates)[8] the separation of eloquence from ethics. The idea of this as a possibility appears in the *De Oratore* only as a view of the *Graeculi* who appear in the dialogue as objects of wonder and scorn.[9] Marcus Cato's definition of the orator as 'vir bonus dicendi peritus' remained a Roman touchstone. To modern ears the phrase seems to be too indefinite to be useful, wavering between a non-sequitur and a tautology (*peritus* = *bonus*). But the contexts in which the idea is rehearsed in Cicero and Quintilian indicate a fairly precise sense. The *bonus* that is required is neither purely instrumental nor purely ethical but basically political.[10] Thus at the beginning of his great work (in the dedication to Marcellus Victor) Quintilian tells us that 'no man can be a complete orator unless he is a good man';[11] for 'if we very often have occasion to treat of justice, fortitude, temperance, and the like virtues (for some matter arises from them in almost every subject that occurs) are we to doubt that the orator makes the principal figure, wherever the force of genius and the force of eloquence is required? These accomplishments (as Cicero has evidently proved), as they are linked together by man's nature, are connected by his duty'. The 'good' orator is one who is able 'to understand social duties, how to manage public and private concerns. to govern cities with wisdom, regulate them by laws, improve them by institutions'. In Book XII (1.14–16) he defends Cicero and Demosthenes against the charge that they cannot (by his definition) be good orators because they were not good men; his answer is that both were patriots. This Roman view is closely connected, of course, with the idea that rhetoric is the source of civilisation. In Book II (16.9ff.) we hear that 'I think it is owing to eloquence, all-powerful eloquence, that the founders of cities have prevailed with dispersed multitudes to form themselves into one incorporate body; nor without exerting the most commanding powers of speech could legislators have persuaded so lordly a creature as man to submit to the dominion of law.'

Inevitably, the recovery of Roman rhetoric by the humanists came accompanied by these Roman views of rhetorical goodness and truth. Salutati and Bruni, successively chancellors of Florence, seem to have seen *eloquentia* as a precondition of *libertas* and thought (like Quintilian) that command of language was a command of political possibility. It is a measure of the distance we have travelled from the Roman position that a critical war rages now as to whether a politics so deeply embroiled with rhetoric as that of Salutati and Bruni can be taken seriously as real politics.[12] But there was one new factor which the Roman heritage could hardly hope to digest: lodged inside the renaissance effort to recuperate rhetorical politics lay the indigestible fact of Christianity and the consequent redefinition of the good man as not only the politically correct man but (more vitally) the holy or pious man.[13] And this element becomes even more important when we move over the Alps into the lands of Protestantism, where the contradiction between the ethical and the political assumes a still larger importance, so that the rhetoric of good public ends is faced (and eventually faced down) by the rhetoric of private goodness.

The attitudes to rhetoric that descended to the Elizabethan age thus involved a complex and highly unstable mixture, validating rhetorical power for social reasons that go back to Rome (the eloquent good man turns other men into good citizens) but validating also the private virtues of Christianity that require the individual not to be overcome by profane eloquence but always to test the meaning of what is said against the truth of his own Christian heart. In respect of the words of this world the Christian soul was offered only the alternatives of Lutheran abhorrence or Erasmian scepticism.

John Rainolds, whose 1572 Oxford lectures on Aristotle's *Rhetoric* bring the issue very close to the period of Elizabethan drama,[14] quotes with approval Ludovicus Vives's denial[15] of the association between speaking well and virtue: 'Quintilian jumbled things together which are completely separate and imagined rhetoric was an art for thinking and speaking well. Sensibly said, and useful too, if only that might persuade men. But not quite true, for in fact thinking and speaking well are separated by ends and materials and the whole of practice' (p. 165). And again 'the conduct of life we learn from Christ, the conduct of the tongue from Cicero; we read profane writings that we may be eloquent and we meditate on sacred writing that we may go forth good men (*legimus profana ut simus eloquentes, meditemur et sacra ut viri boni evademus)'* (p. 388). Rainolds offers no suggestion as to how these different sources of authority can be coordinated. As far as his words go, the *vir bonus* and the *dicendi peritus* are separated by the distance that separates heaven from earth.

Erasmus is the figure who exemplifies with greatest sophistication the issue I am raising.[16] His understanding of the gap between the world of contingency in which words are spoken and the world of absolutes to which we are bound by faith and hope was of a gap that could not be bridged by rhetoric but which rhetoric could delineate by its power of indirection. The gift of rhetorical power is in these terms a gift of knowing how to evade the destructive antinomy between the sacred and the profane while persuading others that this is a version of the good life that they can pursue without abandoning the world and without ceasing to be Christians. Erasmus's power over the educational systems of Northern Europe and his endorsement of an eloquence of paradoxes and of the plays that can be made between different ethically possible attitudes opens the way, one might think, to drama – the art of persuasion by indirection *par excellence* – the area of play that is serious, of truth-telling that cannot claim to be true.

There can be little doubt, however, that Erasmus himself would have disapproved of the drama of Shakespeare and other popular vernacular playwrights, performed by professional actors before a heterogeneous paying audience. He did translate some plays of Euripides into Latin for use as school exercises; but the furthest he allowed the logic of his rhetorical position to carry him was into that favourite Humanist form, the dialogue. One can see the attraction of the dialogue form.[17] For the humanist dialogue (like the drama) is particularly well adapted to fit into the gap between persuasion and truth. Both forms offer us assertions of truth powerfully argued and eloquently stated but stop short of the determination that only one defined truth can really be true at the end of the process. The flow of to-and-fro discussion in humanist dialogues is not intended to end in unison but to raise, turn around, and speculate on alternative versions of the possible truth, which may well be incompatible but are not pressed to reach that point. The ideally relaxed and indeterminate relation between the participants conveys a sense of a civilised even if temporary mode of life achieved by avoiding confrontation. Examples abound of course – the first book of More's *Utopia*, Starkey's *Dialogue between Pole and Lupset*, Erasmus's

Convivium Religiosum – but we may choose to remember the debate between misogyny and philogyny in Castiglione's *Il Cortegiano*, and how it is defused as often as it is kindled by the repetition of such phrases as *Allor messer Federico, pur ridendo, disse* . . . or *Rise messer Bernardo, poi suggiunse* . . .[18] The point of the book, indeed, is that it should not develop into a crisis. The final speech by Bembo turns the mode from discussion into a poetic vision which transcends rather than resolves the dispute. Everyone present can unite in admiring the rapture of the speaker, and with the coming of the dawn the whole experience is allowed to fade back into the status of the ephemeral social game with which it all began. In this version of catharsis the *Cortegiano* is both like and unlike a play. Many plays end with epilogues or throwaway final lines that transcend by evading the points at issue (the endings of *Love's Labour's Lost* and *A Midsummer-Night's Dream* come to mind); but the continuity of drama imposes a differentiation; its through-composed quality inevitably pushes the action forward to a culminating point in which what we have seen and heard is fulfilled in the mode of judgment, whether in the achievement of further life through marriage (or dynastic continuity) or the termination of a career by death.

The relation between rhetoric in drama and in the dialogue form raises the issue of the *argumentum in utramque partem* as a rhetorical technique particularly apposite to both. Eugene Waith, in *The Pattern of Tragicomedy in Beaumont and Fletcher* (1952) has proved beyond doubt a connection between the *controversiae* in the collection of Marcus Seneca and the plots of Beaumont and Fletcher, and Joel Altman in *The Tudor Play of Mind* (1978) has sought to draw on the technique for a general description of the mode of Elizabethan plays. It is clear that the techniques of orator and playwright are related; the experience of having to construct arguments both for and against a proposition is as valuable a training for a dramatist as for a lawyer, teaching flexibility of mind and inventiveness not necessarily trammelled by ethical considerations. But to read through Seneca's examples or through Aphthonius's school exercises is not to come close to anything like the effect of a play. In a *controversia* each argument is designed as a separate event and the principal effect is the triumph of the orator's skill over his intractable material. There is no interest in the motivation that explains a character's actions yet at the same time gives him freedom to move in unexpected directions, no concern with his

capacity to be 'like us' even when he is moving through manifestly
fictional situations. The 'proof' that a play moves towards is not a
legally defined statement of guilt or innocence nor even a definition
of the rightness of some particular action, but rather a discovery that
the truth of the norms that are present is always compromised by
the qualities of human behaviour.

It is undoubtedly true and must be allowed for that persuasion is
what plays aim at, persuasion that the life we see personated on the
stage is to be judged by standards that we can approve of and share.
As we watch, we see different persons trying to persuade one
another to different actions and different points of view. We in the
audience are not, however, simply persuaded serially by one
person, one argument after another, so that we agree for the
moment with whoever is talking. It is rather that we are able to add
or subtract assent as we listen; but we do not do this because some
characters are more (or less) expert inventors of arguments than
others. Writers on rhetoric from Aristotle onwards tell us that *ethos*
is the greatest power of persuasion that a speaker possesses;[19] if he
can persuade us that he is a good man then we will like and believe
what he tells us. Undoubtedly we respond in the same way to the
ethe of characters in drama. But the *ethos* of the individual character
in drama is never an isolated phenomenon, and does not raise the
same central question that bedevils the issue for the orator: is this
genuine *ethos* or only a pretence, a technical exercise to secure
approval? The characters in drama are inevitably all part of a
pretence, a fiction, and we respond to their actions not in general
and set terms but as they are appropriate to what seems possible
and desirable under the given circumstances of the story.[20] Even in
cases where the play has a clear propagandist intention (as in the
anonymous *Respublica*, Dekker's *The Whore of Babylon*, Middleton's *A
Game at Chess* – and much Jesuit drama) the effect of ethical
polyphony is still present. Indeed it might be said that an author
who seeks to control the natural diversity of the genre by imposing
on us a central voice that tells us how to think has given up
playwriting. Certainly he cannot hope to hold our theatrical
attention for long.

The polyphony of truths and standards that a drama sets before
us is certainly a proper part of the persuasive means the dramatist
uses; but the truth of these standards is always held inside the
emotional processes by which they are stimulated. Thus in *Hamlet*,
as we understand the conflict articulated between Claudius'

argument for state expediency and Hamlet's for individual integrity we have to allow that both are effective counter-weights to one another (they could well be handled as part of a dialogue). But this is not what the play is centrally making out of the dispute. Each intellectual position is exposed as part of a notional personal history, so that we understand that these are not only the things they *should* say to strengthen their positions (as good rhetoricians) but also the things they *have* to say, being the people they are in the situations in which they are placed. *Ethos* again is the central issue, not as a factor under control designed to achieve prescribed ends but as an issue that must be seen as itself a site of struggle between alternatives in a world of moral uncertainty and continual surprises, which mimics the emotional world in which the auditors themselves live.

Rainolds in his Oxford lectures cites Aristotle and Quintilian in support of the proposition that 'arguments are the basic supports of oratory and emotions are only accessory (*argumenta firmamenta, affectus ornamenta orationis*)'. In his later controversy with his Oxford colleagues, Doctors Gager and Gentili, Rainolds says that plays are pernicious because in them these priorities are reversed: intellect can no longer control the emotions, the appetites of fallen man take over and the human being becomes a beast. Gager had produced the standard schoolmaster's defence of drama, arguing that plays which show the eventual triumph of virtue have a positive ethical effect; in other words the *ethos* of the plot controls the *ethos* of the individual character's choices. Very properly, Rainolds will have none of this. He sees that the impact of the moment cannot be wholly dissolved or interpreted away by what happens eventually. Even if the young men had admired the chastity of Hippolytus in Gager's play, was it not probable that 'some elder men did *not* wish themselves as chaste as [Hippolytus] was, but were stirred up by Phaedra's pangs and Pandarus' reasons to [regret] the like motion had not been made to them'.[21] Again, speaking of Gager's Penelope character (in his *Ulysses Redux*): 'could no evil affection be ... stirred in any by seeing a boy play so chaste a part? Happy then would Lucretia have thought herself: but when Tarquin saw her he saw her employed as a most virtuous woman. Yet for all the wonderment he made of her virtue he was *more* inflamed with love of her beauty. Yea, the very sight of her chaste behaviour stirred up his wicked lust.'[22]

All representation calls up emotional identification, Rainolds points out, and such emotional connections easily overthrow any intention of the author or direction of the plot. In this he must be

1. Raphael, *Cartoon for the Tapestry of St Paul Preaching at Athens* (Victoria and Albert Museum, London)

2. Raphael, *The School of Athens* (Stanza della Segnatura, Vatican Palace, Rome)

AEOLVS IMMITTIT VENTOS IVNONE PRECANTE

SOLATVR VENEREM DICTIS PATER IPSE DOLENTEM·

TROIANOSQ VAGOS LIBYCAS EXPELLIT IN ORAS

AENEAM RECIPIT PVLCHRA CARTHAGINE DIDO·

CVI VENVS ASCANII SVB IMAGINE MITTIT AMOREM

3. Marcantonio Raimondi after Raphael, *Quos Ego* (The British Museum, London)

4. Raphael, *The Fire in the Borgo* (Stanza dell'Incendio, Vatican Palace, Rome)

5. Raphael, *The Oath of Leo III* (Stanza dell'Incendio, Vatican Palace, Rome)

6. Raphael, *The Coronation of Charlemagne* (Stanza dell'Incendio, Vatican Palace, Rome)

7. Raphael, *The Battle of Ostia* (Stanza dell'Incendio, Vatican Palace, Rome)

8. Paolo Uccello. *The Flood* (Chiostro Verde, Santa Maria Novella, Florence)

9.   Raphael, *The Transfiguration* (Vatican Museum, Rome)

10. After Raphael, *modello* drawing for *The Transfiguration* (Albertina, Vienna)

acknowledged to be in better touch with the realities of audience psychology than are the defenders of dramatic moralism. Yet he seems to disallow too easily the effect of the *ethos* that the narrative endorses. As we watch Iago persuading Othello of Desdemona's infidelity we are bound to appreciate Iago's rhetorical powers; we are fascinated by his capacity to organise the 'evidence' he needs and especially by the *ethos* that underwrites his persuasions, his role as the rough but guileless NCO, honestly grieved to have to disabuse the high-born idealists around him. It is easy to imagine Rainolds's 'some elder men' responding warmly to the realism that Iago espouses and supposing that this was a proper way to face the world (and there have been professional critics who have thought just that). Certainly the play (while remaining a play) cannot define the 'truth' of human relations in such a way as to rule out such a response. If the world is indeed as Iago thinks it is, then his deeds flow naturally from that premise and we should be persuaded that he is right. But does the play require us to think the world is like that? Iago tells lies; he can be contradicted in terms of facts. But is that the central issue? Might we not think that so self-congratulating an idealist as Othello deserves to be set down a peg? Maybe in truth Desdemona is not unchaste at this point, but must one suppose that she will not revert to the type of the Venetian woman? Facts in plays have to be interpreted as parts of an unstable world before they can be led to the bar of judgment.[23] If Iago's view of the Othello world is to be rejected, it is surely, above all, because of the dazzling goodness of truth as it appears in the minds of Othello, Desdemona and Cassio. If this is a world in which we find there are things worth living (and dying) for, it is so because it is represented by the persuasive point of view of an Othello and a Desdemona, projected of course by the idealising rhetoric of poetry.

Plays operate, like rhetoric, in a world of mere probability, in a world of verisimilitude (the mimetic equivalent of probability in logic) not verity. The truth of *ethos* cannot be turned into a proven truth, and yet it demands stable judgments that make complete sense to audiences on repeated occasions and across a wide range of presuppositions; but this is not a judgment that can be taken out of the purely hypothetical context of the play and argued for as applicable to the 'real' world outside, as if we were listening to a lecturer or a preacher. We in the audience accede to the play-with-truth that the actors engage in because the contract of engagement by which we attend can only be fulfilled under these circumstances.

An important part of the contract is the understanding that there is, outside the theatre walls, or the book that stands for them, a world of experiences that are not play, which must be defined as 'real' in terms of that contract and to which the theatre world bears only a referential relation. For us the nature of this relation is, I fear, mainly unspecific. But for a renaissance audience, trained in the potentials of rhetoric and waiting for the social situation that might actualise it, one can see that the playhouse could act as a kind of rhetorical gymnasium in which oratorical muscles could be flexed and imagined as if at full power.[24] If renaissance rhetorical education was, as I have argued, a preparation for linguistic actualities that seldom appeared, then one may see why the playhouse had a social role of great importance. Today we depend as much as ever on rhetorical means to achieve our social objectives, but the relation of that commonplace use to our organised systems of thought is more distant. We can respond to renaissance plays as patterned exercises of power, but the interrelation of that power with the linguistic excitement of our own search for achievement is largely closed to us. Unless we can suppose that the post-modernist enterprise will turn us all into the rhetoricians of our own beliefs, probably we must be content with what a purely literary approach can achieve. That is no means to be despised, but it does not take us, in any genuine way, into the real rhetorical life of the past.

Notes and References

1. See, for example, 'No Bias, no Merit: the Case against Blind Submission', *PMLA*, vol. CIII (1988), p. 739–48.
2. See C.S. Baldwin, *Renaissance Literary Theory and Practice* (Gloucester, MA, 1957); William Kennedy, *Rhetorical Norms in Renaissance Literature* (New Haven, CT, 1978); Arthur Kinney, *Humanist Poetics* (Amherst, 1986); Gary Waller, *English Poetry of the Sixteenth Century* (London, 1986); Thomas O. Sloan, *The Rhetoric of Renaissance Poetry* (Berkeley, 1974); O.B. Hardison, 'The Orator and the Poet: the Dilemma of Humanist Literature', *Journal of Medieval and Renaissance Studies*, vol. I (1971), pp. 33–44.
3. See Lee A. Sonnino, *A Handbook to Sixteenth-Century Rhetoric* (London, 1968); Richard A. Lanham, *A Handlist of Rhetorical Terms* (Berkeley, 1969). On a larger scale, see Sister Miriam Joseph, *Rhetoric in Shakespeare's Time* (New York, 1962). Marion Trousdale's *Shakespeare and the Rhetoricians* (Chapel Hill, 1982) must be excepted from this generalisation.

4. Fredson Bowers (ed.), *The Dramatic Works of Thomas Dekker*, vol. II (Cambridge, 1955).
5. Compare Anthony Grafton and Lisa Jardine, *From Humanism to the Humanities* (London, 1986), pp. 131ff. Peter Mack, 'Rudolph Agricola's Reading of Literature', *Journal of the Warburg and Courtauld Institutes*, vol. XLVIII (1985) suggests (p. 39) that elements of what we would now call literary criticism can be found inside the rhetorical assumptions of the period.
6. See Catherine Belsey, *The Subject of Tragedy* (London, 1985); Jonathan Dollimore, *Radical Tragedy* (Brighton, 1984); Francis Barker, *The Tremulous Private Body* (London, 1984).
7. See Hayden White, *Metahistory* (Baltimore, 1968) and *The Content of the Form* (Baltimore, 1987); A. J. Woodman, *Rhetoric and Classical Historiography* (Portland, 1988); Clifford Geertz, *The Interpretation of Cultures* (New York, 1973); Donald McCloskey, *The Rhetoric of Economics* (Madison,1985) and *If You're So Smart: the Narrative of Economic Expertise* (Chicago, 1990); Nelson, Megill and McCloskey, *The Rhetoric of the Human Sciences* (Madison, 1973); Alan Gross, *The Rhetoric of Science* (Cambridge, MA, 1990); Bruno Latour and Steve Woolgar, *Laboratory Life: the Social Construction of Scientific Facts* (Beverly Hills, 1979).
8. See *De Oratore*, III.xvi.60.
9. See I. 47, 102, 221.
10. Compare Cicero, who in *De Inventione* (I.v,6) says 'we will classify oratorical ability as part of political science'.
11. I quote Quintilian from the translation of W. Guthrie (1756). The section numbers are those of the modern editions.
12. See Jerrold Seigel, *Rhetoric and Philosophy in Renaissance Humanism* (Princeton, 1968); Hans Baron, *From Petrarch to Leonardo Bruni* (Chicago, 1968); Nancy S. Struever, *The Language of History in the Renaissance* (Princeton, 1970); Eugenio Garin, *Italian Humanism: Philosophy and the Civic Life in the Renaissance* (Oxford, 1965).
13. See Jerrold Seigel, op. cit., pp. 152ff. on Valla's handling of this problem.
14. I am indebted to the edition by Lawrence D. Green, *John Rainolds's Lectures on Aristotle's Rhetoric* (Newark, 1986). I have used Professor Green's translation throughout.
15. *De Causis Corruptarum Artium Libri VII*, Book IV.
16. See Victoria Kahn, *Rhetoric, Prudence and Scepticism in the Renaissance* (Ithaca, 1985).
17. See K. J. Wilson, *Incomplete Fictions: the Formation of the English Renaissance Dialogue* (Washington, DC, 1985); Hannah H. Gray, 'Renaissance Humanism: the Pursuit of Eloquence', *Journal of the History of Ideas*, vol. XXIV (1963), pp. 497–514.
18. *Il Libro del Cortegiano*, ed. by Ettorte Bonara (Milano, 1972), II.lvii, II.lxvii. I have noticed 26 other examples of these formulaic interventions.
19. Aristotle, *Rhetoric*, 1.2. 4–5, Quintilian, 6.2. 18–19, *Rhetorica ad Alexandrum*, cap. xviii, xxix.

20. This means that there is available to us a whole range of possibilities between approval and disapproval. We are perfectly capable of having sympathy for characters whose actions are clearly unethical: Richard III, Vittoria Corombona, Tamburlaine, Macbeth.
21. *The Overthrow of Stage Plays* (1599), pp. 111–12.
22. Ibid., p. 112.
23. What Aristotle says in *Rhetoric*, 1.2.4 seems to be relevant here. Speaking of the power of *ethos* in a speaker he notes that where there is no certainty and there is room for doubt (ἐν οἷς δὲ τὸ ἀκριβὲς μὴ ἐστιν ἀλλὰ τὸ ἀμφιδοξεῖν) ethos will be all-powerful.
24. This is one reason why the theatre was thought to be be so psychologically dangerous for lower-class auditors. The third satire in the first book of Joseph Hall's *Virgidemiarum* (1598) tells of a 'high aspiring swain' who 'doth set his soaring thought/On crowned kings . . . Graced with huff-cap terms and thundering threats/That his poor hearers' hair quite upright sets . . . Now swooping inside robes of royalty/That erst did scrub in lousy brokery'.

7

Rhetoric in Use: Three Romances by Greene and Lodge

Peter Mack

In the last fifty years our knowledge and understanding of the history of rhetoric have advanced immeasurably. But when students of renaissance rhetoric are called on to justify their choice of subject, they/we tend to make the same explanations, and express the same hopes as T. W. Baldwin or Sister Miriam Joseph did in the 1940s.[1] Like them we set out the rhetorical basis of sixteenth century education. Like them we hope that in due course we will be able to achieve new understanding of the great sixteenth century writers, and in particular of their processes of composition. Like them, we take most of our examples from Shakespeare.

In this paper I want to look at a group of works that are not especially fashionable or well known,[2] and to ask how a knowledge of rhetoric and dialectic might help us to understand them. I also want to ask how much the rhetoric or dialectic found in these works involves broad themes of both subjects and how much it relates specifically to renaissance rhetoric and dialectic.

I have chosen to concentrate on three texts: Robert Greene's *Mamillia*, which appeared in two parts (1580, 1583), his *Pandosto* (1588) and Thomas Lodge's *Rosalynde* (1590).[3]

Mamillia was Greene's first published work, evidently written under the influence of, and perhaps partly in reply to Lyly's *Euphues* (1578). The narrative is so often interspersed and augmented with speeches, soliloquies, letters and debates, and these texts are so much longer and more polished than the narrative that one reads the book more as an anthology of short texts than as a story. The narrative frame exists to create situations which require verbal response from the characters. On occasion these situations demand conversation, introductions or verbal display. More usually they produce extreme or divided emotions which the characters respond to in soliloquy or with an impassioned plea. In places the story is an afterthought, so for example, the last paragraph of the first part contains almost as much plot material as the preceding 120 pages. Author and audience are concerned more with the tactics and expression of the successive short texts than they are with the outcome of the plot. Pharicles, the principal male character, has just begun to make progress in his wooing of Mamillia when he is overcome by the beauty of Publia. When he returns home from their first meeting he begins his soliloquy with the following words:

> O Pharicles, Pharicles, what a doubtefull combate dost thou feele in thy minde betweene fancy and fayth, loue and loyaltie, beautie and bountie? shal the flickering assault of fancy ouerthrow the castle of constancy, shall the lightnesse of loue violate the league of loyaltie? shal the shadow of bewtie wipe out the substance of bounty? shall hope bee of more force then assurance? wilt thou vow thee constant to one, and proove thy selfe not stedfast to any? the Turtle chuseth, but neuer changeth; the Swan lyketh, but neuer loatheth; the Lyon after he hath entred league with his make, doth neuer couet a new choyce: these haue but only sense, and I am sure thou hast reason and sense, and art more vnruly: they haue but nature for their guide, and yet art constant: thou haste both nature and nurture, and yet thy minde is mouable: these brute beastes keepe their consent inuiolable, and thou a reasonable creature dost falsifie thy faith without constraint, yea euen breake thine oath without compulsion, whereas nothing is so to be hated, as periury, and a man hauing cracked his credit, is halfe hanged.
>
> Marcus Regulus rather then hee shoulde falsifie his fayth, even to his enemies, suffered a most horrible death. Horatius Secundus being betroathed to Civilia, was rackt to death for his constancy. Lamia a Concubine, by no torments could be haled from the loue of Aristogicon. What perilles suffered Theagines to keepe his credit with Caricha? Pharicles, let these examples moove thee to be loyall to Mamillia: be thou stedfast, and no doubt thou shalt not find her staggering: but if thou wauer, ware thou dost not as the dogge, loose both bones: for deceit deserves deceite, and the ende of tretcherie is to haue small trust.[4]

At the level of style this passage is evidently very rich in rhetorical devices. The first sentence combines apostrophe, antithesis, tricola, alliteration, polysyntedon and rhetorical question. The second involves parison, double alliteration, epanaphora and rhetorical question.[5] We should also notice the way in which the immediately opposed terms of the first sentence are repeated with more elaboration in the questions which follow. Again, the length of the parisons and isocola is varied between the repeated questions, the natural history examples, and the conclusions before the closed isocola give way to the more extended sentence examining his faithlessness, at the end of the first paragraph. At the level of structure one can point out the movement from the question, which expresses his dilemma, to the natural history examples of fidelity, which lead to a comparison and an examination of the contrary state of faithlessness. Then historical and literary examples of human fidelity lead to an exhortation and a warning about the effects of deceit. A full analysis of the passage would explore the way it combines argument with decoration.

For the modern reader, however, the effect of this passage is humorous. The verbal and syntactic patterns seem contrived. There are too many paired qualities and the alliteration is excessive. There are too many examples. But as we laugh we also enjoy and admire the contrivance. The renaissance reader's response might not have been so different,[6] except that he or she would have had a keener appreciation for the skill, and more use for the strings of examples. For that is the second point of the passage. The similes and historical parallels provide a treasure house, or *copia*, of material which the readers can reuse through their commonplace books.[7] A third point is the unpersuasiveness of Pharicles's language. He produces many examples and expressions which induce guilt, but he answers them with almost similar persuasions on the other side.[8] And he concludes the speech by deciding that although he prefers Publia the most prudent course is to maintain an interest in both women.

The excess of the figures, the possible use of the examples as comonplaces, and the unpersuasiveness of the arguments suggest that the audience has a detached attitude to Pharicles's words. Amusement at the excess of his language and examples seasons our condemnation of his dishonesty. It might be objected that this is an unhistorical attitude, but studies of medieval drama and recent productions of renaissance plays suggest that acknowledgement of laughter can enhance tragic or religious feeling.[9] It is the modern need to observe a gulf between laughter and moral response which makes difficulties in these texts. Greene's narrator sees Pharicles as the model lover of his time, resourceful and deceitful, but also the victim of his desires.[10]

The way these short texts build on each other can be illustrated from a sequence of them, two speeches and a soliloquy, which occurs towards the end of the book. Pharicles has been disappointed by a letter from Publia whom he has been wooing. He has gone to visit Mamillia, his former love, with a view to getting engaged to her. Her father, Francesco Gonzaga is delighted to see him, but resolves to test his intentions.

> Pharicles, quoth he, the old Fox that cannot spy the fetch of the young one was neuer crafty himself: the Goose that cannot see the Gosling winke, may seeme to haue a defect of nature: he that cannot see fire in the straw, is surely stone blind: and hee that cannot spy the flame of fancy is but a foole. There is none wil so soone spy one halting, as a cripple: it is hard to couer smoke, but more hard to conceale loue. I my self both haue tryed it, and nowe I likewise find the proofe of it in you, who as closely as you keepe your cloke, yet I spy the lining, for loue kept in secret is like the spark couered with ashes, which at length bursteth into a great flame.[11]

In this passage a large amount of ornament (*Copia* of words and things) is combined with a very clear line of argument. In the first three sentences proverbs, images and personal recollection all lead up to and reinforce the observation that Gonzaga has discovered Pharicles's intentions. In the second part of the paragraph the comparison, the historical authorities, the anthropology and the natural history all back up Gonzaga's main contention: that love which is to last should be based on virtue rather than on beauty or fortune. The line of exposition is so clear because the ornaments are organised like supporting arguments. But they *function* as ornaments. Gonzaga is setting out a position from which he will make further observations. He is not trying to convince any one. His ornaments come from the collections of similes, the handbooks of historical anecdote, and the encyclopaedias of natural history (some of it fanciful) which the Elizabethan student was trained to use.[12]

Gonzaga's speech uses many of the same figures as Pharicles's soliloquy: example, parison, alliteration, comparison, antithesis and distinction. Within this elaborated, or euphuistic framework, however, the stylistic effect of Gonzaga's speech is markedly different: the phrases are on the whole longer, the antitheses pointed less sharply, apostrophe and rhetorical question are avoided. Where Pharicles's language indicated emotional turmoil, Gonzaga's suggests reason and premeditation. In both cases the reader is made conscious of the art involved and is kept at a distance by the wish to evaluate that art.

The passage also contains a self-presentation which is amplified in a later section of the speech. Within the ornaments, it is implied, Gonzaga *is* the old fox, the goose, the man of experience. Equally his whole manner of speech insists on his prudence, and his wide knowledge. In the second paragraph of the speech he characterises men like himself.

> for you knowe olde men are very suspitious, and I my selfe doute by the dreade of others: wee are colde of complexion, and therefore fearefull by nature, and will quicklye spye a padde in the strawe and a snake in the grasse. I perhaps thinke the Moon is eclipsed, when she is but changing: and gesse love is lust, when it is loyaltie.[13]

Gonzaga sets up this *persona* of the old oversuspicious father in order to prepare for the final paragraph of his speech in which he accuses Pharicles of flattery, changeable affections and insufficient love for his daughter.[14] The self-presentation (or *ethos*) serves to prepare for the accusations with which the speech concludes. But it also serves to explain them away. They may after all be no more than unwarranted suspicions typical of an old father. Pharicles's reply shows that he understands very well the kind of test which is being put to him.

> Sir, quoth he, as it is hard to hide the smoake, so were he a foole that would goe about to couer it, and if fancy must needs be spyed, who would seeke to cloake it? . . . But I hope that I shall proue a cunning Pylot, and to shew my selfe so chary in my choyse, what wares I chuse, that I shall bee a good Chapman, and the better I trust, in that I haue your counsel. The Lyons whelp taketh euer the fattest sheepe, when the old sire is by: the fawne neuer makes so good choyse of his feede, as the old Bucke.[15]

He begins by turning round Gonzaga's images and proverbs to assert his own point of view. Since smoke and fancy are hard to hide, it must be clear that he has conducted his courting openly. He supports his own prudence and caution with metaphors from seamanship and business. He flatters Gonzaga by giving examples of young animals profiting from the assistance of their elders. All this enables him to feed Gonzaga's own conclusions back to him.[16]

He goes on to echo Gonzaga's remarks on the transitoriness of love based on beauty with images, proverbs, quotations, natural history and historical instances from his own reading. Pharicles in other words seeks to reassure Gonzaga by showing that he can draw the same conclusions about love and virtue from slightly different, though parallel, instances. It is a bit like writing an essay for a tutor who expects you to reach the same conclusions as he has on the basis of slightly different evidence.

The end of Pharicles's speech also follows Gonzaga's example. Where Gonzaga had presented himself as suspicious, Pharicles protests that he is mistrusted.

> But why doe I seeke to try my selfe loyall, when the hearers doe deeme me a lyar? Why doe I bring in reasons to proue my troath, when my wordes can have no trust, or to debate the matter, when they thinke it daliaunce? well Sir, I can not let you to think: but if I daly, it is in dolour; if I sport, it is in spight; if I jest, it is without joy; and so tract of time shal try it.[17]

Pharicles's resentment of the slur is as put on as Gonzaga's suspicion. And the reader, who has the advantage of Greene's comments on Pharicles's insincerity, is surely impressed not by what he claims to believe but by the rhetorical skill and appropriateness of his reply. The skill which enables Pharicles to pass the test pleases the audience rather in the way that the reader of a medieval romance is sometimes asked to admire the skill with which the hero surmounts a problem of courtesy.

Gonzaga is satisfied by this display and the engagement is arranged. Pharicles then returns home and rereads the letter from Publia. This time the letter which before had appeared so negative seems to be more encouraging. He finds himself overcome by the thought of Publia's beauty but restrained by the promise he has made.

so Pharicles driuen by the force of lust, against the lawes of love, felt dubble dolour, and was so diuersly tormented, that he fel into these tearmes.

Of al euil, which either God or nature hath layed vpon man, there is none so great, but either reason may redres, pleasure asswage, or mirth mittigate, hearbes heale, or by some meanes or other be cured: Loue only excepted, whose furious force is so ful of rancor, that phisick can in no respect prevaile to helpe the patient, deserving not the name of a disease, but of an incurable mischiefe: yet importing such a shew of goodnes, that it so inflameth our desire to purchase it, that we wil not care to buy it at an vnreasonable rate: Which loue hath taken such deepe roote in me, as neither reason can rule, nor wisdom wield: it is so ranckled with rage, and infected with franticke folly, frantick I may well term it, as it seemeth to come without liking: so momentary, as it sheweth no modesty: so vnconstant, that it hath not one iot of continuance: so divers, as it may well be called divelish: more brittle than broken glass: more wauering then the wethercock: more variable in thought then the Camelion in hue: more changable in deede then the nightingale in voyce: now liking, now lothing: now fire, now frost: colde before I am hot: and hot at the first dash. O fickle love, fraught with frailty, O traiterous hart ful of trechery. O cursed conscience, altogether careles. O miserable wretch wrapped in wickednes: shal I requit the liberal loue of Mamillia with such disloyalty, returning as the dog to my vomit in liking Publia? shal I deceive the opinion, that both she and her father conceaved in me, with such detestable villainy? shal I return the trust they put in me, with such treason? shal I defile my fayth towards her with such forged falshood? shal I be so new fangle to leave the one so lewdly, and love the other so lightly?[18]

Greene's comments prepare us for an emotional outburst. Against that expectation the opening is surprisingly genial and philosophical - more like an all purpose *exordium* or the beginning of a *dubbio d'amore*. But after ten or fifteen lines the figures indicate a gathering of emotion: the anaphora, isocolon and parison as he describes the changeable nature of love,

> so momentary, as it sheweth no modesty
> so unconstant, that it hath no one jot of continuance
> so divers, as it may well be called devilish

Then, changing the structure but using the same figures,

> more brittle than a broken glass
> more wavering than the weathercock
> more variable in thought than the Camelion in hue
> more changable in deede then the nightingale in voyce

Reasons and images are being packed in very densely here, there is heavy alliteration and the length of the phrases shortens in preparation for the four apostrophes and the rhetorical questions,

> now liking, now lothing
> now fire, now frost:
> colde before I am hot
> and hot at the first dash
> O fickle love, fraught with frailty
> O traiterous hart, full of treachery

Pharicles employs figures which ought to produce an emotional response, but so densely and repetitively that the result is humour. But the humour produces an apt judgement on Pharicles's changeability, and it helps us enjoy Greene's rhetorical games. Here the rhetorical skill results in a display which entertains the audience rather than an outpouring of emotion which drives them to sympathy or to action.

But we must also notice the way in which the soliloquy reasons on both sides of the question. In the section we have just been looking at Pharicles can find all sorts of reasons why it ought to be dishonourable to desert Mamillia.

> shal I be so new fangle to leave the one so lewdly
> and love the other so lightly?

But later in the speech he can easily find equally weighty material supporting the opposite conclusion: the force of destiny, the intervention of the gods, and the stories of Aeneas, Jason and Theseus.[19]

At this point the display of rhetorical skill overwhelms any idea of emotional probability. It was one of the aims of rhetorical education to develop the ability to speak forcefully on both sides of a question, particularly through the emphasis placed on declamation.[20] Disputation serves a similar purpose in the context of dialectic. The divided soliloquy, one of the characteristic features of Elizabethan prose romance,[21] is an opportunity for the display of this skill.

Most of the connections between these three short texts reflect the development of the plot. But there is also a thematic connection. All three discuss the nature of love and the grounds for marriage, subjects which are also raised from different points of view and with different conclusions in Florion's letter to Mamillia, in Castilla's reply, and in Pharicles's discourse on love, among other texts which appear in the first part of *Mamillia*.[22] It would be overstating the case to suggest that the book is organised as an anatomy of love and marriage, but through the relative restriction of theme different voices attempt to discuss a given subject according to their situations and purposes.

At the end of part two, Mamillia herself writes two letters to Modesta advising her on her behaviour towards men.[23] The first is an anatomy of lovers' flatteries which adapts the shape of the formal oration. For the second letter Modesta poses a question in the genre of the *dubbio d'amore* about whether wealth or love should have more weight in choosing a husband. Mamillia's reply takes the form of a fable about Sylvia's dream.[24] In both letters, then, Mamillia organises her material according to forms provided by rhetoric. It is only fair to add that most of the other short texts do not fit easily into these expected patterns. In comparison with the attention given to the short texts, the plot seems to be relatively unimportant to author and readers. The same could be said of character. Characters' actions are said to be typical of their sex or age. Wherever Greene feels obliged to explain Pharicles's changes of heart, he takes the opportunity to remind his gentlemen readers of the deceitfulness of men in love.[25]

If plot and character are not independently interesting to Greene, both serve the purposes of amusement and teaching which also inform the speeches, soliloquies and letters. The short texts teach in that they gather together and pass on images, quotations and fables which the reader can reuse via his or her commonplace book. They entertain because of their display of skilful invention, disposition and style. The plot teaches through its moral structure, and it entertains through surprise and by producing unlikely and bizarre situations.

In *Pandosto* the weight of interest has shifted decisively in the direction of the plot, and in particular towards patterning of the plot. The surprises and the bizarre situations are created within a structure of parallelism and reversal. Pandosto's expulsion of his daughter is echoed by Egistus's inadvertent exiling of his son.[26] Egistus's advice that Dorastus should marry and the son's refusal are paired with the son's discovery of Fawnia and Egistus's rejection of the marriage he will eventually welcome.[27] The meetings and conversations of Fawnia and Dorastus are carefully interspersed with paired soliloquies at each stage.[28] The providential pattern by which the errors of the older generation are unwittingly put right by the affections of the young people provides a satisfying moral framework for the plot as a whole. As Wolff discovered, Greene had been supplementing his imitation of Lyly with a study of Heliodorus and Achilles Tatius,[29] probably also with a study of classical comedy.

In comparison with *Mamillia* there are many fewer speeches and they tend to be shorter and less ornamented. In several places *Pandosto* offers a summary of a character's thoughts where *Mamillia* would have provided a full soliloquy. This is Pandosto reflecting on the friendship developing between Bellaria and Egistus.

> First, he called to mind the beauty of his wife Bellaria, the comeliness and bravery of his friend Egistus, thinking that love was above all laws and, therefore, to be stayed with no law; that it was hard to put fire and flax together without burning; that their open pleasures might breed his secret displeasures. He considered with himself that Egistus was a man and must needs love, that his wife was a woman, and therefore, subject unto love, and that where fancy forced, friendship was of no force.
>
> These and such like doubtful thoughts, a long time smothering in his stomach, began at last to kindle in his mind a secret mistrust, which, increased by suspicion, grew at last to a flaming jealousy that so tormented him as he could take no rest.[30]

This looks like the outline from which a longer speech could be elaborated. It contains factual observations that could be gathered into a chain of reasoning; axioms, proverbs, even hints for passages of alliteration. Although it is made clear to us that Pandosto is incorrect in his suspicions, the effect of the summary is to show how the separate observations are put together into a logical argument in order to reach his conclusion. Where *Mamillia* showed the young man's rhetorical skill misleading the concerned father about the state of his feelings, *Pandosto* shows how logic and passion can combine to make a man believe something that is untrue. This habit of logical enumeration comes across even more strongly in Greene's summary of Franion's attempt to persuade Pandosto not to murder Egistus.

> His cupbearer, either being of good conscience or willing for fashion sake to deny such a bloody request, began with great reasons to persuade Pandosto from his determinate mischief, shewing him what an offence murder was to the Gods: how such unnatural actions did more displease the heavens than men, and that causeless cruelty did seldom or never escape without revenge: he laid before his face that Egistus was his friend, a king, and one that was come into his kingdom to confirm a league of perpetual amity between them; that he had and did shew him a most friendly countenance; how Egistus was not only honoured of his people by obedience, but also loved of the Bohemians for his courtesy, and that if he now should without any just or manifest cause poison him, it would not only be a great dishonour to his majesty, and a means to sow perpetual enmity between the Sicilians and the Bohemians, but also his own subjects would repine at such treacherous cruelty.[31]

This is the skeleton plan for a fairly lengthy argument. We notice that it is organised as an argument, not as an oration in its own right. The reasons are grouped in approved dialectical fashion: first arguments against murder in general, then general arguments against the murder of Egistus (personal relations, protected position, purpose of his visit). Next the argument that the murder would be especially treacherous because of Pandosto's friendly behaviour towards Egistus. Then the likely effects of the poisoning under the headings of personal affection for Egistus, injustice, dishonour, and the likely reaction of the people of both countries. Franion's dialectical invention and his organisation of his arguments is skilful and economical. But the main narrative point of the passage lies in the argument's lack of effect. Pandosto's reason has lead him to the point where rage and fury have taken over. Rage and fury have made him impervious to the counter arguments Franion offers. Indeed the counter arguments, strong though they

are, do not address what is for Pandosto the main point, the
supposed adultery of Bellaria and Egistus.

Greene's pessimism about the effect and the effectiveness of
reason extends also to the relationship between speech and
intention. Although he outlines the arguments which Franion
makes, he will not commit himself on his motivation,

> either being of a good conscience or willing for fashion sake to
> deny such a bloody request.

As with Pharicles, the ability to produce the arguments need not
imply a personal commitment to the view expressed. Even in the
debate soliloquies so typical of the genre the sense is of a mind
setting out the arguments, proverbs and imagery on each side rather
than of a division within the self.[32] Within the soliloquies the
sentences are more tightly controlled, less elaborated and repetitive
in *Pandosto* than in *Mamillia* in spite of the more serious situations.[33]
In comparison Bellaria's speech of defiance in the trial has a higher
proportion of content to decoration, and uses a more varied group
of figures. Bellaria's reasonableness, trying to master her passion in
order to present a balanced account, gives her words strength and
conviction.

> If the divine powers be privy to human actions – as no doubt they
> are – I hope my patience shall make fortune blush, and my
> unspotted life shall stain spiteful discredit. For although lying
> report hath sought to appeach mine honour, and suspicion hath
> intended to soil my credit with infamy, yet where virtue keepeth
> the fort, report and suspicion may assail, but never sack: how I
> have led my life before Egistus' coming, I appeal, Pandosto, to the
> gods and to thy conscience. What hath passed betwixt him and
> me, the gods only know, and I hope will presently reveal: that I
> loved Egistus I cannot deny; that I honoured him I shame not to
> confess: to the one I was forced by his virtues, to the other for his
> dignities.[34]

In *Pandosto* more extreme language works better in less tense
situations: when Dorastus is accusing himself for loving Fawnia or
when they trade examples on the clothing of lovers.[35] In Pandosto's
soliloquy about the attractions of Fawnia the excess and
conventionalness of the proverbs lends an appropriate sense of

distance.[36] *Pandosto* has far more plot interest than *Mamillia* and it creates more serious situations. The more decorated speeches on occasion seem inadequate to their situations. The dialectical outlines portray the thoughts of the characters without reducing the awkwardness of the relations between reason, reality and fortune. In *Pandosto* probability is often the enemy of truth, and fortune can produce tragedy from innocence, and joy from catastrophe. At the end of the book, with the reunions complete and the providential marriage accomplished, Pandosto kills himself.

> But Pandosto, calling to mind how first he betrayed his friend Egistus, how his jealousy was the cause of Bellaria's death, that contrary to the law of nature he had lusted after his own daughter, moved with these thoughts, he fell into a melancholy fit, and to close up the comedy with a tragical stratagem, he slew himself.[37]

This can be seen as one more twist in a plot structure driven by surprise and reversal, but it also reinforces the moral uncertainty of the book and its distrustful attitude to reason.

Lodge's *Rosalynde* is better known than *Mamillia* and *Pandosto*. It draws on the same materials as the others and observes the same conventions, but the end product is more playful, more comic and more favourable to love.

Like many of Greene's works, *Rosalynde* alludes to *Euphues*, claiming to be Euphues's last advice to Philautus for the benefit of his sons. Like many of the romances it begins with an older man's sage advice to his sons.[38] The preface, the legacy and the conclusion insist on the moral purpose of the book, to uphold virtue and friendship. The preface announces that the book is an anatomy of love, and John of Bordeaux's speech particularly warns his sons against love and against women. This theme and the related subject of the prodigal son, both of them very common in the romances, are broached at the beginning of the book, but negated in what follows.[39] Like the other romance writers, Lodge makes much use of the common stock of comparisons and proverbs. *Rosalynde* contains many short texts: soliloquies (particularly divided soliloquies), orations, letters and many poems.

It differs from the other romances in being more patterned and more focused on the subject of love. Like *Pandosto*, the plot incorporates repetition and reversal. Various characters soliloquize about their love or make addresses or write poems to their beloveds. Phoebe receives conventional love poems from Montanus and writes one (a translation of Petrarch's Sonnet 189) to Ganymede.[40] Rosader's two-part soliloquy on discovering his brother sleeping beside the lion is an inversion of Saladyne's soliloquy on their father's death - in each case the division is between a Machiavellian devotion to fortune and a recollection of their father's remarks about brotherly love.[41] The contrasts between the characters' experiences of love and the way in which resolution in one plot is set against complication in another would recall the structures of classical comedy even if we could forget what became of *Rosalynde*.

Just as events recur so also do themes. Most of the characters reflect on the vicissitudes of fortune.[42] Many of them speak of love's worthiness and its changeability, of virtue as its proper object, or of the need for women to be suspicious of men.[43] Rosalind uses the same quotation from Horace twice,[44] her soliloquy about Rosader covers the same ground as the eclogue between Montanus and Corydon, and the same division between the torments of love and the attractions of the lover recurs in a later speech of Aliena.[45] In one way this involves the viewing of a given subject from different angles and in different styles - in another it represents a use and reuse of a common treasury of thought and language, as when Rosalind's distinction between love and the rapid growth of the herb spattania repeats a comparison which Pharicles had made in *Mamillia*.[46] In spite of the differences between their situations, Rosalind's first soliloquy, on falling in love with Rosader, uses similar arguments and images to Bellaria's first soliliquy, in prison wondering how to react to Pandosto's accusations.

Alas, Bellaria, how unfortunate art thou, because fortunate! . . . Thou seest now, Bellaria, that care is a companion to honour, not to poverty; that high cedars are crushed with tempests, when low shrubs are not touched with the wind; precious diamonds are cut with the file, when despised pebbles lie safe in the sand.

Infortunate Rosalynde, whose misfortunes are more than thy years, and whose passions are greater than thy patience! . . . Ah Rosalynde, what cares wait upon a crown! what griefs are incident to dignity! what sorrows haunt royal palaces! The greatest seas have the sorest storms, the highest birth subject to the most bale, and of all trees the cedars soonest shake with the

wind: small currents are ever calm, low valleys are not scorched
in any lightnings, nor base men tied to any baleful prejudice.
Fortune flies, and if she touch poverty it is with her heel, rather
disdaining their want with a frown, than envying their wealth
with disparagement. O Rosalynde, hadst thou been born low,
thou hadst not fallen so high, and yet being great of blood thine
honour is more, if thou brookest misfortune with patience.[47]

Although her situation is less extreme, Rosalind's speech is more
strongly patterned than Bellaria's. She employs far more parison,
isocolon and anaphora. She favours comparisons and three-phrase
sentences (tricola) but she makes less use of antithesis. She
introduces the oppositional wordplay passions/patience that
recurs in the extract below. But the figures here are signs of art
rather than bearers of emotion.

To some extent then the features of *Rosalynde* that I have
mentioned so far are an intensification of trends present in other
romances. What really marks it out is a difference of tone: the
greater playfulness, the acting of parts, the sense of witty
conversation. When Rosalind (as Ganymede) talks to Rosader she
uses her disguise to mock what she also cherishes.[48] When she first
hears his poems in praise of her she ridicules the poses and tactics of
love poetry.

I can smile, quoth Ganymede, at the sonettos, canzones,
madrigals, rounds and roundelays, that these pensive patients
pour out when their eyes are more full of wantonness, than their
hearts of passions . . . . If they find women so fond, that they will
with such painted lures come to their lust, then they triumph till
they be full-gorged with pleasures; and then fly they away, like
ramage kites, to their own content, leaving the tame fool, their
mistress, full of fancy, yet without even a feather. If they miss, as
dealing with some wary wanton, that wants not such a one as
themselves, but spies their subtlety, they end their amours with a
few feigned sighs; and so their excuse is, their mistress is cruel,
and they smother passions with patience.[49]

Once Rosader begins describing his feelings, however, she and
Aliena are full of rapt attention, drinking in his praise and his
wisdom.

'I will tell thee, swain, if with a deep insight thou couldst pierce into the secret of my loves, and see what deep impressions of her idea affection hath made in my heart, then wouldst thou confess I were passing passionate, and no less endued with admirable patience.'

'Why,' quoth Aliena, 'needs there patience in love?'

'Or else in nothing,' quoth Rosader; 'for it is a restless sore that hath no ease, a canker that still frets, a disease that taketh away all hope of sleep. If then so many sorrows, sudden joys, momentary pleasures, continual fears, daily griefs, and nightly woes be found in love, then is not he to be accounted patient that smothers all these passions with silence?'

'Thou speakest by experience,' quoth Ganymede, 'and therefore we hold all thy words for axioms.'[50]

The treatment of Montanus and Phoebe also involves a shift from satire to sympathy. When we first encounter it, Montanus's praise of Phoebe is egotistical and absurd, but just before the revelation of Rosalind, Gerismond treats Montanus as the model of a true lover.[51] When Phoebe first falls in love with Rosalind as Ganymede, her misfortune is a comic judgement on her pride.[52] The letter she writes (with her sonnet) is serious, though, and although Ganymede laughs at first, eventually she pities Phoebe.[53] This movement between jest and seriousness is, in a way, very Chaucerian, but it is also a development of the idea about the gap between the truthfulness and the effectiveness of speech. As though Lodge can use rhetoric to show language as a mask, to be tried on and laughed at without impairing the possibility of using it and believing in it.

Part of the point of my analysis of all three romances has been to show the appropriateness (and the usefulness) of a rhetorical approach to these texts. The 'fine writing' in which these romances self-consciously abound is concentrated in the short texts. The linking narrative puts us in a position to compare these short texts with each other and with the situation, audience and intentions of their speakers. The rhetorical approach offers us a way of understanding these short texts, a way into the mixed tone of these works, and a way of analysing the variations of expression and effect within what would normally be termed 'euphuism'. In spite of my attempt at artlessness the three romances illustrated a range of rhetorical doctrines.

At the higher level of rhetorical organisation, *Mamillia* contained an adaptation of the four-part oration, an example of peroration, a fable and some exploitation of the idea of self-presentation or *ethos*. *Pandosto* had sketches of dialectical invention and an example of dialectical organisation.

Mamillia included examples of *copia* of words and things, of the use of renaissance reference books and of the exploitation of a common stock of argumentative and illustrative material. I suggested that this material, some of which was shared between *Mamillia*, *Pandosto* and *Rosalynde*, fulfilled the function of teaching because it was being offered to the readers for further use through the medium of the commonplace book.

Some of the extracts from *Mamillia* illustrated interplay between argument and ornament, with ornaments being used argumentatively, and arguments being used for display rather than persuasion. Some renaissance theorists were coming to the conclusion that the figures and the places of invention had a good deal in common.[54] In this they were developing some comments of Quintilian.[55] I also analysed the use of different mixtures of figures, and the effect of this use in different situations.

At a more theoretical level the texts touched on problems about the reliability of dialectic, the persuasiveness of argument and the gap between rhetorical competence and sincerity. I drew attention to the use of argument on both sides and declamation. I suggested that part of the pleasure for the audience of these books lay in observing the skilful use of the resources of rhetoric.

How much of what I have discussed belongs specifically to the renaissance, and how much is part of the broader tradition of rhetoric?

Some aspects were available in the standard classical handbooks which the middle ages and the renaissance shared: the structure of the oration, the peroration, the fable, the tropes and figures. Some aspects belong to classical rhetoric but were revived in the renaissance: the interest in *ethos*, discussion of the philosophy of rhetoric, and the conception of arguing on both sides. More particularly renaissance would be the various ideas involved with the rapprochement between rhetoric and dialectic, and the ideas involving *copia*, the new reference books and the commonplace book. So quite a large proportion of the rhetorical ideas mentioned could be thought of as belonging to renaissance rhetoric. But I have treated those ideas in a rather generalised way. It would be harder to say with certainty that one particular aspect comes from Agricola and another from Melanchthon.

How much of this would have been unknown to George Hunter and Grahame Castor thirty years ago - or to William Ringler twenty years before that?[56] They knew much less about medieval rhetoric than we do today.[57] Many of John Monfasani's articles would furnish them with new material.[58] They knew much more about Ramus than they did about Agricola and Melanchthon. But the classical texts, a good knowledge of renaissance education and a keen eye led them to many of the same sorts of observation that rhetorical criticism makes today. Not that there are no differences of emphasis but that the differences are not at all commensurate with the discoveries and publications of the intervening years.

If this is true, there may be a good reason for it. It may be that for a good writer a few basic rhetorical ideas are more useful and more exploitable than any elaborate theory about the whole subject. Or it may be that the general claims made by the pioneers of the historical study of rhetoric were larger than subsequent scholarship has been able to justify. It is quite possible for the critics to be ahead of the historians.

But there may also be consequences. Perhaps we should tell our literature students that the general ideas will be more useful to them than the detailed history. Perhaps we should concentrate our historical studies more on the development of particular rhetorical theories and be more cautious about the broad cultural claims. Perhaps we should be looking for the applications of particular theories in family archives and state papers rather than in consciously literary works.

Notes and References

1. T. W. Baldwin, *William Shakspere's Small Latine and Lesse Greeke* (Urbana, 1944), pp. vii, ix–xi; Sister Miriam Joseph, *Shakespeare's Use of the Arts of Language* (New York, 1947), pp. 3–4.
2. The most important studies are: S. L. Wolff, *The Greek Romances in Elizabethan Prose Fiction* (New York, 1912); G. K. Hunter, *John Lyly* (London, 1962); Walter Davis, *Idea and Act in Elizabethan Fiction* (Princeton, 1969); Nancy R. Lindheim, 'Lyly's Golden Legacy: *Rosalynde* and *Pandosto*', *Studies in English Literature*, vol. xv (1975), pp. 3–20; R. Helgerson, *The Elizabethan Prodigals* (Berkeley, 1976); A. C. Hamilton, 'Elizabethan Romance: the example of prose fiction', *ELH*,

vol. XLIX (1982), pp. 287–99; A. C. Hamilton, 'Elizabethan Prose Fiction and Some Trends in Recent Criticism', *Renaissance Quarterly*, vol. XXXVII (1984), pp. 21–33; P. Salzman, *English Prose Fiction 1558–1700* (Oxford, 1985); G. M. Logan and G. Teskey (eds), *Unfolded Tales* (Ithaca, 1989); Caroline Lucas, *Writing for Women* (Milton Keynes, 1989).

3. R. Greene, 'Mamillia', in A. B. Grosart (ed.), *Life and Complete Works of Robert Greene*, vol. II (reprinted New York, 1964); 'Pandosto', in J. H. P. Pafford (ed.), *The Winter's Tale* (London, 1963), pp. 181–225; T. Lodge, *Rosalynde*, edited by W. W. Greg (London, 1907).
4. *Mamillia*, ed. cit., pp. 90–1
5. The best sources for the tropes and figures are: *Rhetorica ad Herennium*, book 4; Quintilian, *Institutio oratoria*, books 8–9; H. Lausberg, *Handbuch der literarischen Rhetorik* (Munich, 1960); Lee Sonnino, *A Handbook to Sixteenth Century Rhetoric* (London, 1968); B. Vickers, *Classical Rhetoric in English Poetry* (London, 1970). G. K. Hunter, *John Lyly*, (note 2 above), pp. 260–79 has an excellent discussion of Lyly's style and its influence, with bibliography on the origins of euphuism.
6. Quintilian, *Insitutio oratoria*, 9.3.4. warns of the dangers of excessive use of the figures.
7. The method of using a commonplace book is described in R. Agricola, 'De formando studio', in *Lucubrationes* (Cologne, 1539), pp. 193–201 (198–9); D. Erasmus, 'De copia', edited by Betty Knott, in *Opera omnia*, ord. I, vol. 6 (Amsterdam, 1988), pp. 258–69. Ann Moss is currently preparing a book on renaissance commonplace books.
8. *Mamillia*, pp. 91–2.
9. V. A. Kolve, *The Play Called Corpus Christi* (Stanford, 1966), pp. 124–44; the RSC productions of *Titus Andronicus* (Deborah Warner) and *The Jew of Malta* (Ron Daniels).
10. *Mamillia*, pp. 94–5.
11. Ibid., pp. 108–9.
12. See T. W. Baldwin (note 1 above), vol. I, pp. 74–117; W. Ong, 'Commonplace Rhapsody: Ravisius Textor, Zwinger, and Shake-speare', in R. R. Bolgar (ed.), *Classical Influences on European Culture AD 1500–1700* (Cambridge, 1976), pp. 91–126.
13. *Mamillia*, p. 110.
14. 'For you, Pharicles, professe loue to my daughter, and I thinke it is but dissimulation: you faigne faith, and I doubt of flattery; you seeme to offend in excesse, and I feare you faint in defect', ibid., pp. 110–11.
15. Ibid., pp. 112–13.
16. Compare ibid., pp. 109, 113.
17. Ibid., p. 115.
18. Ibid., pp. 120–1.
19. Ibid., pp. 122–3.
20. Aristotle, *Topica*, 101a35; T. W. Baldwin (see note 1 above), vol. II, pp. 355–79; D. Russell, *Greek Declamation* (Cambridge, 1983); M. van der Poel, *De Declamatie bij de Humanisten* (Nieuwkoop, 1987).
21. For example 'Euphues', in R. W. Bond (ed.), *The Complete Works of John Lyly*, vol. I (Oxford, 1902), pp. 205–7, 208–11. The antithetical soliloquy is also found in Achilles Tatius.

22. *Mamillia*, ed. cit., pp. 37–9, 40–5, 78–84.
23. Ibid., pp. 253–66, 267–97.
24. The fable is the first of the *progymnasmata*, a set of short composition exercises widely used in Elizabethan schools. See Baldwin, D. L. Clark, 'The Rise and Fall of Progymnasmata in sixteenth and seventeenth century Grammar Schools', *Speech Monographs*, XIX (1952), pp. 259–63; Aphthonius, 'Progymnasmata', edited by H. Rabe, in *Rhetores Graeci*, vol. X (Leipzig, 1926), pp. 1–51; R. Nadeau, 'The Progymnasmata of Aphthonius in Translation', *Speech Monographs*, XIX (1952), pp. 264–85.
25. *Mamillia*, ed. cit., pp. 20, 35, 94–5, 103, 119, 134.
26. *Pandosto*, ed. cit. (note 3 above), pp. 193, 212.
27. Ibid., pp. 202–3, 217, 222.
28. Ibid., pp. 205–7, 209–10, 220–1.
29. S. L. Wolff, *The Greek Romances* (note 2 above), pp. 367, 376–457.
30. *Pandosto*, ed. cit., p. 186.
31. Ibid., p. 187.
32. E. g. ibid., p. 188.
33. Ibid., pp. 191–3.
34. Ibid., p. 197.
35. Ibid., pp. 205, 210–11.
36. Ibid., p. 219.
37. Ibid., pp. 224–5.
38. *Rosalynde*, ed. cit. (note 3 above), pp. 2–6.
39. In general John of Bordeaux's warnings have surprisingly little relevance to the story which follows.
40. Ibid., pp. 35–8, 49–50, 116–17, 118–19, 137.
41. Ibid., pp. 9–10, 94–6.
42. Ibid., pp. 24–5, 32–3, 57–9, 74.
43. Ibid., pp. 38, 80–1, 110, 118–19, 126, 130.
44. *Epistles*, I.1.53–4; *Rosalynde*, pp. 26, 113. The issue of wealth as a motivation for marriage is also raised in Sir John's schedule and Saladyne's jealousy, pp. 7, 159.
45. Ibid., pp. 24–7, 40–5, 110.
46. *Rosalynde*, p. 144; *Mamillia*, p. 23.
47. *Pandosto*, pp. 191–2; *Rosalynde*, pp. 24–5.
48. Rosalind's assumption (as Ganymede) of male attitudes is equally playful, pp. 36–8, or her 'who knows not, but that all women have desire to tie sovereignty to their petticoats, where, if boys might put on their garments, perhaps they would prove as comely' (p. 72).
49. *Rosalynde*, pp. 80–1.
50. Ibid., pp. 82–3.
51. Ibid., pp. 151–5.
52. Ibid., pp. 121–3 (cf. p. 156).
53. Ibid., pp. 136, 138, 144.
54. R. Agricola, *De inventione dialectica* (Cologne, 1539 reprinted Nieuwkoop, 1967), pp. 197–201 (and the chapters on Agricola in my forthcoming *Renaissance Argument*). For Melanchthon's view on the same issue see K. Meerhoff's chapter in this volume.
55. *Institutio oratoria*, 9.2.100.

56. G. K. Hunter (note 2 above); G. Castor, *Pléïade Poetics* (Cambridge, 1964); W. Ringler, *Stephen Gosson* (Princeton, 1942); W. Ringler (ed.), *Oratio in laudem artis poeticae by John Rainolds* (Princeton, 1940).

57. J. O. Ward, 'From Antiquity to the Renaissance: Glosses and Commentaries on Cicero's Rhetoric', in J. J. Murphy (ed.), *Medieval Eloquence* (Berkeley, 1978), pp. 25–67; idem, 'Renaissance Commentators on Ciceronian Rhetoric', in J. J. Murphy (ed.), *Renaissance Eloquence* (Berkeley, 1983); idem, *Artificiosa Eloquentia in the Middle Ages* (unpublished PhD dissertation: Toronto, 1972); K. M. Fredborg, 'The Scholastic Teaching of Rhetoric in the Middle Ages', *Cahiers de l' institut du moyen age grec et latin*, vol. LV (1987), pp. 85–105, with bibliography.

58. J. Monfasani, *George of Trebizond* (Leiden, 1976); 'The Byzantine Rhetorical Tradition and the Renaissance', in Murphy, *Renaissance Eloquence*, op cit., pp. 174–87, 'Humanism and Rhetoric' in J. Rabil (ed.), *Renaissance Humanism: Foundations, Form and Legacy*, vol. III (Philadelphia, 1988), pp. 171–235.

8

Rhetoric, Ideology and the Elizabethan World Picture

David Norbrook

I

The Elizabethan World Picture is frequently pronounced dead, yet it has remarkable powers of resurrection. Fifty years ago, E. M. W. Tillyard demonstrated how often defenders of the Elizabethan regime appealed to the analogy of the order of nature: monarchy and hierarchy were universal features of the cosmos, and any attempt to overthrow them was a perversion of a divine order.[1] Somewhat more recently, the belief that the early modern period was particularly susceptible to arguments from natural analogy was strongly reaffirmed by Michel Foucault in his highly influential book *The Order of Things*.[2] And some revisionist historians, concerned to demonstrate that the radical political ideas of the mid-seventeenth century were fundamentally alien to English culture, have recently been reiterating some of Tillyard's arguments.[3]

The problem with all such generalising readings of the renaissance mentality is that they are philosophical rather than rhetorical. They locate deep structures of thought which are held inescapably to shape early modern conceptions of the universe; and they thus exaggerate the uniformity of the age's thought and minimise the possibility of contending viewpoints. Recently, however, critics have begun reading renaissance defences of natural analogy rhetorically, as strategies of persuasion with very palpable designs, and hence open to challenge. What is produced from such analogies is not a static world picture but an ideology – a set of representations designed to legitimise specific social interests. I propose in this article to reexamine key texts of the Elizabethan world picture by Davies and Shakespeare in rhetorical terms, drawing on recent work on the history and theory of rhetoric. My emphasis is slightly different from some recent accounts of rhetoric and ideology, which have tended to see rhetoric in post-structuralist terms as an ineluctable counter to linear rationality. On that model, rhetoric is a subversive force which reveals the arbitrariness of all structures of meaning. It is thus intrinsically opposed to ideology, whose role is to naturalise such structures.[4] It is then possible to see texts like *Troilus and Cressida* as subverting rather than reinforcing the Elizabethan world picture.[5] The ease with which the play can be transformed from a deeply conservative to a radically subversive text is a little disquieting: I would suggest that a sharp binary opposition between rhetoric and ideology, between artifice and naturalisation, is inadequate to the complex processes of resistance and reaction in the early modern period.[6] Paradoxically, the more rhetoric is seen as subverting ideology, the more ideology comes to be seen as a unified essence, and it becomes necessary to reinvent a static world picture in order to demonstrate its subversion. And the more rhetoric is defined in terms of pure subversion, the harder it becomes to imagine how it could ever remain stable enough to occupy a place in society from which opposition could be organised: subversion tends in much recent analysis of early modern culture to collapse into containment.[7] Both consent and resistance, however, normally involve more pragmatic and material factors which are amenable neither to total domination nor to instant subversion. I shall try to show that rhetoric in the early modern period was indeed a critical political force: Hobbes was not being overly alarmist when he complained that the study of classical oratory fomented discontent with monarchy.[8] Yet that force lay not so much in direct subversion of monarchical rhetoric – which was not in itself taken all that seriously – as in encouraging a general pressure toward wider debate and discussion of public issues.

II

For the renaissance, rhetoric involved a challenge to scholastic logic but certainly not to all forms of rational argument. In stimulating an interest in debate, rhetoric helped to lay the foundations for some forms of challenge to political authority. In their critique of scholastic reasoning, renaissance humanists shifted their attention from the demonstrative proof of the syllogism to the more pragmatic proofs of dialectic, a mode of argument which offered practical effectiveness rather than necessary truth. They thus took a more favourable view of the provisional forms of argumentation traditionally located in rhetorical manuals, modes of 'invention' such as the lists of 'topics'.[9]

In such provisional modes of argument, analogy and comparison might play very prominent parts. But it is important to note the universal awareness of their limitations. Rudolph Agricola insisted both that similitude was useful to an orator and that it could not force assent:

> Of all the topics from which arguments are drawn almost none has less strength against a resisting hearer [*renitentem auditorem*] than similitude, on the other hand there is none more suitable for the hearer who follows it willingly and shows himself apt to be taught . . . it is not so frequently used for proving things but it is often used by orators for exploring and illuminating things, and even more often used by poets. In spite of this, similitude often has an appearance of proving in itself because it shows how something is.[10]

Agricola's analysis draws attention to the power of similitude, and he backs it up with an example from Lucan's *Pharsalia* (v. 336ff) in which Caesar uses a simile to talk down a mutiny. But Agricola is also aware that similitudes can be resisted: even in a political context, analogy is a tool of persuasion, not a mystical window on transcendental reality.

A similar view of analogy can be found in the most influential of all renaissance rhetorical works, Erasmus's *De copia* (1512). Erasmus offers a whole series of kinds of comparison: example, *homoiosis*, parable, simile, fable – such as Menenius Agrippa's fable of the belly and the body politic – *eikon*, paradigm and illustration. Erasmus insists that such examples amount less to proof than to amplification – a strategy especially appropriate for demonstrative rhetoric. Erasmus points out that some material may serve not only diverse but contrary uses. For example, analogies from the order of nature can be used either to praise or to condemn changeableness. Erasmus lists a dazzling variety of similes that image the fickleness of the inconstant man, including the changing colours of the moon, the ebbing and flowing of the sea, the chameleon, and quicksilver. He then suggests that if you were 'praising a man for all seasons, endowed with a versatile and dexterous mind, you could dip into your "inconstancy" cupboard' and point out that the bending reed was a better model than senseless rocks and the brute earth.[11] Erasmus complemented *De copia* with his *Parabolae,* a massive compilation of analogies in the form 'as a is to b, so c is to d', which he described as 'nothing more than a metaphor writ large'.[12] His book shows the ingenuity with which the rhetorician can build on 'natural history' to illuminate other areas of experience: the link between cosmic and human concerns is a constructed rather than a natural one.

Erasmus's influence on renaissance discourse can hardly be over-estimated; and readers of his texts were in no frame of mind to take analogies between the monarchy and the natural world too literally. Timothy Raylor has shown that the bee analogy favoured by absolutist theorists (and at one point by Erasmus)[13] was open to a bewildering variety of different political appropriations. At various times renaissance writers claimed that bees were ruled by a king, that they were ruled by a queen, that he or she did or did not consult with his or her people; bees could be invoked as a model by monarchists, Cromwellians and republicans.[14] Inconveniently for monarchists, beehives were found to be ruled by a female only after the death of Queen Elizabeth, so that hives provided an adequate pattern neither for Elizabeth nor for James. Such diverse appropriations perhaps contributed to the general scepticism in which the republican Algernon Sidney could dismiss stories of bees as 'fit only for old women to prate of in chimney-corners', while the absolutist Hobbes pointedly observed that bees were irrelevant as a pattern for human commonwealths since they lacked language, the source of conflict and dissension amongst men.[15] If bees did not provide an unambiguous pattern, neither did the body: once it had been granted that the state was like a body, there remained much room for debate about the relative locations of soul, head, and other members – even the New Model Army might be presented as the head of the body politic.[16] In renaissance rhetorical theory, there was no gainsaying the partiality of all analogies. This does not mean that natural analogies altogether lacked authority. Then as now, analogies from nature were at once common in political discourse and liable to be treated with scepticism.[17] The major difference was perhaps that the renaissance was far more self-conscious about the processes of its rhetoric.

That self-consciousness meant that analogies would always be advanced in the full awareness that they could be mustered in a different cause. Erasmus declared that the true rhetorician should be as open to differing circumstances as Homer's Odysseus, who is described as *polytropos*, and his own writings formed a manual for a new polytropic man. Commenting on the *Parabolae*, Gabriel Harvey observed that 'Erasmus, & Dr. Perne will teach a man to Temporise & Localise at occasion'.[18] In invoking the notoriously time-serving Dr Perne, Harvey drew attention to one possibility of this 'polytropic' approach: that it might generate a cynical indifference to any political principle. Many recent critics have concentrated on rhetoric as an instrument of courtly self-advancement; and it certainly had that function, not least in Harvey's own case.[19] But rhetoric could also provide a basis for resistance to any power which illegitimately claimed its authority to be natural. Erasmus cited with approval Achilles's epithet for King Agamemnon at the start of the *Iliad*: 'People-devouring'.[20]

III

The polytropic Odysseus and the world of the *Iliad* were to be much invoked in sixteenth-century discussions of political order. At the opening of the *Iliad*, there is general disillusion with the leadership of Agamemnon. He resolves to rally his troops by a stratagem: he tells them that they should abandon the siege of Troy and go home, but does so in such terms as to indicate that this would be shameful. Odysseus is then brought in to counter this speech. He does so in strongly class-divided terms. If he encounters a prince or gentleman, he lets him into the secret of Agamemnon's stratagem. If any soldier shows signs of flight, however, Odysseus beats him with the royal sceptre, declaring that he is unfit to pass opinion on his betters and that one man alone must take decisions in the realm. He runs into opposition from the malcontent Thersites, who rails against Agamemnon. Odysseus retorts that lesser men are not fit to dispute what kings say, and beats him until the sceptre draws blood. Thersites appears no longer in the poem; with the last oppositional voice thus silenced, Odysseus, Nestor and Agamemnon rally the troops.

Classical and renaissance commentators devoted a lot of attention to this episode as a set-piece in political rhetoric, an elaborate trick in which the troops are pulled first in one direction then the other. Alexander Pope was writing in this tradition when he commented:

'It is indeed hardly possible to find any where more refin'd Turns of
Policy, or more artful Touches of Oratory.'[21] There was particular
admiration for Agamemnon's speech to the troops which, as one
commentator pointed out, put the normal skills of oratory into
reverse, trying to make the course of action he was ostensibly
recommending seem subliminally as unattractive as possible.[22] It
was then Odysseus's role to bring out the latent sense of shame
beneath the oration's overt praise of peace. This was, however, a
somewhat dangerous precedent to be invoked by monarchists, for it
seemed to centre royal authority in artifice and deception,
reinforced by violence in the graphic image of the mace flaying
Thersites, rather than any kind of natural order.[23]

To some readers Odysseus's tactics doubtless seemed praise-
worthy, a necessary strategy in the face of otherwise certain defeat.
The *Iliad* could be read as a strongly monarchist text; it also
contained a celebrated passage where Zeus lets down a golden
chain from heaven, an image that was linked by later commentators
with the great chain of being which connected natural and social
hierarchies (viii.19). But other readers read Odysseus's role in this
episode as a betrayal of the true rhetorician's love of liberty.
Estienne de la Boétie, who in general takes the natural order as
embodying freedom, not hierarchy, and Odysseus as a model of
those free spirits who never lose sight of man's natural liberty, finds
it profoundly disturbing that Odysseus should have justified
monarchy.[24] Monarchy could not really be called a political system
at all, 'for it is hard to believe there is any such thing as politics
when everything is in the hands of one man'.[25] What Odysseus
should have said was that if having several lords was bad, so was
having one lord. Odysseus's wielding of Agamemnon's mace is for
la Boétie a classic instance of a phenomenon all too familiar in the
renaissance: the intellectual doing the dirty work for the monarchy
and in return basking in the reflected glory of royal power. This
cord of coercion which links the tyrant to his people, says la Boétie,
is the real meaning of Zeus's golden chain in Homer. And yet la
Boétie is prepared to make excuses for his monarchism: 'He made
this utterance at a time when a mutiny in the army had to be
quelled, and it seems to me that this circumstance had more
influence upon him than the objective truth did.'[26] Odysseus was
guided in the short term by rhetorical expediency; but a proper
analysis will look behind the rhetoric to rational and universal
principles of justice.

Some scholars argue that la Boëtie's tract should not be taken too seriously since it is merely a rhetorical declamation, part of the pedagogical discipline of arguing *in utramque partem*; but even arguments advanced hypothetically nevertheless become available for serious political discourse. Rhetorical declamations could acquire a sharp political edge even on such ultra-respectable occasions as royal visits. When Queen Elizabeth visited Cambridge in 1564, she was entertained with a series of disputations, one of which was on the theme of whether monarchy was the best form of government. The case was put by Thomas Byng, who defended monarchy by comparing it first with the rule of God and then with the order of Nature; he also cited Odysseus's speech in defence of rule by one man. Several of the subsequent speakers, however, tore into Byng's arguments, pointing out various drawbacks in monarchy, taking issue with Odysseus's speech, and praising the Roman republic.[27] The most celebrated respondent was Thomas Cartwright, already becoming known as a leader of the Puritans. Cartwright attacked the first part of Byng's argument by complaining that it was insolent for mortal and fallen man to compare himself in any way with God. Then he took issue with the argument of analogy from nature: the principle of imitating Nature gets us nowhere because nature produces all kinds of prodigies and monsters, we need a prior principle by which we can decide what parts of nature to imitate. And in any case, if we are to imitate nature on political matters, surely the logic should be communism, for in nature nothing is private. Cartwright suggested that drawing analogies from the lower creatures in fact demeaned man rather than glorifying him. Like la Boëtie, Cartwright insisted that Odysseus's speech on monarchy should be read rhetorically, within a specific context, rather than being advanced as a timeless absolute. The *Iliad*, he argued, also illustrated the value of cooperation and sharing, as in the way Diomedes needed a companion in going behind the enemy lines. In any case, he would prefer to follow the Homer of philosophers, Aristotle, who preferred republican to monarchical government.

This exchange confirms that there was a well-established cluster of arguments around Odysseus, natural analogies and rhetoric, long before Shakespeare wrote his degree speech, and that natural analogies could be used to argue on opposite sides of the case. The fact that it was considered possible to attack monarchy before the Queen presumably testifies to the element of ritualised rhetorical exercise in such speeches. Nonetheless, the speeches do testify to the lively interest in republican ideas in mid-century Cambridge. One of the disputants, Thomas Preston, is later to be found reading Machiavelli's republican *Discourses* with Gabriel Harvey.[28] Patrick Collinson has argued that a belief in strictly limited monarchy was so deep-seated as to constitute England, for some leading councillors, as effectively a 'monarchical republic'.[29] It remains true that criticisms of monarchy, if publicly professed, were not likely to lead to advancement in the state. If we ask who won the argument at Cambridge about the best form of government, the answer is in one sense clear enough: the following year Byng was made Public Orator while Cartwright left Cambridge for Ireland, and such exchanges are not found in later royal visits.[30]

Natural analogies in political discourse, then, were attended with an awareness that they were rhetorical constructs with evident palpable designs on their audience. In poetry and drama, the significance of context is still more to the fore: in these genres, an unusually close scrutiny of the relations of discourse to motive or interest was possible. This is certainly the case with the texts by Davies and Shakespeare which Tillyard took as exemplifying the Elizabethan World Picture.

IV

Sir John Davies's *Orchestra* (first draft 1594, published 1596) tells how, while Ulysses is away on his travels, his wife Penelope is urged by her suitor Antinous to dance. When she protests that dancing is immoral, Antinous runs through the places of nature, arguing that all things dance and therefore so should she. As Tillyard points out, he clinches his argument by giving her a magic glass in which he can see Queen Elizabeth surrounded by dancing courtiers. Natural analogy vindicates monarchical order; and according to Tillyard, the poem 'has no qualms or doubts about the order it describes'.[31]

It happens that we have a rhetorical analysis of this poem by a contemporary, John Hoskyns, in his *Directions for Speech and Style* of c. 1599.[32] Hoskyns's treatise concentrates on *copia* in an Erasmian spirit, and he offers many different kinds of analogy, all of which are seen as ways of heightening an argument and making it more vivid rather than a basic part of its logical structure. He lists metaphor, similitude, allegory, emblem, fable and myth (or 'poet's tale') under the category of 'varying', comparison under 'amplifying', and division variously under 'amplifying' and 'illustrating'. Amplification was held to be especially appropriate for demonstrative rhetoric, for ceremonial praise, as opposed to deliberative or persuasive rhetoric, because of its relative lack of argumentative rigour. Moreover, the more Hoskyns draws attention to the rhetorician's role in inventing or varying such analogues, the harder it is to see them as representing some timeless natural order. On the contrary, Hoskyns constantly draws attention to the secular, time-bound character of figurative language. Metaphor, he writes, appeals to 'the compassing sweetness of men's minds, that are not content to fix themselves upon one thing but they must wander into the confines' (p. 8). Throughout his treatise Hoskyns emphasizes this mutability: 'I have used and outworn six several styles since I was first Fellow of New College' (p. 39).

Hoskyns classifies *Orchestra* under the strategy of division, one category of *copia*. Under comparison he includes the following example:

Shall a soldier for a blow with his hand, given in war to a captain, be disgraced, and shall a lawyer, for the bastinado given in a hall of Court to his companion, be advanced? (p. 22)

This is a reference to an incident which sits oddly with Davies's reputation as a paragon of order: in 1598 he marched into the Middle Temple hall where Richard Martin, his rival for leadership of the Christmas revels, was dining, and beat him over the head until his stick broke. This was one of many unruly incidents which had got Davies in trouble. Shortly after recalling this incident, Hoskyns moves on to the figure of division, and he stays with Davies: 'This only trick made up J. D.'s *Poem of Dancing*: all danceth, the heavens, the elements, men's minds, commonwealths; and so by parts all danceth' (p. 23).

Hoskyns writes of this figure as a 'trick' in response to Bacon, who had included in his 'Colours of Good and Evil', published along with the *Essays* in 1597, an account of the fallacy of division, by which things seem greater if they are divided up into small parts. Bacon writes:

So when a great moneyed man hath deuided his chests and coines and bags, hee seemeth to himselfe richer then hee was, and therefore a way to amplifie any thing, is to breake it, and to make an anatomie of it in seuerall partes, and to examine it according to seuerall circumstances.[33]

'He said true,' comments Hoskyns. 'It is like the show which peddlers make of their packs, when they display them; contrary to the German magnificence that serves in all the good meat in one dish' (p. 22). The emphasis on display links the strategy with demonstrative rhetoric; Hoskyns says that Bacon 'took' this colour 'out of the rhetoricians' (p. 22), and indeed he was taking up hints offered by Aristotle's *Rhetoric*.[34] As Bacon puts it,

the perswaders labor is to make things appeare good or euill, and that in higher or lower degree, which as it may be perfourmed by true and solide reasons, so it may be represented also by coulers, popularities and circumstances, which are of such force, as they sway the ordinarie iudgement either of a weake man, or of a wise man, not fully and considerately attending and pondering the matter.[35]

Bacon does add that colours may also strengthen true arguments, but there is no guarantee that they will be deployed on the side of truth. It is with such sophisms that Hoskyns groups Davies's *Orchestra*: divisions, he writes, 'need not be strictly tied to the rules of logic', even though some of its principles are covered by logical categories (pp. 44–5). The figures of accumulation and division 'skilfully and fitly used, do amaze an adversary of mean conceit' (p. 32); those not of a mean conceit, then, as long as they remain attentive, may take pleasure in their ingenuity but will not necessarily be impressed by the reasoning. Like Agricola, Bacon and Hoskyns leave a space for the resisting reader.

Hoskyns alerts us to read Davies's poem as a display of sophistry rather than as a transcendent vision: its original subtitle was 'Judicially prooving the true observation of time and measure', and it was dedicated to Richard Martin, whom Davies associated with Suada, the goddess of persuasion. As R. J. Manning has pointed out,[36] the poem's praise of dancing is a highly interested pleading by the suitor Antinous against the ever-constant Penelope, and the high-flown invocation of cosmic harmony is marshalled in a rhetoric of seduction. Antinous in Homer is a violent and unattractive character; though Davies gives him a courtly gloss, the fact remains that if he wins the argument in favour of cosmic dancing he may also end up by making Ulysses a cuckold. In his penultimate stanza Davies invokes Sir Philip Sidney, whose 'supple Muse Camelion-like doth change': Sidney had presented his own sonnet sequence as an attempted but unsuccessful seduction of a Penelope, the 108 sonnets reflecting the number of unsuccessful suitors in Homer.[37] There may be a glance at this numerical symbolism in the original version of Davies's poem, which also has a break at the 108th stanza where Antinous shows signs of being swayed by Penelope's chastity, after which Davies exchanges his 'light Muse' for the heavenly muse Urania. But up to that point the poem celebrates rhetorical variety rather than political unity. We have seen how Erasmus and Hoskyns link *copia* with changeableness, and the poem is close to Erasmus's marshalling of examples of mutability to demonstrate *copia*. As Manning points out, Antinous's cosmic dance is really a celebration of Fortune dancing on her slippery wheel (stanza 59), and it subverts conventional patterns of cosmic order, celebrating competitive emulation and making even gender roles appear arbitrary as Caenus dances in and out of a male role (stanza 82). It is notable that Antinous links dancing with the turnings of language:

> And when you speake, so well she dauncing loves,
> That doubling oft, and oft redoubling new,
> With thousand formes she doth her selfe endew:
>> For all the words that from your lips repaire,
>> Are nought but tricks and turnings of the aire (stanza 44).

The defence of rhetorical turning is elaborated later in the poem:

> For Rhetorick clothing speech in rich aray
> In looser numbers teacheth her to range,
> With twentie tropes, and turnings every way,
> And various figures, and licentious change (stanza 93).

If he persuades Penelope to dance, Antinous will have out-troped the many-troped Ulysses.

Reading the poem as a straightforward celebration of Tudor orthodoxy, then, is radically misleading: in fact the praise of

Elizabeth as the new Penelope whose court will redeem chaste dancing was added after the poem's first composition, and it caused some difficulties in its moral scheme: invoking Elizabeth as a moral exemplar that may persuade Penelope to dance will involve cancelling the poem's earlier reserve about Antinous. There are ways, however, in which the royalist reading may not be so inappropriate. First of all, in defending dancing Davies was vindicating a favourite target of the Puritans. Moreover, Davies's personal quarrels may to some degree have reflected differences of political outlook. Hoskyns's somewhat dismissive reference to the poem probably reflects the immediate aftermath of Davies's quarrel with Martin, but their breach had been building up for some time: Davies had been mocked during the revels and a host of epigrams against him have survived. They focus on his ugliness and lack of grace: a particularly cruel epigram presents him as especially apt to be a *homo rhetoricus* precisely because his complete lack of social attractiveness has pushed him through the natural and back again: his pock-marked face is so hideous that he

> masking needes no vizard weare,
> Who for a face doth still a vizard beare (p. xxxiii)

Davies was ridiculed as 'wadling with his arse out behinde as though he were about to make every one that he meetes, a wall to pisse against' (p. xxxiii). If there is a degree of fantastic identification in Davies's presentation of Antinous the ideal dancer, there is also an ambivalence toward such glibness. And Davies had political as well as personal differences from many of his contemporaries: he became allied with the Cecils in the increasingly polarised political world of the 1590s, and he had come under attack for 'sawcy imitation' of one of the entertainments in which Essex wooed the Queen.[38] After Essex's fall from court favour, when the Essex faction were plunged into political gloom, Davies praised the queen most extravagantly in his *Hymnes of Astraea*. Davies was to become a strong defender of the royal prerogative, dying just before he took up his appointment by Charles I as Lord Justice of the King's Bench. Hoskyns's close friend James Whitelocke was thankful that 'God prevented so inconvenient an intention to the common wealthe.'[39]

But it would be wrong to overstress party groupings in this period. Davies and Hoskyns were part of a common legal and rhetorical culture, and they shared literary interests such as an admiration for Sir Philip Sidney. Sidney's legacy was, however, itself an ambiguous one, ranging from loyal courtiership to political rhetoric placed in the service of Protestant militancy. Sidney had donated his sword to Essex, and the Essex faction tended to claim him as their own. The *Arcadia*, with its critical analysis of the dangers of an irresponsible monarchy, could be read as offering a warning to England, and at least one contemporary annotator drew extensive parallels between the *Arcadia* and Tacitus's *Annals*.[40] John Hoskyns based his rhetorical manual on the *Arcadia*, and he read Sidney in a highly politicised way. Rhetoric had got him in trouble from an early stage in his career: after graduating at Oxford he had been made 'Terrae Filius', an orator privileged to make satirical speeches, but he was expelled from his fellowship shortly afterwards for overstepping acceptable bounds. It is possible that the speech in question was an attack on the queen's favourite, Sir Christopher Hatton, whose lavish tomb was contrasted by many with the failure to erect a proper monument for Sidney.[41] The *Directions* may have been addressed to Robert Harley, who became a leading Puritan politician.[42]

Though primarily concerned with the written word, the treatise also envisages situations of public speaking. In the copy of the *Arcadia* which accompanied his treatise, Hoskyns marked not only particular figures of rhetoric but also 'policy generally in all particular actions' (marked as 'pc') (p. 42). He writes for an audience who, as he says, are fond of gathering 'scraps of policy . . . out of Polybius and Tacitus' (p. 35).[43] 'Policy', of course, had equivocal meanings in the sixteenth century, hovering between intelligent planning and dubious manipulation; Hoskyns does not make a clear distinction between them, and he blurs the boundaries between ethics and rhetoric:

> The perfect expressing of all qualities is learned out of Aristotle's ten books of moral philosophy; but because, as Machiavel saith, perfect virtue or perfect vice is not seen in our time, which altogether is humorous and spurting, therefore the understanding of Aristotle's *Rhetoric* is the directest means of skill to describe, to move, to appease, or to prevent any motion whatsoever (p. 41).

Hoskyns notes that Sidney had translated the first two books of Aristotle's *Rhetoric* – significantly, the books concerned with rhetorical argumentation rather than figures. Sidney had drawn

on Tacitus for his own 'scraps of policy'; he had also studied Livy –
and probably Machiavelli – with Gabriel Harvey.[44] The *Discourses*
were widely read in the 1590s; there readers could find a sceptical
view of political analogies, such as the caustic comment that when
the Romans found that the monarchy, the head of the body politic,
was diseased they took the obvious course and cut it off.[45]

In keeping with these political interests, Hoskyns offers examples
suitable for the Parliamentary debater. For instance, under the
heading of comparison he offers a contrast between English policy
towards Ireland and Spanish policy towards the Netherlands (p. 20).
He illustrates synecdoche by the example of 'the Earl is gone into
Ireland' for 'E[arl of] E[ssex]' (p. 11).[46] The figure of 'division' is
illustrated by the following example:

> All men exclaim upon these exactions. Nobles, gentlemen,
> commonalty, poor, rich, scholar, merchants, peasants, young,
> old, wise, ignorant, high, low, and all cry out upon the hard
> impositions of these burdens (p. 31).

The question of impositions and other suspect means of bolstering
royal finances was to become central in Parliamentary debates
under James I. Hoskyns took up a position opposite to Davies, who
believed that Parliament should not have been allowed to discuss
the question of impositions.[47] Hoskyns became famous for his wit
and his forceful analogies, as in an anti-Scottish fable recounted by
Aubrey of 'a conduit, whereinto water came, and ran-out afarre-off.
"Now," said he, "this pipe reaches as far as Edinborough"'.[48]
Hoskyns vigorously championed the Commons against men like
Bishop Richard Neile, who criticised its outspokenness. Hoskyns
argued (prophetically, as it was to turn out) that if the bishops went
too far they would be overthrown: '*Scotland* and *Germany* hath swept
away greater Myters than his'.[49] Such provocativeness led to his
being thrown in jail in 1614. He advised his son on the dangers of
political rhetoric:

> Keepe [your tongue] in thral whilst thou art free:
> Imprison it or it will thee.[50]

Hoskyns's case became a *cause célèbre* and was to be taken up again
when Parliament reassembled in 1621.[51] How far was freedom of
speech a right, as it had been in the classical *polis*, and how far was it
a grace handed down by the king? Sir Henry Wotton took an

interest in Hoskyns's fate: after all, it had been he who had shown Hoskyns his copy of Sidney's translation of Aristotle's *Rhetoric*. He commented that such speeches were 'better becoming a Senate of Venice, where the treaters are perpetual princes, than where those that speak so irreverently are so soon to return (which they should remember) to the natural capacity of subjects'.[52] Wotton had recently returned from Venice and he was in a good position to assess the balance of monarchical and political elements in the English constitution: Hoskyns and his allies, he felt, were pushing their demands for the right to speak out so far that they were undermining the constraints a monarchy must necessarily place upon public oratory. Wotton commented that one of Hoskyns's fellow-prisoners, Christopher Neville, was 'a young gentleman, fresh from the school, who having gathered together divers Latin sentences against kings, bound them up in a long speech, and interlarded them with certain Ciceronian exclamations'.[53] The study of classical rhetoric was becoming a powerful incentive for political outspokenness; and this was already causing concern. In the 1614 Parliament the Earl of Northampton anticipated Hobbes's anxieties about the role of humanist education in stirring up political dissension, lamenting the diffusion of 'new opinions' when 'the scum are sent out of the university'.[54] He cited Menenius Agrippa's fable of the discontented body politic and Virgil's fable of the bees. He compared the House of Commons with a theatre: a place for demonstrative rather than deliberative rhetoric, for the king's views to be applauded rather than subjected to critical scrutiny. Though Northampton shared some of Hoskyns's scholarly interests, the two men had sharply divergent political outlooks.[55]

V

I have been jumping forward chronologically in order to suggest some of the political implications of the lively interest in rhetoric in Hoskyns's Inns of Court milieu in the 1590s. It is possible that Shakespeare's *Troilus and Cressida* was specifically written for this milieu.[56] A number of critics have pointed out the difficulty of taking the degree speech as a straightforward expression of an official world picture.[57] My more specific purpose here is to show some of the connections of the degree speech with the rhetorical and Homeric motifs of the debates about monarchy and natural order.

We have seen that a defence of monarchy by Odysseus was an expected part of rhetorical debates about politics, and that differing views of his arguments were likely to be taken. There is evidence of a reciprocal relation between the degree speech and successive versions of Odysseus's speech to the multitude in Chapman's translation of Homer.[58] There are possible links via contemporary politics: Chapman explicitly linked his Achilles with Essex, and it has been suggested that Shakespeare may have become concerned that his Nestor and Ulysses could be taken as glancing at Essex's arch-rivals, the Cecils.[59] Like Homer's Odysseus, Shakespeare's Ulysses is involved in a series of somewhat devious rhetorical strategies to secure the unity of the Greek forces; in Shakespeare's case the deviousness is much greater and there is a gap between the lofty vision of natural harmony invoked by Ulysses and the speech-act he is performing, of persuading the leaders to engage in a shabby tactical trick. Thersites, far from being banished at an early stage, haunts the whole play with his cynical vision. The situation encourages us to be self-conscious about Ulysses's rhetorical strategies.

The argumentative structure of Ulysses's speech is simple: the 'specialty' of rule is degree, and the Greeks are failing because this has been neglected. Having said this, he merely proceeds to amplify it at length, following the kinds of strategy discussed by Hoskyns. He uses the figure of division, working through the places of natural order, from the beehive to the movement of the planets. We have been alerted by the examples of Hoskyns and Davies not to be too mesmerised by the cosmic examples themselves but to observe the specific uses to which they are put. Here the cosmos is used to illustrate not the more grandly transcendental qualities of love or order but the more drily managerial concept of degree, an emphasis appropriate to the rationalistic Ulysses.[60] Ulysses is particularly fond of what Hoskyns describes as the third part of amplification, accumulation, 'heaping up of many terms of praise or accusing, importing but the same matter without descending to any part' (p. 24). Thus to amplify a sedition, suggests Hoskyns, we may speak of

Tumults, mutinies, uproars, desperate conspiracies, wicked confederacies, furious commotions, traitorous rebellions

and a whole list of synonyms – though he adds that this example is 'somewhat too swelling'. Ulysses is especially fond of this device:

> What plagues and what portents, what mutiny,
> What raging of the sea, shaking of earth,
> Commotion in the winds, frights, changes, horrors,
> Divert and crack, rend and deracinate
> The unity and married calm of states
> Quite from their fixure . . . (I.iii.96–101)[61]

And at the end of his second speech he heaps up his resentment at Achilles:

> All our abilities, gifts, natures, shapes,
> Severals and generals of grace exact,
> Achievements, plots, orders, preventions,
> Excitements to the field, or speech for truce,
> Success or loss, what is or is not, serves
> As stuff for these two to make paradoxes (179–84).

This multiplication of synonyms has a potentially equivocal effect: it at once powerfully evokes disorder and risks itself enacting the 'swelling' loss of order and control to which Ulysses' speech points. Bacon had declared that this figure was most effective if presented in a disorderly way, 'for confusion maketh things muster more . . . if it be without order, both the minde comprehendeth lesse that which is set downe, and besides it leaueth a suspition, as if more might be sayd then is expressed'.[62] Hoskyns disagreed: method and order would heighten the effect of amplification (*Directions*, p. 22). There is a reflexivity in Ulysses' heaping up of figures of disorder: he is poised between distancing himself from that disorder and himself re-enacting it.

There is a comparable reflexivity in another prominent means of amplification in Ulysses' speech, the figure of climax or *gradatio*:

> Then everything includes itself in power,
> Power into will, will into appetite (119–20).

> The general's disdained
> By him one step below, he by the next,
> That next by him beneath: so every step,
> Exampled by the first pace that is sick
> Of his superior, grows to an envious fever
> Of pale and bloodless emulation. (129–34)

Rhetoricians noted the etymology of *gradatio* as the figure of the ladder: it is the figure of climbing by degrees. Hoskyns's example is as follows:

> You could not enjoy your goodness without government, nor government without a magistrate, nor magistrate without obedience, and no obedience where every one upon his private passion doth interpret the doings of the rulers (p. 12).

This was one of several references in Hoskyns to Pyrocles's address to the rebels in the *Arcadia*, a situation laden with irony in which order is vindicated with heavy moralism by a protagonist who has disguised himself as a woman in order to seduce a member of the royal family. In Ulysses's speech the irony centres rather on the structure of the figure of *gradatio*: in describing degree as 'the ladder to all high designs', Ulysses draws attention to the fact that what you can do with a ladder is climb up it (the Quarto has the slightly less blatant 'ladder *of* all high designs'). How, we may ask, did the leaders get where they are except precisely by that process of climbing and emulation which Ulysses is condemning? Once they have climbed the ladder, they try to kick it away and naturalise it with euphemising names: perhaps it is they who really engage in vizarding degree.[63]

The possibility that degree may be a vizard, an artifice, rather than a link with natural hierarchies, plays also around the speech's diction. It is full of words that are *OED* first or very early usages, occasionally even unique words – 'insisture' (I.iii.87), 'deracinate' (99), 'fixure' (101), 'dividable' (105), and 'primogenitive' as noun (106; Quarto gives 'primogenity', an equally odd form). *OED* datings, of course, are extremely fallible, but such a dense clustering does link the play with that world of Inns of Court wits who delighted in coining new words: Hoskyns, as we have seen, claimed to have outworn six styles by 1599. Such a multiplication of words constantly endangered any attempt at a fixity or fixure in meaning: and when fixity is lost, as Ulysses says, right and wrong 'lose their names'. And yet in invoking fears of what will happen if planets start to wander, he reminds us that according to their names that is exactly what they do anyway: 'planet' derives from the Greek for 'wanderer'. Again, there is a potential reflexivity in which the ordering in question is as much rhetorical as divine. Such doubts hover around much writing of the late 1590s: in Fulke Greville's *Mustapha*, a priest who denounces his monarch as using illegitimate artifice to stay in power looks at the heavens and asks if 'thou fayre orderlye confused planettes' are 'more then ornaments'.[64] Doubts about the basic structure of the cosmic order contributed to an unfixing of easy analogies between secular and cosmic orders. The fact that the cosmos was being reinterpreted in new ways might be seen as a challenge rather than, as it is for Ulysses, a source of despair: Hoskyns, who was a strong Copernican, had located men's love of metaphor precisely in their wandering minds. William Drummond was to invoke the planets' wandering as a precedent for religious toleration.[65] Similar tensions between natural and artificially imposed order can be found in the nonce-word 'insisture', whose etymology could suggest either standing still or following on. The word may in this context refer to a point of apparent stasis at a star's outward curve, in which case it carries on the sense of tension and difficulty in maintaining natural and social orders in stasis.[66]

Thus Ulysses's speech would have seemed to a rhetorically trained audience to be calling attention to the difficulty of sustaining a transcendental vision of monarchical order. The difficulty is highlighted when Ulysses turns to the threat presented by Achilles and Patroclus, who parody the monarch and his followers and thus present political order as rhetorical artifice rather than natural harmony. And it is significant that the analogue which Ulysses chooses for this process is that of acting: drama demystifies the rhetoric of the ruling authorities. Jonathan Dollimore has argued that *Troilus and Cressida* is a key example of the way in which the Elizabethan theatre could subvert the dominant ideology by exposing the artifice of social relations. It can indeed be argued that the emergence of the public theatre marked a significant new chapter in the political history of rhetoric by bringing debates previously confined to a narrow academic audience before a wider public (though *Troilus and Cressida* itself does not seem to have been performed on the public stage). If the actors' role as King's Men could be naturalised into that of traditional members of a noble household, at the same time their role in court festivities potentially revealed the whole apparatus of monarchy as an arbitrary 'vizarding'.

It may be misleading, however, to read the degree speech as straightforwardly 'subversive'. By now it will have become clear that the belief that monarchy was part of the order of nature was by no means so single-mindedly accepted that its questioning would

lead to the total collapse of the political universe; only a literal-
minded acceptance of the analogies of the great chain of being could
have been vulnerable to such an easy attack. Moreover, scepticism
about theories of natural order did not necessarily lead to
republican or democratic sympathies. Ulysses' vision is in the end
a radically nominalist one, in which arbitrary force and cunning are
needed to keep in check a world of otherwise atomised individuals
locked in an internecine struggle for power. No gradations are
offered between monarchical order and utter chaos. Such a proto-
Hobbesian vision was arguably more likely to foster absolutism
than constitutionalism; as W. R. Elton has argued, the degree speech
has affinities with contemporary Machiavellian theories of reason of
state and the artifice of power. At the same time, the speech does
attempt to establish a distance between its own discourse and the
self-consciously subversive 'paradoxes' of Achilles and Patroclus.
Patroclus's subversion in fact amounts to boosting the ego of a sulky
aristocrat. What the many-troped Ulysses is doing is more complex:
he is parodying Patroclus's parody, trying to warn his leaders of
their own egotism but also to salvage their project. The speech
registers the difficulty of that task, of trying to build a heroic
language out of an already discredited currency, but a humanist
audience may have been expected to feel an element of sympathy
for Ulysses's position. His role as rhetorician is that of a humanist
trying through all the accompanying frustrations to persuade
conservative and none too intellectual aristocrats to act for the
common good rather than remaining locked in their own egos,
trying to inspire them to a dignity they intrinsically lack. To what
extent such a strategy represented capitulation was something much
debated by humanists from the *Utopia* onward. La Boëtie, while
critical of Ulysses's service of Agamemnon, could sympathise with
his uphill struggle to keep a centrifugal political body together. For
Cartwright, what the Troy story was really concerned with was not
a specific form of government but the always-important skill of
working together for a common goal. If Ulysses's role to some
degree figures that of Shakespeare's own dramatic company, what it
suggests is not simply a Patroclean subversion, but rather a more
long-term process of creating and responding to a demand for
public participation in the process of arguing about political
legitimacy. If men like Northampton were trying to turn Parliament
into a theatre, there were others who were trying to turn the theatre
into something not a little like a Parliament – or even a senate.

VI

Rhetorical analysis of the Elizabethan World Picture, then, reveals it as something less monolithic than the term 'ideology' suggests: it was a field in which the rhetorician could indulge in ceremonial amplification. This is not to deny that the figures of natural harmony had a powerful emotional appeal in a nation fearful of internal sedition or foreign invasion. But that appeal was always open to rational criticism. Cultural historians need to take account of the phenomenon of the resisting hearer or reader; which means that they need to be resisting readers themselves.

Notes and References

1. E. M. W. Tillyard, *The Elizabethan World Picture* (1943; reprinted, Harmondsworth, 1963).
2. Michel Foucault, *The Order of Things* (London, 1970), pp. 35ff. On Foucault's account of the renaissance *episteme*, see J. G. Merquior, *Foucault* (London, 1985), pp. 57ff.
3. Kevin Sharpe, *Politics and Ideas in Early Stuart England* (London, 1989), pp. 3–71. For a different view, emphasizing scepticism about arguments from analogy, see Johann Sommerville, *Politics and Ideology in England 1603–1640* (London, 1986), pp. 48–50
4. See for example Paul de Man, *Allegories of Reading: Figural Language in Rousseau, Nietzsche, Rilke, and Proust* (New Haven, 1979), p. 10, and *The Resistance to Theory* (Minneapolis, 1986), p. 11. But on the radical narrowing of the rhetorical tradition involved in de Man's privileging of figure over persuasion, see Brian Vickers, *In Defence of Rhetoric* (Oxford, 1988), pp. 453ff.
5. For an important analysis of the functioning of rhetorical terms in concepts of political order, see Patricia Parker, 'Motivated Rhetorics: Gender, Order, Rule', in *Literary Fat Ladies: Rhetoric, Gender, Property* (London, 1987), pp. 97–125; cf. Jonathan Dollimore, *Radical Tragedy* (New York, 1989), pp. 42–50.
6. On the limitations of theories of ideology as naturalisation, see Terry Eagleton, *Ideology: An Introduction* (London, 1991), pp. 58–61.
7. For a rhetorician's argument that a sustained challenge to ideology is impossible, see Stanley Fish, *Doing What Comes Naturally* (Oxford, 1989), pp. 214–46, 471–502, and for a critique, see Eagleton, *Ideology*, pp. 167ff. The issues here parallel an earlier debate between Gadamer and Habermas on rhetoric and ideology: see Hans-Georg Gadamer, 'Rhetoric, Hermeneutics, and the Critique of Ideology: Metacritical Comments on *Truth and Method*', in Kurt Mueller-Vollmer (ed.), *The Hermeneutics Reader* (Oxford, 1986), pp. 274–92, and Jürgen Habermas, 'On Hermeneutics' Claim to Universality', ibid. pp. 294–319.

8. *Behemoth*, in *The English Works of Thomas Hobbes*, edited by William Molesworth, 11 vols (London, 1839–45), vol. VI, p. 168.
9. See Lisa Jardine, 'Humanistic Logic', in *The Cambridge History of Renaissance Philosophy*, edited by Charles B. Schmitt *et al.* (Cambridge, 1988), pp. 173–98.
10. Rudolph Agricola, *De inventione dialectica* (Cologne, 1539), p. 142, quoted and translated in Peter Mack, 'Rudolph Agricola's Topics', in Fokke Akkeman and A.J. Vanderjagt (eds), *Rodolphus Agricola Phrisius, 1444–1485* (Leiden, 1988), pp. 257–69 (267).
11. Erasmus, *De copia*, trans. Betty I. Knott, in *Collected Works of Erasmus*, vol. 24, edited by Craig R. Thompson (Toronto, 1978), pp. 641–6; *Opera omnia*, I.6, edited by Betty I. Knott (Amsterdam, 1988), pp. 263ff.
12. Erasmus, *Parabolae*, translated by R. A. B. Mynors, in *Collected Works of Erasmus*, vol. 23 (Toronto, 1978), p. 130; *Opera Omnia*, I.5, edited by J.-C. Margolin (Amsterdam, 1975), p. 90.
13. Ibid., p. 260.
14. Timothy Raylor, 'Samuel Hartlib and the Commonwealth of Bees', in Michael Leslie and Timothy Raylor (eds), *Culture and Cultivation in Early Modern England: Writing and the Land* (Leicester, 1992), pp. 91–129.
15. Algernon Sidney, *Discourses Concerning Government*, third edition (London, 1751), II.8, p. 95.
16. James Daly, 'Cosmic Harmony and Political Thinking in Early Stuart England', *Transactions of the American Philosophical Society*, vol. LXIX (1979) pp. 16ff; Richard Overton, *An Appeale from the Degenerate Representative Body* (1647), in Don M. Wolfe (ed.), *Leveller Manifestoes of the Puritan Revolution* (New York, 1944), p. 184.
17. On the scepticism see Brian Vickers, 'Analogy versus Identity: the Rejection of Occult Symbolism, 1580–1680', in Brian Vickers (ed.), *Occult and Scientific Mentalities in the Renaissance* (Cambridge University Press, 1984), pp. 95–163.
18. *Gabriel Harvey's Marginalia*, edited by G. C. Moore Smith (Stratford-upon-Avon, 1913), p. 138.
19. See for example Frank Whigham, *Ambition and Privilege: The Social Tropes of Elizabethan Courtesy Theory* (Berkeley, 1984).
20. Erasmus, 'Scarabeus aquilam quaerit', in Margaret Mann Phillips (ed.), *Erasmus on his Times* (Cambridge, 1967), p. 51.
21. *Translations of Homer: The Iliad*, edited by Maynard Mack in *The Poems of Alexander Pope*, 11 vols (London, 1940–69) vol. VII, p. 143 (note to II, 348).
22. The standard edition of the later sixteenth century, *Homeri quae extant*, edited by Johannes Spondaeus (Basel, 1583), p. 31, describes Agamemnon's speech as 'Artificiosa'.
23. Spondaeus describes Odysseus as prevailing 'uerbis & uerberibus' (p. 32); the people must be coerced 'non rationibus, sed mera authoritate' (p. 33).
24. Estienne de la Boëtie, *Slaves By Choice* (*Discourse de la servitude volontaire*), translated by Malcolm Smith (Egham, 1988), pp. 53–4.
25. Ibid., p. 37.
26. Ibid., p. 37.

27. J. Nichols (ed.), *The Progresses and Public Processions of Queen Elizabeth*, 3 vols (London, 1788–1805), vol. III, pp. 63ff (not reprinted in the 1823 edition). A. F. Scott Pearson, *Thomas Cartwright and Elizabethan Puritanism* (London, 1925), pp. 419–21.

28. Lisa Jardine and Anthony Grafton, ' "Studied for Action": How Gabriel Harvey Read His Livy', *Past and Present*, vol. CXXIX (November 1990), pp. 30–78 (43).

29. Patrick Collinson, 'The Monarchical Republic of Queen Elizabeth I', *Bulletin of the John Rylands Library*, vol. LXIX (1986), pp. 394–424.

30. There were similar debates about natural analogy in Scotland, with the Presbyterian David Hume retorting to a bishop who used the bee analogy that the same similes could be used to 'inferre the plaine contrare': one could equally well argue that kingship was unnatural by appealing to sheep or horses. See Stewart R. Sutherland, 'The Presbyterian Inheritance of Hume and Reid', in R. H. Campbell and Andrew S. Skinner (eds), *The Origins and Nature of the Scottish Enlightenment* (Edinburgh, 1982), pp. 141–3.

31. Tillyard, op. cit., p. 129.

32. Quotations in the text are from *Directions for Speech and Style*, edited by Hoyt H. Hudson (Princeton, 1935), pp. 114–66. There is another edition by Louis O. Osborn, *The Life, Letters and Writings of John Hoskyns 1566–1638* (New Haven, 1937). Baird W. Whitlock, *John Hoskyns, Serjeant-at-Law* (Washington, DC, 1982), supersedes Osborn in most respects.

33. *A Harmony of the Essays, etc. of Francis Bacon*, ed. Edward Arber (London, 1871), p. 143. Lisa Jardine, *Francis Bacon: Discovery and the Art of Discourse* (Cambridge, 1974), pp. 161, 196–7, 207ff.

34. Ibid., pp. 219ff.

35. Ibid., p. 138.

36. R. J. Manning, 'Rule and Order Strange: A Reading of Sir John Davies' *Orchestra*', *English Literary Renaissance*, vol. XV (1985), pp. 175–94. Ian Sowton, 'Hidden Persuaders as a Means of Literary Grace: Sixteenth-Century Poetics and Rhetoric in England', *University of Toronto Quarterly*, vol. XXXII (1962–3), pp. 55–69 (65–68); John Huntington, 'Philosophical Seduction in Chapman, Davies, and Donne', *ELH*, vol. XLIV (1977), 40–59.

37. *The Poems of Sir John Davies*, edited by Robert Krueger (Oxford, 1975), p. 125 (further citations will be from this edition); Alastair Fowler, *Triumphal Forms: Structural Patterns in Elizabethan Poetry* (Cambridge, 1970), p. 175.

38. Philip J. Finkelpearl, *John Marston of the Middle Temple* (Cambridge, Mass., 1969), pp. 48ff. Jeanie R. Brink, 'Sir John Davies's *Orchestra*: Political Symbolism and Textual Revisions', *Durham University Journal*, vol. LXXII (1980), pp. 195–202, gives a different political reading from Manning, arguing that the text is pro-Essex and critical of Elizabeth.

39. *Liber Famelicus of Sir James Whitelocke*, edited by John Bruce (London, 1858), p. 105. On Davies's political views see Hans Pawlisch, *Sir John Davies and the Conquest of Ireland* (Cambridge, 1985) and Sommerville, op. cit., pp. 37, 89–90, 162–3.

40. Folger Shakespeare Library, STC 22540, copy 1.

41. Whitlock, op. cit., pp. 77–82; the oration against the extravagant tomb of 'D.H.', cited in *Directions*, p. 26, probably refers to Hatton.
42. Whitlock, op. cit., pp. 137–8; Osborn, op. cit., pp. 106–7.
43. Hoskyns cited Tacitus in a Parliamentary speech criticising royal policy on 23 November 1610, cited in Whitlock, op. cit., p. 372; he presented a copy of Tacitus to the Hereford Cathedral library (ibid., p. 582).
44. Jardine and Grafton, 'How Gabriel Harvey Read His Livy', p. 36; for Sidney's praise of Machiavelli see p. 39.
45. This figure was made notorious in the 1590s by Robert Parsons's tract on the succession, which excited many indignant refutations: see J. E. Phillips, *The State in Shakespeare's Greek and Roman Plays* (New York, 1940), pp. 67ff.
46. Annabel Patterson, 'All Donne', in Elizabeth D. Harvey and Katharine Eisaman Maus (eds), *Soliciting Interpretation: Literary Theory and Seventeenth-Century English Poetry* (Chicago, 1990), p. 48, exaggerates the subversiveness of this sentence by reading 'E.E.' as 'E.R.' and taking it to allude to the Queen.
47. Sir John Davies, *The Question Concerning Impositions* (London, 1656), dedication, and cf. pp. 76, 101.
48. John Aubrey, *Brief Lives*, edited by Andrew Clark, 2 vols (London, 1898), vol. I, pp. 421–2.
49. Speech of 25 May 1614, cited in Whitlock, op. cit., p. 448.
50. Whitlock, op. cit., p. 469. On Hoskyns's political role see also Patterson, 'All Donne', pp. 54–60.
51. Christopher Thompson, *The Debate on Free Speech in the House of Commons in February 1621* (Orsett, Essex, 1985).
52. *Life and Letters of Sir Henry Wotton*, edited by Logan Pearsall Smith, 2 vols (Oxford, 1907), vol. II, p. 37.
53. Ibid., vol. II, pp. 37–8.
54. Peck, op. cit., pp. 179, 183; *Proceedings in Parliament, 1610*, edited by Elizabeth Read Foster, 2 vols (New Haven, 1966), vol. 1, p. 79.
55. Ironically enough, allegations were made that Hoskyns was bribed by Northampton to make his inflammatory speech, but see Peck, pp. 208–10, and Whitlock, p. 429. His close friend James Whitelocke had recently been imprisoned at Northampton's instigation; Whitelocke felt unable to express himself freely on paper until after the death of the Earl, whom he described, with an ambivalence Hoskyns probably shared, as 'my il affected frend' (*Liber Famelicus*, p. 39).
56. W. R. Elton is exploring this issue fully in a forthcoming study; cf. his 'Shakespeare's Ulysses and the Problem of Value', *Shakespeare Studies*, vol. II (1966), pp. 95–111.
57. Brian Vickers, *The Artistry of Shakespeare's Prose* (London, 1968), p. 253, argues that the degree speech 'in its dramatic context and in its portentously diffuse style' should be taken 'as a specious politic manipulation of those ideas'. Frank Kermode, '"Opinion" in *Troilus and Cressida*', in Susanne Kappeler and Norman Bryson (eds.), *Teaching the Text* (London, 1983), pp. 164–79; T. M. Burvill, 'Ulysses on "Degree": Shakespeare's Doctrine of Political Order?', *Parergon, N.S.*,

vol. II (1984), pp. 191–203. But see Charles and Michelle Martindale, *Shakespeare and the Uses of Antiquity: An Introductory Essay* (London and New York, 1990), pp. 91–120.

58. These are traced by T.W. Baldwin in his appendix to Harold N. Hillebrand (ed.), *Troilus and Cressida*, New Variorum Edition of Shakespeare (Philadelphia, 1953), pp. 399 ff. The 1598 version reads (as cited by Baldwin):

> The rule of many is absurd, one Lord must leade the ring:
> Of far resounding gouernment.

This is changed in 1610 to

> The rule of many is absurd; degrees in euerie thing
> Must be obseru'd.

The 1611 edition reads

> We must not all be kings: the rule, is most irregularre
> Where many rule; one Lord, one King, propose to thee.

59. Ernest A. J. Honigmann, 'The Date and Revision of *Troilus and Cressida*', in Jerome J. McGann (ed.), *Textual Criticism and Literary Interpretation* (Chicago, 1985), pp. 38–54.
60. Baldwin, New Variorum *Troilus and Cressida*, pp. 391, 408, 410.
61. Quotations are from Kenneth Palmer's New Arden edition (London and New York, 1982), which draws heavily on the Quarto text.
62. Bacon, op. cit., p. 144.
63. On the political implications of *gradatio*, see Parker, *Literary Fat Ladies*, p. 99.
64. *The Poems and Dramas of Fulke Greville*, edited by Geoffrey Bullough, 2 vols (Edinburgh and London, 1939), vol. II, p. 241.
65. William Drummond, *Irene* (1638), in Robert H. MacDonald (ed.), *Poems and Prose* (Edinburgh and London, 1976), p. 186.
66. Baldwin, New Variorum *Troilus and Cressida*, p. 402, argues that 'insisture' comes from 'institiones' in a 1573 edition of Cicero's *Tusculan Orations*.

9

Raphael and the Rhetoric of Art

Patricia Rubin

In 1759 there appeared an edition of engravings after the heads in Raphael's tapestry cartoons, at that time displayed at Hampton Court (now in the Victoria and Albert Museum). Titled *The School of Raphael* or *The Student's Guide to Expression in Historical Painting*, this drawing book was intended to supply examples from the 'inimitable Cartoons of Raphael' useful both to experienced painters and to novices to 'encourage the study of the most profound part of Painting, the *Characteristics of the Passions*'.[1] The index lists the various passions and their subdivisions in alphabetical order, indicating the plate number of the appropriate head from the cartoons. Ranging from affection to zeal, they include 'Arrogance, dejected', three types of surprise and six forms of fear. Occupying a distinct place in the histories of eighteenth century sensibilities and artistic practices, these engravings are also emblematic of Raphael's position in the history of visual eloquence. In the first extended account of the artist, Vasari's biography of 1550, he is characterised as 'always seeking to represent histories as they are written' and his compositions are described in terms that both establish and emphasise the connection between painting and writing.[2] As part of his strategy for the advancement of the visual arts, Vasari adopted a rhetoric of appreciation that placed Raphael in the 'discourse of letters'. His lengthy descriptions of Raphael's works further served to chronicle and confirm their place as examples for imitation and emulation. Subsequent writers and subsequent artists accepted this canonical role for Raphael as the supreme master of narrative expression. In his dialogue, *L'Aretino* (1557), Lodovico Dolce described him as master of history who 'imitated the writers to such a degree that the judgment of connoisseurs is often stirred into crediting this painter with having depicted the events better than the writers had described them, or at least into considering that the two compete together on equal terms'.[3] He is presented as superior to Michelangelo in the divisions of painting: invention (with its parts: *l'ordine e la convenevolezza*), design and coloring.[4] A century later, according to an entry in John Evelyn's *Diary*, the wall paintings in the papal apartments in the Vatican, the Stanze, were known as the *Accademia dei Pittori*.[5] For Giovanni Pietro Bellori, who wrote an exhaustive account of the frescoes in the Stanze in the 1690s, it was Raphael, 'the Urbinate Apelles', who had captured the 'essence of painting' - the imitation of human deeds.[6] And in his *Essay on the Theory of Painting* published in 1725, the painter/connoisseur Jonathan Richardson wrote of the figure of St Paul preaching (Plate 1) that

> no Historian, or Orator can possibly give me so great an Idea of that Eloquent, and Zealous Apostle as that Figure of his does; all the fine things related as said, or wrote by him cannot; for there I see a Person, Face, Air, and Action, which no Words can sufficiently describe, but which can assure me as much as Those can, that that Man must speak good Sense, and to the purpose.[7]

Raphael's paintings provided a rhetoric of images, a figurative vocabulary and narrative structures that were the basis for pictorial communication for over three hundred years. The writings that promoted his reputation borrowed their terms, concepts and subdivisions from the rhetorical tradition. The construction of the historical figure of Raphael was in itself Ciceronian – for Raphael, already Apelles during his lifetime – soon was 'set before the eyes' of posterity as that 'perfect specimen' used to express 'the character and magnitude' of his art's essential nature, in the fashion of the ideal orator in *De Oratore*.[8] The reasons for this are to be found in the history of the discussion of the visual arts in the renaissance. Classical rhetorical treatises provided the critical language and conceptual bases for humanist writing about painting.[9] Alberti noted the completion of his work on painting in 1435 in his copy of *Brutus*.[10] Rhetorical language gave writing about art credibility as well as coherence. It also conditioned a sensitivity to style, order, ornament, decorum and invention and reinforced the notion of progressive development in the arts. The parallels drawn between orators, painters and sculptors further allowed the topos of fame to be applied to artists, creating a cultural space for artistic accomplishment. It is in that space that Raphael's activity may be viewed.

This paper will consider the relation of rhetorical concepts to Raphael's career and compositional practices. The role of eloquence as an instrument for encoding and enhancing pictorial messages will be examined through an analysis of some of the works Raphael produced between his arrival in Rome in 1508 and his sudden death on Good Friday in 1520. Raphael's figurative language as it developed there was addressed to a particularly restricted audience. His Bible – the New Testament of the Sistine tapestries or the Old Testament of the Pope's private loggia, for example – far from serving the illiterate or ignorant of the Gregorian dictate, was a visual text for the most learned men of the day.[11] The question is to what extent did ideas from rhetoric influence the vocabulary of viewing? How might they have conditioned the perception and reception of those texts? Also to be considered is how the exchange between verbal and visual means is registered in Raphael's historical image as it was formed in early accounts by Paolo Giovio and Giorgio Vasari. Is the rhetoric of the objects received by the rhetoric of their descriptive record? The answers to these questions are not precise. Many relate to poetry as much as to prose and to what might be called rhetorical culture rather than rhetoric itself. They involve the wider implications of that culture in the assimilation, adaptation and reformulation of ancient models to modern purposes.

Pietro Bembo devoted the opening paragraph of Book III of his dialogue on the vernacular to a statement about the importance of classical models to those who wished to write 'well and gracefully' (*bene e leggiadramente*). He starts by describing the artists who came to Rome from far and wide to study the ancient remains scattered about the city and treasured in private collections. The more they sought to be praised for their new works, he says, the closer they tried to make them to the ancient ones, because they recognised that the ancient ones more nearly approached the perfection of art'.[12] Michelangelo and Raphael above all, he says, had done this with such diligence and had achieved such excellence and fame that it was easier to say how close they were to the great masters of antiquity than which of them was the greater and better artist. Inevitably as Bembo develops the comparison of visual and verbal arts, writers are given the greater glory and prestige, but important here is the place held by artists, and specifically Raphael, in the formal consciousness of the day.

Raphael probably met Bembo in Urbino after Bembo moved there in the summer of 1506. He is identified as the artist Bembo calls a 'great master of painting' in a letter dated 6 May 1507 about a work commissioned by the Duchess, Elisabetta Gonzaga.[13] Bembo's correspondence documents his subsequent interest in Raphael's career.[14] Raphael made a group of engravings in which he sought to publish his identity as a rival or new Apelles by means of the direct restoration and imitation of ancient types and subjects. The print known from its central scene as the *Quos Ego* (Plate 3) derives its format from a specific type of Roman relief showing scenes from Homer.[15] Here Roman epic replaces Greek, the panels show ten scenes from Book I of the *Aeneid*. They are not in order, so the 'reader' must create a text from a previous knowledge of the poem. In another such print, the *Judgement of Paris*, references to classical sculpture are manifest and determine the stylistic idiom.[16] These prints can be seen as conscious attempts to use the study of relief sculpture to discover a style of painting that was properly antique. All make antiquarian learning evident (and posit a learned, *litterato* public) in the choice and arrangement of subjects and in the use of Latin inscriptions. Indeed the inscriptions, which paraphrase and do not quote Virgil, necessarily involved consultation with a man of letters. There are many candidates: Raphael's friends included Tommaso Inghirami, Baldassare Castiglione, Andrea Navagero and Agostino Beazzano (all of whom he portrayed), to name but a few of the eminent humanists with whom he can be associated. But Bembo's place in this project of purposeful imitation deserves particular consideration here as providing a general conceptual model.

In 1512–13 Bembo engaged in an epistolary debate with Gianfrancesco Pico della Mirandola on the question of imitation. Bembo's view was that 'the activity of imitating, is nothing other than translating the likeness of some other's style into one's own writings and to cultivate that very temperament present in him who you have chosen as a master'.[17] The master for prose was Cicero, for poetry Virgil. The acquisition of style required long study to absorb the model. Only after this was it possible to equal or surpass that model. Imitating Cicero, Bembo used examples from the visual arts.[18] In style, Raphael's prints are set-pieces of such close imitation. And in subject the choice of Virgil for two of Raphael's classicist manifestoes is perhaps not coincidental. In these prints matter and style (*res* and *verba*), invention and composition (*inventio* and *dispositio*) are suitably matched to express the artist's excellence. Following Bembo's ideas, artistic perfection depends upon the quality of its sources – here Raphael's imagery is Virgil's. As poetic subjects they also explain his claim to particular respect for creativity by exploiting the much-repeated simile *ut pictura poesis*.

It has been argued that Raphael placed himself among the poets in his fresco of *Parnassus* behind Homer and Virgil.[19] Drafts of sonnets, suitably Petrarchan, on drawings for the *Disputa* show him seeking to establish literary credentials soon after his arrival in Rome, becoming a painter/poet even as he drafted the picture phrases and places that would best express the nature of the painting's subject – theology.[20] The frescoes in this first room show him formulating an artistic identity in association with learning and letters, and in the mode of Roman revival appropriate to the aspirations and imperial imagery of Julius II's pontificate and its rhetoric.[21] He included himself in the great basilica of learning. Standing near Euclid, Ptolemy and Zoroaster, the artist looks out towards the viewer from the far right-hand corner of the fresco known as the *School of Athens* (Plate 2).

Raphael's compositions for these subjects are almost unprecedented. He elaborated a scheme of disciplines and representatives – as in the *School of Athens*, or Philosophy – in terms of a series of dialectical relationships and particular settings. In the process of responding to the simple task of exemplification he invented new subjects through amplification. The project for the room probably envisioned a traditional matching of personified Arts and Virtues (Theology, Poetry, Philosophy and Justice in the vault) with representatives below.[22] As such it would have been seen as a suitable replacement for the Room of the Liberal Arts recently decorated for Pope Alexander VI by Pinturicchio in the apartments below the Julian Stanze. Alexander's suite had been vacated by Julius because he refused to live where he would be subjected to the sight of his predecessor's portrait, as he told his master of ceremonies in no uncertain terms.[23] His dislike of the patron did not extend to the painter or his decorative inventions, however. Even as Raphael worked in the Stanze, Pinturicchio was employed by Julius to paint the vault of the choir of Santa Maria del Popolo. Another contemporary precedent for such a scheme was the cycle showing cardinal virtues with exemplars painted by Raphael's teacher, Perugino, in the Collegio del Cambio at Perugia. Typically, Raphael was not content to repeat the formula, even when this might have been all that was required or expected. Instead he reinvented the subject. He did this in a characteristic fashion, through the understanding and exploitation of the narrative potential of his subject and also through a command of both pictorial and metaphorical spaces. The temple of philosophy, classical and grandiose, is a convincing perspectival fiction that alludes to Julius II's and Bramante's scheme for the new St. Peter's, for example. In all the frescoes he translated static images into narratives and the notion of *storia*, particularly as articulated by Alberti whose treatise Raphael probably knew, carries within it many of the terms of rhetoric.

As Raphael progressed through the papal apartments from the frescoes in the first room, painted for Julius II between 1508 and 1511, to those of the third room, decorated for Leo X between 1514 and 1517, he acquired skills, enriched his vocabulary and developed an increasingly articulated artistic identity. The Virgilian prints are almost programmatic in declaring that identity. And the group in the corner of the *Fire in the Borgo* (Plate 4), for example, which Vasari recognised as 'shown in the same way that Virgil describes Anchises being carried by Aeneas', is both a simile for filial piety and a form of signature of the artist/poet whose epic history is composed in imitation of the ancient master.[24]

The frescoes of the first room may delight and instruct. They certainly project idealised realms and mediate between the real space of the room and the propagandastic visions of its patron, but they are less directly dependent upon the viewer to understand and to be moved by their messages than the later frescoes. They are closed structures, complete in their meaning. The later frescoes are generally more demanding, their various figured topics require recognition to complete their meanings. The difference is in part due to a sort of innate competitiveness in Raphael's creative personality. Not only was each work he produced meant to be better than that of any predecessor or competitor, but usually better than any previously produced by Raphael. The difference is not only internal to Raphael's development, however, it can be related to a change in the notion of audience. It was a consequence both of Raphael's successful translation of cultural values to viewing modes and of the tastes and interests of his particular viewers: Leo X and his court.

Raphael's friends and supporters in the Pope's entourage were among those most gravely afflicted by the disease diagnosed by Erasmus in his dialogue the *Ciceronianus* – *zelodulean,* style mania. Pietro Bembo's place in the debates on imitation is proof of this. Castiglione sent for his copy of *De Oratore* when he began to work on the *Courtier*.[25] The prefatory letter to the Aldine edition of Cicero's rhetorical works issued in 1514 is addressed to Navagero and pairs him with Bembo. In 1514 Navagero wrote the dedication of his edition of Virgil's work to Bembo and later addressed the prefatory letter of Book II of his edition of Cicero's orations to Bembo. The dedicatory letter to Book I is to Leo X and Book III to Sadoleto, so the whole is framed by reference to the Pope and his two secretaries, a celebration of the cult of eloquence furthered by Leo X, who had also set Raphael and Andrea Fulvio the task of systematically studying the ruins of Rome.[26] One result of that study was the letter Raphael addressed to Leo X on the project of an archaeological plan of Rome. Among the other novelties in this letter is the first application of stylistic analysis to Roman sculpture and architecture.

A version of the text, *una minuta,* is in Castiglione's hand and it has been assumed that he drafted the letter with Raphael.[27] Castiglione had previously supplied Raphael with an *inventione* for a painting, acknowledged in a letter dating from 1514, where Raphael also records his regret that his friend was not in Rome to help him select among beautiful ladies, a necessary prerequisite to painting them. He concluded 'but lacking both good judges and beautiful women I will make use of a certain Idea that comes to my mind'.[28] His artistry is constructed in terms of its recognition and praise from his learned friend and their collaboration as connoisseurs of beautiful ladies. It is also set into commonplace frameworks offered by painting (the choice of Zeuxis) and philosophy (the neoplatonic Idea).[29] The latter may well be as much Ciceronian as Platonic. In the passage in the *Orator* about 'delineating the perfect orator', Cicero considers the nature of the ideal. He refers to the examples of sculpture and painting:

> Surely that great sculptor [Phidias], while making the image of Jupiter or Minerva, did not look at any person whom he was using as a model, but in his own mind there dwelt a surpassing vision of beauty; at this he gazed and all intent on this he guided his artist's hand to produce the likeness of the god. Accordingly

as there is something perfect and surpassing in the case of sculpture and painting – an intellectual ideal by reference to which the artist represents those objects which do not themselves appear to the eye, so with our minds we conceive the ideal of perfect eloquence, but with our ears we catch only the copy. These things are called . . . ideas by Plato, that eminent master both of style and thought[30]

Raphael may well be fashioning himself not only in imitation of the great artists of the past, but in accordance with ideals of perfect eloquence.

The ideals of eloquence certainly seem to inform Raphael's attitude to the operation of history painting by about 1514, as is indicated by the scene on his *Aeneid* engraving showing Aeneas before the temple of Juno (Plate 3, bottom left panel). There Aeneas 'noticed a series of frescoes depicting the Trojan war' and was moved to tears. Aeneas 'fed his soul on those insubstantial figures' and Virgil uses them to give a vivid synopsis of the Trojan war as the past becomes doubly present – to Aeneas and to the reader.[31] In the print Raphael, rather than depict Aeneas in the 'deep trance of attention', shows the moment of his encounter with his own past, pointing out the pictures, turning to his companion Achates in a pose of demonstration and dialogue. The relationship of Aeneas to the frescoes – of viewer to image – is rendered as a discursive one. Their sense is enhanced by appreciation, by reaction and reflection and consists in the recognition of that meaning and its implications. Words complete the understanding of the painted text and that understanding is a connective link between the painting and the viewer in a continuous process whereby visual and verbal images complement and complete one another. Embedded in Virgil's description are the familiar, fundamental aims of rhetoric to move, delight and instruct and they are also accepted in Raphael's illustration as he shows Achates fixed in a posture of wonder while Aeneas gives voice to the lessons recorded in the painted stories.

These goals are equally apparent in the histories Raphael painted for Leo X between mid-1514 and the spring of 1517 in the room that takes its present name, the *Sala dell'Incendio*, from one of Raphael's frescoes, the *Fire in the Borgo* (Plate 4). The four scenes chosen for this room show episodes from the pontificates of Leo III and Leo IV, in a scheme that is simple, but not simplistic. As a Medici, Leo was acutely aware of the power of names and Leo's purposeful imitation of his papal predecessors and adoption of lion-like virtues (fortitude, *pietas*, magnanimity) were staples of the rhetoric and imagery of his rule.[32] The paintings show Leo IV quelling a fire in the Borgo (in 847) by making the sign of the Cross (Plate 4), Leo IV's victory against the Saracens at Ostia (Plate 7), Leo III swearing an oath before Charlemagne (Plate 5) and the subsequent coronation of Charlemagne by Leo III in the basilica of St Peter (Plate 6). Beneath, in the dado, rulers and emperors literally support these scenes affirming the position of the papacy and the Pope's role as guarantor and propagator of peace and as the true ruler of the *imperium Christi*. This position is sanctioned by the divinely appointed order represented in the scenes of the vault painted by Perugino for Julius II in 1508 and incorporated into this subsequent scheme. Contemporary events are wed to illustrious precedents by the conspicuous portrayal of Leo X as Leo III and IV. Here the oratorical injunctions that those popes be imitated by Leo in his actions are recognised and realised. So Leo IV's coronation of Charlemagne echoed the actual meeting of Francis I and Leo X at Bologna in December 1515. The scenes celebrate the Pope and the papacy through their mutual history. The particular historical episodes chosen function as rhetorical examples, meant to be paradigmatic and persuasive.[33] They are topical and typical, and through them Leo X's actions become models for future occupants of these rooms (and Peter's throne). This scheme can be taken as a visual oration in praise of Leo X. Not only does it illustrate the themes of panegyrics dedicated to Leo, but it adapts their purposes and formal principles as the viewer is urged to understand and participate in the celebration of the Pope, and the Pope is encouraged to act in imitation of his illustrious predecessors.

The rhetorical notion of praise not only informs the examples chosen – the subject matter of his histories (their inventions), but also their arrangement and style. The choice of style was obvious, the greatest powers of persuasion and those appropriate to praise belong to the grand style meant to move the viewer to acclaim the subject. The contrivance of Raphael's paintings in this room is a remarkable as their historical subtlety, where truth and semblance of truth are manipulated to enlist the sympathy and wonder of the spectator. Just as Aeneas could recognise himself on Dido's temple to Juno, the bishops and cardinals of Leo's court could see themselves in Raphael's *Coronation of Charlemagne* (Plate 6). The terms are obviously the most impressive possible – those of the *maiestas papalis.* To depict the chapel in full regalia was to display a splendor whose every detail was a symbol for the power and glory of the Church.[34] The Doric order used in the setting was itself a metaphor of the Church's authority. The columns conspicuously placed in the background over Charlemagne's bowed head recall the order of Bramante's altar house over Peter's tomb and the temple he designed at San Pietro in Montorio for the site of the saint's martyrdom.[35] According to Vitruvius, temples to Minerva, Mars, and Hercules should be Doric, for on account of their might (*virtus*) it was decorous that those buildings be erected without embellishments.[36] Doric severity is the parallel mode to rhetorical gravity.[37] According to Raphael in his letter to Leo X, the Doric was the most ancient of the orders and characterised by its strength and unadorned proportion.[38] Here the order expresses the strength of Peter's church, as architecture and as an institution.

Raphael has also made ingenious use of the facts of his story to produce an effective arrangement for his narrative. This meaningful artifice becomes clear in comparing the *Coronation* with the adjacent scene of the *Oath* (Plate 5). To the hieratic centrality of oath-taking is contrasted the diagonally constructed space of the coronation. In the first, an episode chosen to assert the doctrine of papal supremacy, the viewer is made to venerate the Pope's action. His glance then directs the gaze to the vault, with its depictions of God the Father and Christ. The centrally placed martyrdom of St Catherine on the altar frontal is a reminder of how (according to the *Golden Legend*) 'the edifice of pride was destroyed by her humility' and her speaking of truth, one rung in her ladder to Heaven.[39] In both scenes Raphael has observed, respected and recorded the details of papal ceremony, so dear to Leo X, but in the *Coronation* sequence and circumstance are elaborated. The process and ritual of imperial submission to papal authority are emphasised. The magnificent hierarchy of the Church is displayed, as is the tribute brought by Charlemagne. In the *Oath* Raphael used the natural focus of the centre to lead the viewer to the message of the scene. In the *Coronation*, the viewer's glance is directed by the pointing figure in armour in the centre foreground. The viewer is urged to look towards Leo IV and Charlemagne, present in the guise of Leo X and Francis I, with young Ippolito de' Medici as the emperor's page. The arrangement of the whole composition is exhortatory. It is angled to include the onlooker's space. The devices of amplification are employed: repetition in the outward glancing figures, placed in a line reinforced by the pointing hand of the armoured figure; antithesis in the contrasting foreground groups – the diagonally ordered rows of gorgeously attired cardinals opposed to the contorted, or rather 'difficult' postures of the porters. The seeming lapse from grandeur of this group is actually just the kind of relief advised by Quintilian: 'our style need not always dwell on the heights: at times it is desirable that it should sink. For there are occasions when the very meanness of the words employed adds force to what we say'.[40]

The *Fire in the Borgo* (Plate 4) is differently arranged. It has been analysed in terms of Aristotle's *Poetics* and treated as though its construction were more contrived than that of the other stories in this room.[41] It is, indeed, different from the *Coronation* and from the *Oath* and again from the *Battle of Ostia* (Plate 7). The differences among them are a product of Raphael's desire to be copious in invention, various in the figures and structures employed and to be decorous in each composition. In each case arrangement and stylistic idiom are particularly appropriate to the subject. So the frieze-like format of the *Battle* is a direct and obvious imitation of the reliefs of Trajan's column – a military subject takes a military form, which is also part of its historical reconstruction. In the case of the *Fire* the arrangement follows the sequence of its story. The foreground events are those that occurred first: the outbreak of fire, the unsuccessful attempts to put out flames blown higher by the winds, and then, later, in resolution, in the background, the Pope is shown making the sign of the Cross and extinguishing the fire. Time is expressed in space. Danger is expressed through disorder in the varied postures of the figure groups shown in flight (left), futile attempts to put out the fire (right) and piteous appeal (centre). To these clusters and curvilinear rhythms, graceful in themselves, however horrible the subject, are opposed the insistent diagonals of the pavement and architecture – indicative of the underlying order of the papal realm and leading to the solid architecture of the Pope's loggia.

The scene has been called theatrical and related to the scenic perspectives of the early sixteenth century, but it has also been pointed out that the actual view into the Borgo was an architectural perspective.[42] As with the papal court in the *Coronation*, empathetic reality is invoked and points of contact between past and present established. Raphael also displays the 'fullest possible supply of facts' necessary to oratory.[43] Another possible source for the

Raphael and the Rhetoric of Art

construction of the scene, and one reinforcing the decorum of representation is Paolo Uccello's fresco of the *Flood* in the large cloister of Santa Maria Novella in Florence (Plate 8). Uccello's *Flood* was a striking instance of a disaster scene, playing the order of perspective against the disorder of panic and death. Surely the man clinging to the wall of the burning house in Raphael's composition was inspired by the one hopelessly gripping the side of the ark in Uccello's mural. This would be a case of the painter working within the medium of his art, by visual associations, to arrive at the effective power of the other arts of imitation.

These frescoes can be related to multiple systems of meaning. Raphael can be shown to be thinking as an historian, an archaeologist, an architect, a servant of the papal court, a poet, an orator, and above all as a painter. These are very studied compositions and their design process was necessarily influenced by many factors. They register Raphael's curiosity about the antique, about anatomy and artistic precedent (like the Florentine painters of previous generations such as Paolo Uccello and Domenico Ghirlandaio) as well as current novelties, such as the prints of Albrecht Dürer, with whom he exchanged letters and drawings at this time.[44] Still an analysis of the compositions indicates the rhetorical values operating in their conception – in their particular persuasive relationship to the viewer, in their exhortations to admiration and in the decorum and devices of style employed. The delight in artifice was a feature of the artistic production of Leo's court, much of it supervised by Raphael. It was inspired by and depended upon a responsive audience, those for whom style was also substance, those like Bembo, who valued beauty and grace of expression above all else.[45]

This mode conditioned devotional works as well, with far-reaching consequences for the development of religious art. The most dramatic instance is the *Transfiguration* (Plate 9), which Raphael painted for Cardinal Giulio de' Medici in competition with Sebastiano del Piombo. His preliminary project, known from a *modello* now in Vienna (Plate 10) answered the commission in a straightforward manner, presenting a simple illustration of the text and a closed statement of faith.[46] It is a surface for the projection of contemplative ideals – meditation, prayer, intervention. As such it is a direct descendant of altarpieces produced by his teacher, Perugino. The order of Perugino's altarpieces was typically fixed by the hierarchies represented – absolute in their symmetry. In its final form the *Transfiguration* instead opens the mind to doubt, to contradictions. The spectator/worshipper must arrive at the truth by experiencing the drama depicted in the confusion of the agitated crowd in the foreground of the painting. The conclusion will be inevitable: it is in the dawn of the new day and the illumination of Christ.[47] This altarpiece is not a narrative taken from consecutive passages in the Gospel of Matthew (XVII:1–9). It is a form of epideictic sermon on the topic of faith, delivered in suitably ornate style. It takes from the vocabulary of those sermons the prompts to look, view, gaze upon and contemplate (*intueri, videre, aspicere, ante oculos ponere, contemplari*).[48]

Raphael's *Transfiguration*, like his history paintings participates in an exchange of visual and verbal means of argumentation. The rhetorical nature of the expression involves an important shift in the awareness of both artist and viewer. One is deliberately and directly, with all possible skill and artifice, addressing the other. The viewer is meant to be impressed and moved by the skill of the author as well as by the power of the argument. It is painting of eloquence, of skilled and learned address intended to elicit admiration and delight.

The match of Raphael's inventive practices and figural language to Castiglione's ingratiating *grazia*, to Bembo's notions of beauty, Dolce's subdivisions of painting and Vasari's descriptions results from their mutual origins in the circle that sponsored and admired his works.[49] Bembo and Castiglione composed epitaphs at Raphael's death and the first biographical notice of Raphael was written by Paolo Giovio just a few years later. Its second sentence, devoted to the topic of 'gifts of character', describes his intimacy with the powerful achieved through an all-conquering charm: 'so that he never lacked the opportunity to demonstrate his splendid artistry'.[50] The character of the artist was matched by the character of his painting, of which Giovio says 'it never lacked that particular beauty (*venustas*) that is called grace (*gratiam*)'.[51] Giovio is here conflating Pliny and Quintilian. Pliny says that Apelles's 'art was unrivalled for graceful charm' (*venustas*); the distinction *venustas/gratia* is one made by Quintilian.[52] Giovio implicitly made Raphael the new Apelles by describing and succumbing to this charm.

Giovio was Vasari's principal adviser in the 1540s when Vasari wrote the *Lives*. Vasari accepted and developed Giovio's portrait of the gracious artist. Vasari's biography is an exemplary Life for an exemplary painter.[53] As such it conspicuously employs rhetorical devices, particularly in its opening paragraph or *exordium*, which Vasari uses to establish the topics of praise for the *Life*. These are found in the excellence of Raphael's character. As the model artist Raphael is also endowed with the qualities of the model orators of Cicero's and Quintilian's treatises – goodness, modesty and application to study – and his works with those of model orations – beauty and grace. Much of Raphael's *Life* is given over to a demonstration of his visual eloquence in numerous lengthy descriptions. In these Vasari is particularly aware of Raphael's skill at what he calls 'the inventions of compositions'.[54] He finds parallels with writers of histories and the practices of poetry.[55] And he constantly repeats his praise for the way Raphael 'finds figures' for his subjects (*figurare*) – a word that neatly relates to the human forms found and their expressive functions within each composition. He is also sensitive to Raphael's 'fine sense of decorum', as in the *Disputa* where 'he showed old age in the expressions of the holy patriarchs, simplicity in the apostles and faith in the martyrs'.[56] He employs his own sense of decorum in the vivid and varied passages he devotes to the paintings.

Vasari's appreciation of Raphael owes much to the literary conventions and conversations of his day. Indeed their conspicuously literary quality is part of their message. But those conventions also helped Vasari to be particularly sensitive to the devices that determine the communicative power of Raphael's works. Vasari repeatedly points out what 'one sees', what 'is demonstrated', what should be 'recognised' in a combined language of sight and insight that mediates between images and words. As a form of translation of experience it is a neat inversion of Raphael's procedure as a painter. Vasari wrote in complete sympathy with Raphael's strategy of exhortation, accepting and furthering the goal of prompting admiration for the artist and his artistry. For Raphael was not only outstanding in the invention of compositions, as Vasari states, but in the composition of the inventive self of the modern period.

Notes and References

1. B. Ralph and N. Dorigny, *The School of Raphael: or, the Student's Guide to Expression in Historical Painting* (London, 1759), p. 1.
2. G. Vasari, *Le vite de' più eccellenti pittori scultori e architettori nelle redazioni del 1550 e 1568*, vol. IV, edited by P. Barocchi and R. Bettarini (Florence, 1976, hereafter BB) pp. 179–80: 'cercando di continuo figurare le storie come elle sono scritte.'

3. M. Roskill, *Dolce's 'Aretino' and Venetian Art Theory of the Cinquecento* (New York 1968), p. 161.
4. For the origins of Dolce's divisions in ancient rhetorical theory see Roskill's introduction, op cit., particularly pp. 22–3. S. Serlio, *Regole generali di architetture . . . sopra le cinque maniere degli edifici* (Venice, 1537–40), used rhetorical terminology to lament the early death of the 'divin Raffaello', whose memory will be 'lagrimosa per color che sanno qual sia disegno perfetto, invenzione, leggiadria, dispositione giuditiosa et colorir accomodato', quoted by F. Mazzini, 'Fortuna storica di Raffaello nel Cinquecento', *Rinascimento*, vol. IV (1953), p. 68.
5. F. Mazzini, 'Fortuna storica di Raffaello nel sei e settecento', *Rinascimento*, vol. VI (1955), pp. 145–62.
6. G. P. Bellori, *Descrizzione delle Imagini Dipinte da Raffaello D'Urbino* (1695) (Farnborough, Hants, 1968), p. 4.
7. J. Richardson, *Essay on the Theory of Painting* (Menston, Yorks, 1971), pp. 96–7.
8. Cicero, *De Oratore*, III, xxii.85.
9. M. Baxandall, *Giotto and the Orators: Humanist Observers of Painting in Italy and the Discovery of Pictorial Composition 1350–1450* (Oxford, 1971); B. Vickers, 'Rhetoric and the Sister Arts', *In Defence of Rhetoric* (Oxford, 1988), pp. 340–74, with further references. See also G. Le Coat, *The Rhetoric of the Arts* (Frankfurt, 1975).
10. Biblioteca Marciana, Venice, Cod. Lat. 67 cl XI: 'Die Veneris ora xx 3/4 quae fuit dies 26 Augusti 1435 complevi opus de Pictura Florentiae', see L. B. Alberti, *Opere volgari*, edited by C. Grayson, vol. III (Bari, 1973), p. 305.
11. J. Shearman, *Raphael's Cartoons in the Collection of Her Majesty the Queen and the Tapestries for the Sistine Chapel* (London, 1972); K. Andrus-Walck, *The 'Bible of Raphael' and Early Christian Antiquity*, (PhD Diss., University of North Carolina, Chapel Hill, 1986), pp. 72–168; L. Duggan, 'Was art really the "book of the illiterate"?', *Word and Image*, vol. V (1989), pp. 227–51.
12. P. Bembo, *Prose della volgar lingua*, edited by M. Marti (Padua, 1955), pp. 97–8.
13. V. Golzio, *Raffaello nei documenti, nelle testimonianze dei contemporanei e nelle letteratura del suo secolo* (Città del Vaticano, 1936), pp. 15–16. The painting of the *Agony in the Garden* is now lost. A Flemish diptych owned by Bembo's family provided the model for the landscape elements of Raphael's *St. George and the Dragon* of ca 1506; see D. Brown, *Raphael and America* (National Gallery, Washington, 1983), pp. 153–7 for this connection between Raphael and Bembo, and L. Campbell, 'Notes on Netherlandish Pictures in the Veneto in the Fifteenth and Sixteenth Centuries', *Burlington Magazine*, vol. CXXIII (1981), pp. 467–73 (p. 471).
14. Golzio, op cit., pp. 42, 43, 48. For his print *Il Morbetto*, illustrating *Aeneid*, III, 140, Raphael consulted the illustrations in a late antique manuscript of the *Aeneid* which belonged to Bembo. D. Wright, *Vergilius Vaticanus. Vollständige Faksimile-Ausgabe im Originalformat des Codex Vaticanus Latinus 3325 der Biblioteca Apostolica Vaticana* (Graz,

1984), p. 13; P.N. Pagliara, 'La Roma antica di Fabio Calvo. Note sulla cultura antiquaria e architettonica', *Psicon*, vol. III, nos 8–9 (1976), pp. 65–88, n. 40, p. 74; I.H. Shoemaker and E. Broun, *The Engravings of Marcantonio Raimondi*, exhibition catalogue, Spencer Museum of Art (University of Kansas, Lawrence, 1981), no. 31, pp. 118–19.

15.   Ibid., no. 32, pp. 120–1.
16.   Ibid., no. 43, pp. 146–7.
17.   T.M. Greene, *The Light in Troy. Imitation and Discovery in Renaissance Poetry* (New Haven, 1982), p. 174.
18.   G. Santangelo (ed.), *Le epistole 'De Imitatione' di Giovanfrancesco Pico della Mirandola e di Pietro Bembo* (Florence, 1954), p. 41. See also C. Hulse, *The Rule of Art. Literature and Painting in the Renaissance* (Chicago, 1990), pp. 93–103 for a discussion of the relevance of the debate for Raphael.
19.   In his 1695 *Descrizzione* Bellori was the first to claim that this figure, depicting either Statius or Ovid was based on Raphael. See P. F. Watson, 'To Paint Poetry: Raphael on Parnassus', in M.C. Horowitz, A.J. Cruz and W.A. Furman (eds) *Renaissance Rereadings: Intertext and Context* (Urbana, 1988), pp. 113–41.
20.   Fragments of sonnets are on drawings in the British Museum, London (Ff. 1–35), the Ashmolean Museum, Oxford (545, 546, 547), Musée Fabre, Montpellier (3184) and the Albertina, Vienna (Bd. IV, 205). For illustrations, see P. Joannides, *The Drawings of Raphael* (London, 1983) nos 207r, 209, 218r, 220v, 221v, 225r. The texts of the sonnets are in Golzio, op cit., pp. 183–7.
21.   E. Kai Kee, *Social Order and Rhetoric in the Rome of Julius II (1503–1513)*, (PhD diss., University of California, Berkeley, 1983) and J. O'Malley, 'Fulfillment of the Christian Golden Age under Julius II', *Traditio*, vol. XXV (1969), pp. 265–335.
22.   E. Gombrich, 'Raphael's *Stanza della Segnatura* and the Nature of its Symbolism', *Symbolic Images. Studies in the Art of the Renaissance* (London, 1972), pp. 85–101 for this tradition and its relation to Raphael's scheme.
23.   Golzio, op cit., p. 14: '1507. In die coronationis. Hodie papa incepit in superioribus mansionibus habitare, quia non volebat videre omni hora, ut mihi dixit, figuram Alexandri praedecessoris sui, inimici sui, quem marranum et judaeum appellabat et circumcisum'. For illustrations of the Liberal Arts by Pinturicchio, see E. Carli, *Il Pinturicchio* (Milan, 1960), plates 86, 87.
24.   BB, p. 193.
25.   V. Cian, 'Nel mondo di Baldassare Castiglione', *Archivio storico lombardo*, vol. IX (1942), pp. 3–97, (34–5).
26.   A. Nesselrath, 'Raffaello e lo studio dell'antico nel Rinascimento', in C.F. Frommel, S. Ray, M. Tafuri (eds), *Raffaello architetto*, (Milan, 1984), pp. 407 ff. Raphael painted a double portrait of Andrea Navagero and Agostino Beazzano. Now in the Galleria Doria Pamphili, Rome, it was in Pietro Bembo's house at Padua until 1538 when he conceded it to Beazzano. See R. Jones and N. Penny, *Raphael* (London, 1983), p. 162 and plate 173.

27. Generally dated 1519. For dating, authorship, further references, see C. Thoenes, 'La "Lettera" a Leone X', *Raffaello a Roma, Il Convegno del 1983* (Rome, 1986), pp. 373–81.
28. Golzio, op cit., pp. 30–31: 'Ma essendo carestia e di buoni guidici, et di belle donne, io mi seruo di certa Idea, che mi uiene nella mente'. This letter was published as by Raphael in letter collections by L. Dolce (1554, 1559) and B. Pino (1574, 1582). Its attribution has been doubted. Like Raphael's other formal letters it is likely to have been drafted by someone with literary training, but not by Aretino to whom it is normally attributed. Aretino only reached Rome in 1517.
29. For an interpretation of this, see also Hulse, op cit., pp. 86–9.
30. Cicero, *Orator*, translated by H. M. Hubbell (Cambridge, Mass., 1971), iii, 9–10, pp. 310–13.
31. *Aeneid*, I, 443 ff. Raphael probably referred to Bembo's Virgil manuscript here as well, the form of the temple and its relation to the figures is similar to that of the manuscript's illustration of the temple of the Latins, *pictura* 41.
32. J. Shearman, *Raphael's Cartoons in the Collection of Her Majesty the Queen and the Tapestries for the Sistine Chapel* (London, 1972), pp. 18–19 for Leo's choice of name and its attendant associations and R. Quednau, 'Päpstliches Geschichtsdenken und seine Verbildlichung in der Stanza dell'Incendio', *Münchner Jahrbuch der bildenden Kunst*, vol. xxxv (1984), pp. 83–128, 84, 95 for instances of panegyric based on Leo's imitation of his predecessors.
33. J. D. Lyons, *Exemplum. The Rhetoric of Example in Early Modern France and Italy* (Princeton, 1989), pp. 6–14.
34. G. Durandus, *The Symbolism of churches and church ornaments: a translation of the first book of the 'Rationale divinorum officiorum'*, translated and edited by J. M. Neale, and B. Webb (Leeds, 1843).
35. J. Onians, *Bearers of Meaning. The Classical Orders in Antiquity, the Middle Ages and the Renaissance* (Princeton, 1988), p. 254 and plates 132, 139 for illustrations of the Tempietto at San Pietro in Montorio and the altar house in St Peter's.
36. Vitruvius, *On Architecture*, I.2.5.
37. For the relation of Vitruvius's notion of decorum to rhetorical ideas, see Onians, op cit., pp. 37–8.
38. Golzio, op cit., p. 91: 'di tutti [ordini] Dorico è il più antico, il quale fu trovato da Doro Re di Achaia edificando in Argo un tempio a Junone. Di poi in Jonio, facendosi il tempio di Apolline misurando le colonne Doriche con la proportione del homo, onde servò simitrie et fermezze et bella misura senza altri ornamenti'.
39. For a discussion of the intricate cross-references disguised by the simple composition, see Quednau, op cit., pp. 86–9.
40. Quintilian, *Institutio Oratoria*, VIII, 3.22.
41. K. Badt, 'Raphael's *Incendio del Borgo*', *Journal of the Warburg and Courtauld Institutes*, vol. xxii (1959), pp. 35–59 and J. Rasmus Brandt, 'Pity and Fear. A Note on Raphael's "Incendio del Borgo"', *Institutum Romanum Norvegiae. Acta ad Archaelogiam et Artium Historiam Pertinentia*,

vol. I (1981), pp. 259–74. Poetics and rhetoric are not mutually exclusive, certainly not in the sixteenth century. Dolce cites the *Poetics* as an authority in discussing propriety in disposition of the narrative, Roskill, op cit., p. 121.

42. Quednau, op cit., p. 96.
43. Cicero, *De Oratore*, III, 24.32.
44. For a consideration of some of the influences operating here see, K. Oberhuber, 'Die Fresken der Stanza dell'Incendio im Werk Raffaels', *Jahrbuch der Kunsthistorischen Sammlungen in Wien*, Neue Folge, vol. XXII (1962), pp. 23–72.
45. *Prose della volgar lingua*, M. Marti (ed.) (Padua, 1955), p. 4.
46. Vienna, Albertina Z. G. Bd. VI, 193, brush and wash, white heightening, dark grey wash, 398 x 268 mm. For this drawing and a discussion of the genesis of this painting, see K. Oberhuber, 'Vorzeichnungen zu Raffaels *Transfiguration*', *Jahrbuch der Berliner Museen*, vol. IV (1962), pp. 116–49.
47. For a more detailed discussion of this, see P. Rubin, 'Il contributo di Raffaello allo sviluppo della pala d'altare rinascimentale', *Arte cristiana*, vol. LXXVIII (1990), pp. 169–82.
48. J. O'Malley, *Praise and Blame in Renaissance Rome* (Durham, North Carolina, 1979), pp. 44, 63.
49. For the importance of this with respect to Petrarchan notions of beauty, see E. Cropper, 'On Beautiful Women, Parmigiano, "Petrarchismo", and the Vernacular Style', *Art Bulletin*, vol. LVIII (1976), pp. 374–94.
50. Translated from Golzio, op cit., pp. 191–2. For an important consideration of Giovio's place in renaissance art theory and its relation to oratorical treatises, see T. C. P. Zimmerman, 'Paolo Giovio and the Evolution of Renaissance Art Criticism', in C. Clough (ed.), *Cultural Aspects of the Italian Renaissance* (Manchester, 1976), pp. 406–24.
51. Ibid., p. 192: 'Caeterum in toto picturae genere numquam eius operi venustas defuit, quam gratiam interpretantur'.
52. Pliny, *Natural History*, XXXV, 36.79; Quintilian, *Institutio oratoria*, XII, x.6.
53. BB, p. 211: 'Ora a noi, che dopo lui siamo, resta imitare il buono anzi ottimo modo da lui lasciatoci in esempio.' For a detailed analysis of this Life, see the chapter on Raphael in P. Rubin, *On Reading Vasari* (Yale University Press, forthcoming).
54. BB, p. 179: 'Laonde veramente si gli può dar vanto che nelle invenzioni dei componimenti, di che storie fossero, nessuno già mai più di lui nella pittura è stato accomodato et aperto e valente'.
55. BB, pp. 179–80, 183.
56. BB, p. 172: 'senzaché egli riservò un decoro certo bellissimo, mostrando nell'arie de' santi Patriarci l'antichità, negli Apostoli la semplicità e ne' Martiri la fede'. For an illustration, see Jones and Penny, op. cit., p. 75, plate 87.

Index of Names

Index of Rhetorical Terms and Issues